The Baltimore
Black Sox

The Baltimore
Black Sox

A Negro Leagues History, 1913–1936

BERNARD McKENNA

McFarland & Company, Inc., Publishers

Jefferson, North Carolina

This book has undergone peer review.

LIBRARY OF CONGRESS CATALOGUING-IN-PUBLICATION DATA

Names: McKenna, Bernard, 1966– author.
Title: The Baltimore Black Sox : a Negro Leagues history, 1913–1936 /
Bernard McKenna.
Description: Jefferson, North Carolina : McFarland & Company, Inc.,
Publishers, 2020 | Includes bibliographical references and index.
Identifiers: LCCN 2020020177 | ISBN 9781476677712 (paperback) ∞
ISBN 9781476640198 (ebook)
Subjects: LCSH: Baltimore Black Sox (Baseball team)—History. | Negro
leagues—Maryland—Baltimore—History. | Baseball
teams—Maryland—Baltimore—History. | African American baseball
players—Maryland—Baltimore—Biography. | Baseball—United
States—History—20th century. | Baltimore (Md.)—Social conditions. |
United States—Race relations.
Classification: LCC GV875.B154 M34 2020 | DDC 796.357/64097526—dc23
LC record available at https://lccn.loc.gov/2020020177

BRITISH LIBRARY CATALOGUING DATA ARE AVAILABLE

ISBN (print) 978-1-4766-7771-2
ISBN (ebook) 978-1-4766-4019-8

Front cover: The 1925 Baltimore Black Sox team photo (Penn Studio)

Printed in the United States of America

*McFarland & Company, Inc., Publishers
Box 611, Jefferson, North Carolina 28640
www.mcfarlandpub.com*

To Lisa
and the kids
(Aedin and Christopher)

"Their ability astonished me."
—Roger Pippen, *Baltimore News*

Table of Contents

Preface

When the 135th Street YMCA opened in Harlem in 1932, the director organized a membership campaign under the title of the "World Series." Eight teams of workers would compete against one another for the title. Each group took the name of a "well known Negro ball team." Half of the teams had local ties, such as the Lincoln Giants, the Cuban Stars, the Bacharachs, and the Harlem Hellcats. Others were teams with a national following: the Homestead Grays, the Hilldales, the Crawfords, and the Baltimore Black Sox.[1] In retrospect, it might be difficult to appreciate the level of prominence the contest signified. Such distinction is certainly a testament to the clubs' owners who invested their time and money into building their teams' reputations, but it is even more of a testament to the men who played for those teams. They performed with such skill and professionalism as to be a marker of pride for the national African American community. For the Baltimore Black Sox, such prominence fulfilled the ambition of the men who shaped African American professional baseball in the city as the sport served as a marker for community pride and accomplishment, not just on the local level but on a national level. The Black Sox and those other clubs had become symbols for a brand of "colored professionalism" both on and off the field. Such distinction carried with it a special responsibility.

The owners and players were no longer just operating and playing ball for themselves. They had become stewards of an institution that meant much more than athletic excellence. "Negro ball teams" were on the front lines of the battle for racial equality. As Daniel Nathan, a history professor at Skidmore College, points out, "the Baltimore Black Sox matters because the team provides us with an opportunity to consider a specific time and place, and complicated relationships that helped define the cultural moment."[2] Such arguments certainly justify a book-length study of the Black Sox, and this work explores aspects of that "cultural moment." I examine, where possible, the lives of the men who were associated with the Black

Sox and their struggle within a racially hostile social and political climate. Although resources are notoriously thin, much can be learned through census data, military records, and digital archives. As James Bready, author of *Baseball in Baltimore*, notes, "the phase of Baltimore baseball that calls out the loudest for closer inspection, is the Baltimore Black Sox. Without surviving players to interview, without business records to examine, the best hope for recovering box scores and game-by-game highlights is probably the nation's array of African-American periodicals."[3] Digitized databases offer easy access to those national periodicals, enabling researchers to accomplish in hours what used to take days or weeks. They have also enabled more thorough searches, bringing to light accounts of games, biographical details of players, and even accounts of the business of African American professional baseball that had hitherto eluded research. As illustrated by the New York YMCA's choice of teams, records for the Baltimore Black Sox can be found in not just the local but also the national record, and this book utilizes not just the Baltimore papers but also periodicals from New York, Harrisburg, Pittsburgh, Washington, New Jersey, and other places to help write the story of the team.

Even as the picture of a club with national prominence emerges, it is important to note that the story of the Black Sox is also a regional and even local history. Far too often, "local" and "regional knowledge" have been "disqualified as inadequate."[4] On the contrary, as Richard Kearney, professor of philosophy at Boston College, notes, it is through these far too often disqualified local stories that "human selves discover an ethos binding them to others in a community" and in a "tradition."[5]

Chapter 1 studies aspects of Baltimore's communities and traditions at the turn from the nineteenth into the twentieth century. I explore how athletics, particularly boxing and baseball, became a central component of the city's life and how they became entwined in the racial conflicts of the day. The chapter also examines some of the men and teams who laid the foundations for the Black Sox. In particular, the chapter focuses on Joe Gans, the Baltimore native and boxing champion, who was also an influential owner of and a talented player for local semipro baseball clubs.

Although a social and political context is important (Nathan's "cultural moment"), the story of the team is the story of a series of struggles, season by season, to build a successful baseball club. That effort provides the focus for this volume. What emerges is, in part, a tragedy: The Black Sox left the city and all but faded from living memory within a generation or two. However, the year-by-year accounts offer additional perspectives.

Chapter 2 explores the formation and early years of the team that would become the Black Sox. Founded by Wallace Smith, who had been born a slave, the Weldons established themselves as the premier semipro team in the city. The team then rose to regional and national prominence, becoming a member of the National Association of Colored Baseball Clubs and taking the name the Baltimore Giants. Even as they rose to prominence, the team became pawns in a racial battle for control of semipro baseball in the city. The players left the club when white ownership decided to "take over" the franchise in 1912.

Chapter 3 begins with the newly christened Baltimore Black Sox and the players from the Giants coming back together for the 1913 season. The team's new owner, Howard Young, was a prominent African American pharmacist and civil rights organizer. The club's secretary, John R. Williams, saw the team's potential to advance the rights of African Americans in the city. As a baseball club, they were at first a success but eventually experienced difficulties. By the end of the 1917 season, the Black Sox were no longer a dominant force. They found themselves existing on the margins of the city's semipro circuit and playing their home games at the Simpson and Doeller Oval on the east side of town, far from their fan base and situated in an area not well served by public transportation.

Chapter 4 picks up the story in late 1917, when Charles Spedden bought the team. Spedden moved the Black Sox into the Westport Baseball Grounds, which he, as an employee of the B&O Railroad, was responsible for leasing. Spedden and his business partner, William Brauer, worked to reestablish the Black Sox as a competitive club. They also worked to restore the team to regional prominence. By 1920, Rube Foster, owner of the Chicago American Giants and co-founder of the Negro National League, had taken notice of the Black Sox and of Baltimore. Their future in an eastern Negro League was a strong possibility.

Chapter 5 tells the story of Charles Spedden's efforts to ensure that the Black Sox would be a member of an African American professional league in the East. He put the team on a firm financial footing, assembled a talented club, and built a new ballpark. In 1922, he also gained a new financial partner, George Rossiter, the son of Irish immigrants and owner of pubs and restaurants in the city.

Chapter 6 begins with the 1923 season and the Black Sox as a charter member of the Eastern Colored League (ECL). Spedden was able to establish Baltimore as an integral part of the new league, hosting games for the 1924 and 1926 Negro League World Series. The Black Sox, however, were a disappointment. Despite the presence of Jud Wilson and John Beckwith in the heart of their lineup, the Black Sox barely played .500 ball in the first four years in the ECL, and before the 1927 season started, the league asked for Spedden's resignation. He had been embroiled in a controversy over the ECL's share of gate receipts for World Series games.

Chapter 7 examines George Rossiter's tenure as principal owner. His story is a mirror opposite of Spedden's. Unlike his predecessor, Rossiter neglected to maintain the club's home grounds, Maryland Park. Unlike Spedden, Rossiter maintained a difficult relationship with the African American community, but he also assembled an exceptionally talented baseball team, winning the 1929 American Negro League championship. The chapter also explores Rossiter's efforts to field a club with the onset of the Depression. As it became increasingly difficult for him to supply financial support for the Black Sox, he sold majority interest to Joe Cambria.

Chapter 8 tells the story of Cambria's efforts to build a successful ballclub. He gave the team a new home, moving them to Bugle Field, named for Cambria's Bugle Laundry, on the site of the old Simpson and Doeller Oval. In the fifteen years since the Black Sox had been located on the city's east side, public transportation had expanded, roads had been widened, and Bugle Field had been built into a modern ballpark. The team performed well in 1932 but entered a period of decline starting with the 1933 season. Cutting his losses, Cambria sold the team to Jack Farrell, who became their first African American owner since 1917. Farrell's story is one of optimism confronting reality. At first, he tried to keep the Black Sox in Baltimore and to keep them playing on the professional level. Eventually, circumstances forced him to move them to Chester, Pennsylvania, where they became known as the Chester Baltimore Black Sox. They were a semipro ballclub and played their final game in Wilmington, Delaware, in 1936.

Chapter 9 follows the storylines of the men who owned and played for the Black Sox. Many remained in Baltimore. Many remained active in baseball and in the civil rights movement. Ultimately, with their deaths, the team faded from living memory, but their legacy remains. The Black Sox and their predecessors, the Weldons and Baltimore Giants, offer stories of extraordinary success. Baseball gave the men associated with the team opportunities that would have otherwise been denied to them. Those opportunities enriched their local communities and Baltimore city.

Despite their success and national prominence, the history of the Baltimore Black Sox has largely remained untold. Both James Bready and Daniel Nathan have written components of the team's history, as chapters in books that offer the stories of individual seasons or of prominent players. However, a book-length study was not available. To put the need for such a study in perspective, of those eight teams named by the New York

YMCA, all but the Lincoln Giants, the Harlem Hellcats, and the Baltimore Black Sox have had a book or a large portion of a book devoted to their story. The goal of this volume is to fill in that gap in knowledge.

This book is also a deeply personal story. When I was a boy, I had two great passions: Baltimore and baseball. The best moments of my childhood were collecting for the *News American* in the evenings during the summer. I would walk along the row houses between Chesterfield and Brendan avenues, to the west of Belair Road, and listen to Chuck Thompson and Bill O'Donnell call the Orioles games. Their voices carried from house to house through open windows or over transistor radios. If the Orioles were home at Memorial Stadium, I could also hear the cheers from the stands.

My twin passions may have been bred into me. My father grew up on Barclay Street and remembered his father waking him up in July 1944 to see Oriole Park burning.

A great-great uncle, John Andrew Jackson McKenna, sat on the city council for the Tenth Ward and authored the "McKenna Ordinance," legalizing Sunday baseball.

My mother's family grew up on Patterson Park Avenue, a few blocks south of where the Weldons, the team that would become the Black Sox, played their first game against Joe Gans' Nine in 1905. Her uncle, Tony Willinski, told me how he saw Lefty Grove pitch at Oriole Park and about the Orioles teams that won seven straight International League titles. We would spend hours compiling all-star teams of Baltimore ballplayers, combining those International League teams with the old National League Orioles and the modern American League Orioles. When we got to who would be *our* catcher, he said, "Roy Campanella." I told him that Campanella played for Brooklyn, and he told me about the Elite Giants and their ballpark, Bugle Field, near my home in Belair-Edison. He also told me about the Black Sox and how he once saw Laymon Yokely pitch against Lefty Grove "down in Westport."

When I left Baltimore, I still followed the Orioles, by listening to the games when I could or by poring through box scores. My passions never left, but geography, the demands of studying for a PhD and later work as a professor took me far from home. A chance meeting in November 2013 brought me back. I had lunch with David Bennett Stinson at Cubano's Restaurant near his home in Silver Spring. We talked about Baltimore, baseball, and the city's "lost ballparks." He told me about how no one knew the location of Maryland Park or the Westport Baseball Grounds, where the Black Sox played ball.

Oriole Park, located on Greenmount Avenue between 29th and 30th streets, served as the home grounds for the Baltimore Terrapins (Federal League) and for the Baltimore Orioles (International League). The Black Sox also played there when the team's home field proved unsuitable. Oriole Park burned to the ground on July 4, 1944. The photograph shows Baltimore police, fire department, and team officials on the field the morning after the fire. The scorched right-field bleachers are clearly visible. The light stanchion towards the right of the bleachers melted and the scorched left-field turf lies in the foreground.

Playing a hunch, I searched for aerial photos of Baltimore from the 1920s. I discovered the Port Authority's aerial survey from 1925, and on the first slide I checked, I saw Maryland Park, sitting on a peninsula of land just to the north of where the Gwynns Falls flows into the Middle Branch. My passions were reborn. Shortly after publishing my "discovery," I served as an historical consultant for Peabody Heights Brewery, which is located on the site of old Oriole Park, and later for Sagamore Development, for their work in South Baltimore and Westport. I learned the importance of telling stories that can help bring a community together. At the same time, David Stinson and I founded the Baltimore chapter of Society for American Baseball Research. I had come full circle.

My chair at the University of Delaware, John Ernest, put his full support behind my new project, and Charlie Robinson, the Romantics scholar, embraced the idea with his characteristic enthusiasm, reviewing a very early draft of my first chapter. Kevin Kerrane also encouraged me; he too publishes on Irish literature and baseball. In the end, I owe them and, most especially, my wife, Lisa Gonzon, a debt I can never repay. Lisa does not share my passion for baseball but lovingly tolerates it. She tries to understand my love for Baltimore, which is harder to explain.

I am also indebted to the people who built, reported on, and played for the Baltimore Black Sox, from their early days as the Weldons and Baltimore Giants to their emergence as one of the premier professional teams in the nation. I have made an effort to tell their stories in this book with the knowledge that I can never fully understand their circumstances, divided as we are by race and time.

1

Baltimore, Baseball and Race in the Athletic Revival

On May 4, 1913, the *Baltimore Afro-American* published an advertisement confidently announcing the birth of the Baltimore Black Sox. It declares, "Baltimore is to witness for the first time professional colored baseball," and that the club "is composed of some of the best players of Baltimore and the south."[1] Such bravado has an appeal, even if it is not entirely accurate; professional African American baseball clubs in the city had laid the groundwork for the Black Sox. The team drew on the regional reputation those other clubs had established to attract the best players to Baltimore.

Moreover, those teams had carved out a place for black baseball in the city, maneuvering through an often hostile social climate. The Black Sox' antecedents include not only African American professional and quasi-professional teams such as the Baltimore Giants, the Weldons, and Joe Gans' Nine, named after native Baltimorean and lightweight boxing champion, but also numerous amateur and semipro ballclubs. To understand the Black Sox, it is necessary to appreciate the accomplishments of these teams and to understand the context from which they emerged, including the social forces at play in the first decades of the twentieth century. In the city, those social forces shaped athletics and baseball, and set the stage for influential African American teams that emerged in the twentieth century.

Historical Context: The Urban Landscape

On Sunday morning, February 7, 1904, Cardinal Gibbons, the archbishop of Baltimore, told his congregation, "Suffering is a law of human life. No one can escape."[2] As he was speaking, an automatic alarm registered a fire at the Hurst Building, a dry goods warehouse, about a half-mile south of the Basilica of the Assumption. Engine Company No. 15, a hook and ladder truck, and the district chief arrived within minutes; their station house was two blocks away. Firefighters were able to get a line into the basement and started to fight the fire, but seconds later it spread through an elevator shaft and an explosion rocked the upper floors. Flames spread to the surrounding buildings. A street box registered a second alarm at 10:55. Within minutes, a safe, containing sixty pounds of gunpowder, exploded in front of the Finlay, Roberts, and Company Hardware Store. The Baltimore City fire chief, George Horton, recognizing the danger, summoned almost the entirety of the city fire department. Forty minutes later, he asked for help from Washington, D.C., and later from surrounding states.[3]

The responding crews' hoses proved ineffective. The fire burned so intensely that water could not get close enough to cool the flames. Firefighters attempted to create a firebreak by exploding buildings on the perimeter of the flames.[4] The parishioners of St. Leo's in Little Italy processed towards the banks of the Jones Falls, carrying aloft the church's statue of St. Anthony, praying for a miracle. By the time the fire burned itself out, 140 acres and 1,545 buildings had been destroyed. Contemporary and current histories reported that no one had died in the fire.[5] However, Jim Collins, a researcher at Johns Hopkins University, uncovered evidence that an African American man, whose charred remains were found near Bowley's Wharf, was a casualty. Collins speculates that "the dead man fell out of history largely because he was black. He just didn't count.... The fire occurred during the rise of Jim Crow in Maryland. A year earlier, the Democratic candidate for governor, running on a white-supremacy ticket, had called African-Americans 'this ignorant race.' He won. The segregationist Jim Crow laws that devalued African-Americans even in death lasted more than half a century longer."[6] Such was the world into which the Black Sox were born.

Matthew Crenson, writing in *Baltimore: A Political History*, suggests that the "fire proved a fortunate disaster," in that it "unleashed a new era of urban development." Crenson points out that by 1906 "800 new buildings had arisen to replace 1,343 [of the 1,545] destroyed by fire." The buildings were larger than their predecessors, rested on widened streets, and assessed at "$25 million dollars, almost twice the value of the buildings they replaced."[7] The Inner Harbor quickly resumed its role as a center for commerce, travel, and tourism. Along Pratt Street, oyster luggers, schooners, and all sorts of small and medium-sized sailing vessels unloaded their wares.

The Chesapeake Steamship Company's headquarters (ca. 1911), as well as the offices of its rival the Old Bay Line, rested along the Light Street Wharfs. Largely unaffected by the Great Fire, steam packets would deliver passengers and goods from ports along the Atlantic and Gulf Coasts. The Old Bay Line and the Chesapeake SS Company plied their trade on ports along the Chesapeake south to Norfolk (*Baltimore News*).

The Light Street piers hosted the steamship lines and could take passengers to ports along the East and Gulf coasts.

In the decades after the fire, the now familiar Baltimore cityscape began to emerge. The Baltimore and Ohio Building, now the Hotel Monaco, was erected immediately after the fire. The Emerson (Bromo Seltzer) Tower was built in 1911. The Locust Point Grain terminal, now Silo Point, went up in 1924. The Art Deco Baltimore Trust Company Building, now the Bank of America Building, was finished in 1929, the year the Black Sox won the American Negro League championship.

To the east of the burned district, the city funded the Recreation Pier, a public works project, at the foot of South Broadway, adjacent to Brown's Wharf. When the Recreation Pier opened in the summer of 1914, Baltimore City ranked third in the nation for foreign trade and second in imports and was second only to New York as a destination for immigrants.[8] In fact, the area surrounding the new pier was an immigrant community with Polish, German, and Russian more commonly heard than English on the streets of Fells Point. A generation before the pier, and before the waves of Eastern European immigrants, Fells Point was home to a fairly sizable African American population. Isaac Myers established the Chesapeake Marine Railway and Dry Dock Company at the foot of Philpot Street, near the Thames Street Wharf, about a third of a mile from the Recreation Pier.

It was the first African American owned shipyard in the United States. Myers also founded the Colored Caulkers Trade Union Society in Fells Point. Frederick Douglass would succeed Myers as the head of the union in 1872. Douglass, when he was a boy, lived in a house with the Auld family on Aliceanna and South Durham streets, about two blocks from the future site of the Recreation Pier. Joe Gans, the first African American boxing champion, trained nearby and worked shucking oysters in the Broadway Market before his prizefighting career took hold.

The pier's opening was a cause for celebration. On the evening of July 15, 1914, 20,000 people gathered at the corner of Broadway and Thames, "representing a score and more of nationalities."[9] The acting mayor, John Hubert, "turned on the electric switch that lighted up the pier. Then the big gates on Thames Street were opened and there was a yell and a rush of cheers and singing by the crowd that surged through."[10] They made their way to the open deck, where, "[e]xcursion boats flashed their searchlights over the throng and excursionists cheered in return the cheering thousands."[11] In the years that followed, the pier served as one of the city's gateways to the world.

Commercial ships unloaded and loaded their cargos directly on to pier. Steamers arrived from Denmark, Sweden, and the United Kingdom.

The photograph shows the paddle-wheel steamer *Dreamland,* in the bottom right, moored adjacent to the Recreation Pier along Brown's Wharf. It also depicts the range of commercial ships and boats that would dock at the pier to unload and take on passengers, food, and other cargo. The rake-masted schooner at the right of the photograph may be a Baltimore Clipper, and, as such, this would be one of the last images of an active commercial clipper (U.S. Navy, ca. 1920).

Excursion craft, such as the "side-wheeled excursion boat *Dreamland*," would take residents to resorts along the Chesapeake.[12]

In Westport and South Baltimore, areas that would play a prominent role in the history of the Black Sox, the Western Maryland Railroad, the Consolidated Power Company, and the city would change the landscape. Around the time of the Great Fire, the Western Maryland Railroad developed its Waterfront Terminal in Port Covington, building piers to export grain and coal and to import ore and general cargo. Within decades, the railroad had positioned itself as a center of world trade. Grain arrived by rail from the Midwest and left Port Covington by sea to Europe, Africa, South America, and Asia. The Western Maryland Coal Pier incorporated advanced design into its construction in the early 1900s. Graded levels and calculated inclines increased efficiency. In excess of 52,000 tons of coal could be loaded in a day. The newspapers heralded the development as an "awakening" that held the promise for, "commerce of the coming centuries."[13] Across the Middle Branch of the Patapsco River, adjacent to the future home ballpark of the Black Sox, Consolidated Power and Light constructed a power plant in 1905, just south of Clare Street and between Maryland Avenue (now Annapolis Road) and the Patapsco River.

The plant could generate 30,000 horsepower, "equal to the highest demand for power yet made upon the company." It utilized state-of-the-art technology. "Direct driven General Electric alternators will turn out electric current at 13,000 volts." The plant was "capable of almost indefinite extension."[14] To modernize access to residential and commercial areas south of Baltimore, the city built the Hanover Street Bridge, replacing the wooden trestle Long Bridge that had become a hazard. The new bridge would cost almost $1,250,000 but would open residential and commercial traffic between the city and the county.[15] In the wake of the Great Fire, Baltimore was experiencing an industrial "awakening." For all its progressive tendencies, Baltimore also was experiencing an awakening in racial hatred and institutionalized prejudice. African Americans were not full participants in the city's burgeoning economy. The jobs they could hold were restricted. The places where they could live were limited, both by custom and by law. Such were the social forces at work.

Social Context

The Baltimore Black Sox arose out of convergent social movements. The most influential of these was a sense of moral mission, or, stated more

The Baltimore Black Sox

NEW HANOVER STREET BRIDGE OVER PATAPSCO RIVER, BALTIMORE, MD.

The postcard (ca. 1917) shows the newly completed Hanover Street Bridge in the foreground. To the east of the bridge lies the Western Maryland Railway docks. To the west, and across the Middle Branch, sits the Consolidated Power Company's new generating plant in Westport. Just to the plant's south lies the Carr Lowrey Glass Company's headquarters. The postcard also shows the mix of open spaces, row houses, and industry just to the north of the Hanover Street Bridge. Union League Park (in the center of the illustration) hosted the Weldons, the Baltimore Giants, and the Black Sox and was bordered by Charles, McComas, Donaldson, and Light streets. It contains the only known image of the ballfield, which should not be confused with Union Park, the home of the Baltimore Orioles in the 1890s, or with Union Park/Belair Lot, which hosted a team in the Union Association in 1884.

clearly, the demand that society not only improve but purge itself of impurities. The movement's roots lay in the late eighteenth-century Evangelical Revival, which successfully campaigned to purge slavery from American and British society. In the early twentieth century, it took both a secular and religious path. The secular movement sought to advance capitalism, patriotism, and what it saw as the proper conduct for a civil society. The evangelical core focused on campaigns against gambling, alcohol, and Sunday baseball.

However, the desire for purification would take on an insidious mission, in some quarters, after the Civil War when Emancipation opponents hijacked the Evangelical rhetoric and moral philosophy to advance another social movement. Baltimore's *Afro-American* described it with clarity in

1. Baltimore, Baseball and Race in the Athletic Revival

1915: "[I]n the place of slavery of the days before the war, a new slavery has been instituted, a slavery of 'jim crowism,' a slavery of segregation, a slavery of race prejudice, and worse than all, a slavery of disfranchisement."[16] *The Journal of Education* attempted to validate the moral argument, stating that the "races were made distinct by the law of the creator, and it would be impiety to efface the distinction."[17]

Another influential social movement, the athletic revival, arose in the late nineteenth century and continued in force up to the Great Depression. In 1898, the *Baltimore Sun* reported, "Popular interest in athletic sports has grown in America with a rapidity well-nigh amazing."[18] Contemporary magazines observed, "Hundreds of business men ... take their exercise" daily.[19] Football, still in its infancy, attracted an increasing number of participants and fans. Tennis, rowing, cycling, and sailing became common recreational activities. Horseracing drew even more adherents.[20] Interest in boxing began to grow as well, with "Gentleman Jim" Corbett and John L. Sullivan becoming celebrities. African Americans also made names for themselves, with Jack Johnson and Baltimore's own Joe Gans becoming champions. However, for all the popularity of other sports, baseball was the heart and soul of the revival. A newspaper story from 1913, the year the Black Sox played their first game, observed, "Diamond fans can be counted in the millions whereas other classes are restricted to thousands."[21] It was in this period that James Summers, writing in *Journalism*, noted, "Baseball is firmly established as the national pastime, and the prospects of the sport are very bright."[22]

For some, taking pleasure in physical activity was not enough; the athletic revival had to serve a higher goal. To that end, experts touted its benefits, noting that "athletics not only relieve the drudgery of work," they serve a "moral function" and "furnish energy and enthusiasm."[23] Sports would benefit the nation and help to shape the national character. Exercise would create a more productive work force, produce a range of new business opportunities, and increase profits.[24] Norris Arthur Brisco, a professor at New York University, advised businesses to promote athletics: "Wholesome recreation and outdoor exercise are good for health and create the smiling, cheerful face. Athletics may be encouraged in various ways—from contributing to the support of a ball team, to furnishing grounds and equipment, and to permitting the members of the team to take a certain amount of time off for practice."[25] It would also infuse into spectators and participants "moral and social ideals" that could be translated into the workplace and the home.[26] Those values would then carry through into the governance and conduct of the nation and its leaders.[27]

With so much at stake, athletics became then not simply the concern of spectators and participants but also of society's moral watch guards, whose attitudes form a subtext to baseball history in the twentieth century. The response to the Chicago Black Sox scandal of 1919 demonstrated their influence. The Hall of Fame controversies over gambling and performance-enhancing drugs show that a similar sense of moral mission lingers today. One hundred years ago, there were those in baseball and in society who, with equal moral conviction, advocated racial segregation. Consequently, African Americans had to form their own teams. In part, the history of athletics in the period can be read as a struggle between those, such as African Americans, who wanted to participate fully in sports, and those who saw integrated baseball, for example, as a threat to the nation's character.

As baseball commissioner, Kenesaw Mountain Landis put into practice the goals of these social movements. He certainly viewed his mission as a type of moral crusade. With evangelical zeal, he imposed lifetime bans on the eight men implicated in the 1919 World Series gambling controversy. Some give Judge Landis credit for saving baseball, and the major leagues did need to purge themselves of an organized crime element. Nonetheless, for all his moral zeal, Judge Landis chose not to end segregation, and he actively blocked efforts to integrate the game. As a result, the great African American players of the period would not be able to play in Landis's major leagues, and the era's great teams, such as the 1929 Baltimore Black Sox, were not given the opportunity to challenge the best white teams. Judge Landis was nonetheless elected to the Hall of Fame in 1944 because of, in large part, his moral leadership. Moral guardianship then as now can be a self-justifying ideology. The converging values and resulting tensions consequent of both moral guardianship, in all its manifestations, and the love of sport played themselves out across the United States. The establishment of public parks was a notable by-product of the athletic revival.

Public Parks: "4,000 games of baseball"

The progressive movement advocated for green areas in urban centers that served a utilitarian role. They believed that "social reform had to begin by altering the environment of the neighborhood."[28] Jacob Riis, the author of *How the Other Half Lives*, wrote of the need for "a great park with a playground" that would enrich the lives of the urban poor.[29] The first public parks in Baltimore City date to the late 1850s, predating the progressive movement.[30] Parks such as Druid Hill, Paterson Park, Federal Hill Park, and Riverside Park were established as suburban oases, meant to provide a respite for city dwellers. By the early 1880s, progressive ideals were beginning to take shape, and the city government recognized the need to designate specific sections of these parks as athletic fields with the intent to provide Baltimore children a place to play organized sports.[31] Druid Hill Park is, most likely, the first Baltimore City park to include such youth playgrounds, as reported by the *Baltimore Sun*. "Grounds for baseball, lacrosse, football, lawn tennis and other games are assigned, and all that can be done to further the proper athletic sports has received attention."[32] Indeed, Druid Hill Park included what is believed to be the very first professional baseball diamond located in the state of Maryland, and briefly was the home of Baltimore's first professional baseball club, the Excelsiors.[33]

The first public parks servicing South Baltimore were Federal Hill and Riverside Park, although neither park prior to 1900 included a formal baseball field. The area from the Harbor Basin to the Patapsco River was particularly important because, as noted in the *Baltimore Sun*, "there are more young men in South Baltimore than in any other section of the city who would be benefited by such and that the extensive building operations of late have practically crowded the young fellows into the streets."[34] In 1900, the Public Park Athletic Ground Association petitioned the Park Board of Baltimore to include within its public parks athletic fields for Baltimore youth (albeit its focus mainly was on boys).[35] According to the petition, "There are very few places where [young men] can play baseball and other games. Parks are for public use. They are the 'commons' where the facilities should be given for those physical exercises which make men strong and keep them healthy."[36] The petition proved successful and by the summer of 1900, baseball fields were planned for Carroll Park and Clifton Park. The need for a baseball field in South Baltimore was noted as well. A year later, Baltimore mayor Thomas Hayes signed an ordinance requiring the building of an athletic park (to include baseball) in South Baltimore, specifically "south of Hamburg Street and west of Riverside Park."[37]

In 1901, the city selected two sites for the construction of new parks in South Baltimore, the first one east of Port Covington at Locust Point and the second west of Port Covington at Moale's Point.[38] By April 1902, construction of a baseball field at Moale's Point Park was underway, with additional athletic fields for track and tennis planned as well.[39] According to the *Baltimore Sun*, "The new field lies west of Hanover Street at the foot of

McComas Street. It is bounded on the south by Donaldson Street."[40] In May 1902, the *Baltimore Sun* likewise noted, "The approach to the athletic field is by way of McComas street. This street is entirely unpaved from Hanover Street to the boundary line of the field, a distance of about a block and a half. There is a general desire that an ordinance should be introduced in the Council to pave this."[41] Acting mayor Henry Williams officially opened the South Baltimore field in August 1902.[42] At that time, Moale's Point Park included fields for both a baseball and basketball, and was accessible "by either the Curtis Bay or the Light Street and Ferry Bar cars."[43]

In April 1903, the Park Board voted to construct a second baseball field at "the recently acquired Locust Point Park."[44] A gymnasium had been constructed at Locust Point the previous year and plans called for expanding the park to include a track and basketball courts in addition the baseball diamond.[45] In January 1904, the park board agreed to solicit plans from Boston-based landscape artist F. L. Olmsted for developing Locust Point Park and other city parks.[46] The park board also voted "to change the names of Locust Point and Moale's Point Parks. In the future Locust Point Park will be known as Latrobe Park, in honor of ex-Mayor [Ferdinand] Latrobe and a member of the present Park Board, and Moale's Point Park will be called Swann Park, after ex-Mayor [and Governor Thomas] Swann, who is considered the father of the park system."[47]

A 1915 report of the parks board summarizes the interest and use of city parks at that time, including parks located in South Baltimore: "Permits were issued for 4,000 games of baseball and 19,454 games of tennis in the various parks. There were 363 picnics in Druid Hill and Patterson Park. Other park attendance statistics are given as follows: Users of athletic grounds and children's playgrounds at Latrobe Park, Locust Point, 48,750; users of athletic and children's playgrounds at Riverside Park, South, Baltimore, 60,197."[48] A passion for statistics often accompanied the desire for social reform and urban planning. Humor aside, without the green spaces and playing fields built at the turn of the last century, sports, including baseball, may not have taken as much of a foothold in the city.

A "diamond on every open lot"

In Baltimore, baseball was more than a pastime. It was an obsession, and its citizens, both black and white, were full participants in the athletic revival and its controversies. With the exception of segregation, the advocates of moral hegemony played a reactive rather than a proactive role.

1. Baltimore, Baseball and Race in the Athletic Revival

Business and community leaders responded to the athletes' enthusiasm, with the hope of having baseball serve their fiscal and moral aspirations. Racial hatred and prejudice, however, manifested themselves in proactive ways. The teams were not integrated. However, the love of sport and the persistence of those who played ball and organized teams against discriminatory headwinds constituted yet another social movement, a civil rights movement.

In the late nineteenth century, the Orioles captivated the city, winning championships in 1894, 1895, and 1896. Ned Hanlon, a member of the Hall of Fame, managed the team, which included six additional Hall of Famers: John McGraw, Wee Willie Keeler, Wilbert Robinson, Hughie Jennings, Joe Kelley, and Dan Brouthers. They practiced an "aggressive brand of baseball that was despised by the opposition, that was embraced in Baltimore, and laid the foundations for the modern game."[49] The team attracted the attention of society's moral watch guards who felt that such a style of play "legitimized underhand tactics ... and compromised virtue."[50] Taking their logic to its natural conclusion, they saw that "corruption on the ball field, left unchecked, must inevitably dilute the public ethic as well."[51] Within a few years, Baltimore lost first its star players, then its National League team, and, finally, its American League franchise. The moral guardians must have considered that divine justice had been served.

Even such tumult on the professional level could not douse the city's enthusiasm for the game. The *Baltimore American* listed no less than two dozen semiprofessional baseball parks in the city and surrounding areas.[52] Amateur baseball was thriving in Baltimore, with teams and leagues playing formal matches at parks located throughout the city, including Swann Park and Latrobe Park.[53] The team names were often colorful, and included such organizations as the Iola Pleasure Club, the Excelsior Literary and Athletic Club, the Winona Athletic Club, the Piedmont Club, the Barton Athletic Club, the Southern Athletic Club, the Oriental Pleasure Club, the Severn Athletic Club, and the Calvert Athletic Club.[54]

In 1898, *The Sun* reported that "amateur baseball flourished in Baltimore and other Maryland towns," uniting the state and the surrounding communities.[55] Cambridge and Cumberland played against one another and against teams from Clifton and Sparrows Point in the city. Clubs from Delaware, Northern Virginia, and Washington, D.C., also participated. In Baltimore, a "great number of ... athletic clubs among the young men and boys [arose] in every section of the city."[56] Further, teams were not solely based on region. Area athletic and social clubs sponsored membership that crossed neighborhood and community boundaries. For example, the

The Mutual Athletic Club played to a record of 11–2 in 1908. Comprised of boys in their teens or early twenties, the Mutuals competed against semi-pro and corporate teams. The boys took the games very seriously and kept careful records; note the "Official Score Book" at the photograph's bottom right. The players are unidentified.

NELA Park, sponsored by Baltimore's branch of the National Electric Light Association, offered spectators covered grandstands (*NELA Bulletin*).

Mutual Athletic Club and the Calumet Literary Society backed teams. The latter won the city's amateur championship in 1908.[57]

These games attracted widespread interest and enthusiasm. In 1926, "thousands" turned out for a sandlot game in Clifton Park. Companies also sponsored intramural clubs and often more than one semipro team. Following the spirit if not the actual advice of Professor Brisco, ball fields sprouted up throughout the city, many with covered grandstands, such as The Baseball Field at NELA Park, at the southwest corner of Clifton Avenue and Grantley Street.[58]

The National Electric Light Association (NELA) purchased the grounds and clubhouse from the Walbrook Athletic Club for a five-team company intramural league.[59] NELA, like other companies, provided uniforms and equipment. The Baltimore and Ohio Railroad built the Westport Baseball Grounds, future home field for the Black Sox, and sponsored a semipro team and various intramural clubs.

The South Baltimore Industrial League made its home at Union League Park, where teams such as the Western Maryland Railroad played against Crown, Cork and Seal.

The Motor League also hosted games there, where the Baltimore

The photograph depicts the "married men" who beat the "single men" in an intramural game held at the Westport Baseball Grounds in the spring of 1917. The Consolidated Power Plant is visible over the right-field fence. William Brauer, who owned the Black Sox with Charles Spedden, stands third from the left. The others are not definitely identified (*Baltimore and Ohio Employees Magazine*).

21

The BTU (Baltimore Tube Company) finished second in the Industrial League in 1923. Names written on the back of the photograph make it possible to identify some of the men depicted. Callaghan stands in a boater at the left next to the umpire, Allen. Moving to the right are James, Shea, Crothers, Harrell Kesler, Ryan and Kenny. Others depicted include Keilhotz, Hubbard, Benkin, Woodhall, and Curry, but they are not positively identified.

Tube Company team would play teams from its league as well as opponents from the Commercial League and the Insurance League.

Youth baseball also flourished. In 1909, the *Baltimore Sun* reported that "the games going on every afternoon—are legion," and that there was a "diamond on every open lot."[60] In 1915, the youth league championship game drew 2,500 spectators.[61] The city and community organizations encouraged and sponsored summer baseball programs, but they were segregated, both in practice and in coverage. The *Afro-American* reported on the boys "Afro Baseball League."[62] The *Sun* covered white teams.

Opposite, top: B&O Railroad's "Coal and Coke" team was one of many clubs in Baltimore's Industrial League. Standing in the back row from left are Harry Shakespeare (umpire), Schreimer, Landerkin, Finlay, Garrigan, Hartwig, Baker, Walter, Robb and Myers. Kneeling from left are Charles Spedden, Barrett, Knoche, and Barnes. A. H. Lehman and his son sit in the center (*Baltimore and Ohio Employees Magazine*). *Opposite, bottom:* The Crown, Cork, and Seal Company was one of many that competed in the city's variety of industrial leagues. The players depicted in the photograph include Tony Castle, Jimmie Lystin, Johnny Bats, and Joe Bird, but their positions are not indicated.

The *Baltimore Sun* sponsored youth baseball for the city's white community. In this photograph, boys gather outside the walls of Greenmount Cemetery on June 23, 1922, holding banners representing their schools and neighborhood athletic associations (*Baltimore Evening Sun*).

The boys' teams played in fields next to one another in Druid Hill and Carroll Park. There is no record of them playing league against league, but it defies imagination that the boys would not want to test their skills against their league rivals. Adult amateur and semiprofessional clubs, in contrast, would play against one another and in front of black and white spectators. In a city where race relations were becoming increasingly problematic, baseball was a common ground.

"Race conflict"

Youth, amateur, semiprofessional, and professional teams were segregated, but Baltimore was a baseball town. Most fans, regardless of race, would pay to see it played well. In fact, at a game between the Baltimore Giants and the Royal Giants, "two colored baseball teams," at Oriole Park (American League Park) in 1904, "one-fourth"[63] of the fans were white. A game in 1902 between two black amateur teams, also at Oriole Park

(American League Park), attracted a crowd that was almost entirely white, including "crews from the battleship *Indiana* and the United States training ship *Chesapeake*."[64] Players and promoters soon discovered that staging games between black and white teams was lucrative. On the Fourth of July in 1905, a tripleheader drew 1,400 fans. The games were billed as a "race conflict." A white player commented if "we were playing another white team we would have about 30 paid spectators."[65] Semipro black and white teams completed against each other for "the championship of Maryland."[66] In large measure, baseball games between blacks and whites, although the teams themselves were segregated, became a place of peaceful interaction.

Such was not the case in the city as a whole. The culture that allowed racial hatred to flourish came from the government, the private sector, and the press. Rapid urbanization had catalyzed racial tensions. Baltimore's population doubled between 1870 and 1900, rising from 250,000 to 500,000. The city's black population increased at a lesser rate, but rose nonetheless. With the added influx of European immigrants, a housing crunch ensued. In addition, an African American middle and professional class began to emerge, challenging the economic advantages of the majority white population and the discriminatory discourse that kept power in the hands of that majority.[67] Many of those involved in the formation of the Baltimore Black Sox were part of this rising professional class. It was no coincidence that advertisements for the Black Sox, as well as other "Negro" teams nationwide, placed an emphasis on the words *colored professional*. They had to face powerful enemies, however.

Baltimore's mayor and city council passed and enforced a series of laws, between 1910 and 1913, prohibiting black families from moving into white neighborhoods.[68] These laws became a model for segregation laws throughout the country and resulted in the confinement of a growing black population into increasingly congested sections of the city. One such area was the 17th Ward, described as a "filthy slum. Animal excrement and garbage lay in the streets.... Cholera and typhoid were a constant threat, and the district was the tuberculosis center for the city."[69] Prominent members of the African American community fought back. The Black Sox' first president, Howard Young, purchased a home in a white neighborhood, challenging the law.[70] The front page of the *Afro-American* read, "Dr. Young Expects All to Help."[71] A Supreme Court ruling in 1917 made such laws unconstitutional, but de facto segregation lingered for decades. More importantly, because of the city government's actions, discrimination became more acceptable and more widespread. As the *Afro-American* noted,

"Since segregation has been in vogue in the departments [the city government] there have been complaints of discourteous treatment in stores and other places."[72]

Some businesses followed suit, particularly the railroads. The WP&A Railroad and the Baltimore and Ohio Railroad introduced separate cars for "colored" people.[73] Howard Young spoke out against the attempt: "We should make a vigorous protest against it. Once the thing starts we will see no end to segregation in Maryland, and our people will be the only sufferers."[74] Despite resistance, the policy continued, and, in 1916, the railroad's expansion forced 100 African American families into the 17th Ward.[75] The effects of segregation were twofold. The places set aside for African Americans were less desirable and more inclined to deteriorate. In addition, segregation encouraged racism, particularly when sponsored by the government.

The press, outside the *Afro-American,* did not speak out against the city government. On the contrary, the *Baltimore Sun* fomented racial mistrust. "News columns agitated disenfranchisement as a means of controlling the spread of black residential neighborhoods; it published a bogus real estate advertisement and a fake letter to the editor to fan racial panic."[76] The *Sun* also published letters that gave voice to the worst stereotypes of African Americans: that they could not be trusted, that they encouraged and perpetrated criminal acts, and that they smelled bad.[77] Interestingly, the *Sun*'s sports pages did not follow suit. They not only continued to report on games between black and white teams but reported that the games were played with no violence or confrontation on the field or in the stands. In fact, the reporters repeatedly made note of the high quality of play and of professionalism on the field. The racially charged stories from elsewhere in the paper did not gain traction on the sports pages or in the citywide, baseball community. Almost all interracial games were played without incident.

Outside of the city, conflict was often the product of games between black and white teams, and the *Sun* covered those stories in its news pages. In Hagerstown, for example, the local club played a doubleheader against the Brooklyn Giants. The paper sympathetically reported that three of Hagerstown's ballplayers refused to play, and few fans came to see the games: "They would not go to see ... whites associated with Negroes on the diamond."[78] The article quotes a local politician objecting to "any movement that throws the two races together on any basis tending towards social equality."[79] The "official" saw baseball then as part of a larger "movement" towards integration and equal rights. The Giants won both games and that same "official" noted that "the local Negroes are already boasting about the superiority of the negro in baseball. These incidents have a tendency to make the Negro insolent and overbearing."[80] "Colored" professionalism, on the diamond, offered an example of competence and confidence that permeated through the community. As such, it was a threat to perceptions of racial inequity and the enforcement of racial superiority. On the same day it ran the story about baseball in Hagerstown, the *Sun* published a letter on its editorial page, which drew attention to "worthless, good-for-nothing negroes playing ball every afternoon in Druid Hill Park," and asked that "this thing should be stopped. It is a disgrace to the city of Baltimore."[81] On its news and editorial pages, the paper perpetuated the discourse that integration leads to violence and that blacks must be kept separate for the benefit of the entire community.

The *Sun* news and editorial staff, the local official, and the correspondent all understood the power of sports in general and of baseball in particular. Consequently, games between black and white teams became a target, but segregation proponents did not win.

Black and white ballplayers continued to play on the same field at the same time. The crowds continued to be interracial, and the neighborhoods surrounding the ball fields did in fact become peacefully integrated, at least for a short time before, during, and after the games. The *Baltimore Sun's* sportswriters continued to report on games between black and white teams and between "colored" teams. Outside of noting that a team was comprised of "colored" players, the sports pages make no mention of race and often mentioned that the games were "well played."[82] In Baltimore, baseball obsessed as it was, those games and the manner in which they were reported served as powerful civil rights tools. Baseball fields functioned as one of the few places where blacks and whites had the opportunity to congregate together. In a way perhaps unanticipated by the early commentaries on the value of athletics, sports did indeed serve a moral purpose.

Joe Gans and the Giants

Although they could not help but be aware of the social implications of the games, players and fans were most likely motivated by a love for the sport rather than social zeal. They would have to be. It was no easy task to follow, let alone organize, a quality baseball team in such circumstances. Many did, however, and some established a regional reputation. In doing so, they would be forced to leave the relative tolerance of city fields for games in places like Hagerstown, but they would also carve a space for the Black Sox, Elite Giants, and other African American athletes in Baltimore and in the region. The Baltimore Giants were one such team. William Tydings managed the club. He had played for and managed other amateur and semipro teams in the city. William T. Jordan served as the club's president and, presumably, as its main financial support. Jordan owned and operated saloons and a billiard parlor on East Lee Street.[83] The Giants' participation in the Colored Southern Ball League set them apart from other African American-owned teams in Baltimore. There is very little information available about the league. It was apparently a loose organization of baseball teams in Richmond, Portsmouth, Wilmington, Norfolk, Petersburg, Lynchburg, Baltimore and Washington, D.C.[84] However, it did have some lasting effect in that teams from these cities would continue to play other Baltimore-based teams, including the Black Sox, years after the Giants folded.

Those Giants had another legacy, as well. Joe Gans, the first "Colored Boxing Champion," played for them when he was not in the ring.[85] He had managed other clubs, such as the "Dick-de-Doos" and the Norfolk Elites.[86]

Later, he also founded his own team, which was the most influential club of the era. The team was known as the Middle Section Giants or simply as Joe Gans' Nine and later, when the name became available, as the Baltimore Giants. Without his work, the Baltimore Black Sox would not have been able to establish a foothold in the city.

Gans built on the regional connections established by Tydings and Jordan, continuing to play the teams from the old Colored Southern League and expanding into the north, with games against clubs in Wilmington, Delaware; Philadelphia; and Chester.[87] He also expanded deeper into the South, playing teams from North Carolina and Georgia.[88] In doing so, Gans put Baltimore on the map for African American baseball. Of course, his celebrity helped. Fans would come to the games to see the boxing champ.[89] Not only would they catch a glimpse of Gans, the boxer, they would see Joe Gans, the baseball player. The sports pages describe his fielding as "clever" and "brilliant." At the plate, he was "a terror."[90]

Joe Gans's legacy as a boxer and as a ballplayer survived him. His work made the later success of the Black Sox possible. His celebrity, at first, and later his skills as a player, owner, and promoter created a regional reputation for Baltimore baseball in general and for black baseball in the city in particular. His clubs and the other black amateur and semipro teams of the period established a foothold for African American sports in the region.

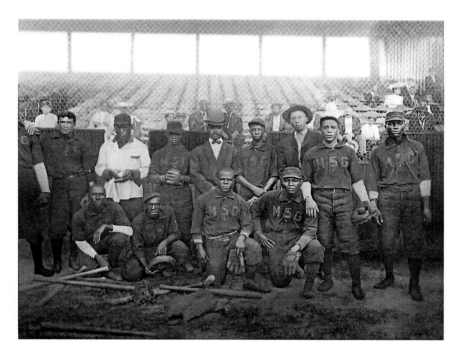

Joe Gans, the first African American boxing champion and a Baltimore native, actively participated in the city's semipro baseball circuit. Pictured here, Gans stands second from right with the Middle Section Giants circa 1905 (courtesy Bryan Alston).

He is also an ideal figure through which to read race and sports in turn-of-the-century Baltimore. A child of the athletic revival, he was a multi-sport athlete, and, as a product of Baltimore, he had a talent and passion for baseball. In both sports, Gans dealt with sometimes-conflicting notions of moral elitism. Many objected to boxing's violence on religious grounds.[91] However, secular moralists saw boxing as a demonstration of a "Manly Art," offering Jack Johnson, an African American, as the example.[92]

Gans also had to deal with racism, prejudice, and hatred. John L. Sullivan and many other white boxers, "never permitted themselves to fight a colored man."[93] Just as in its handling of the ballgame in Hagerstown, the *Baltimore Sun*, in its news pages, saw integrated boxing as contrary to the public good. A headline proclaimed the film of Jack Johnson's championship match, in which he defeated Jim Jeffries, the former champ and a white man, as a "Revolting Show." The paper quoted the president of the police board, who characterized it as "humiliating to white people," and

Introducing Johnson.

Jack Johnson, depicted here in his championship defense against Jim Jeffries, paved the way for African American participation in all sports, including baseball. His cousin would play with the Baltimore Black Sox (Dana Photo Studio).

the police commissioner, who indicated that it would "give rise to racial prejudice" and, consequently, create a public disturbance.[94]

The author of *Joe Gans*, Colleen Aycock, writes, "Both baseball and boxing cut across racial and economic divides."[95] As in its coverage of baseball, the *Sun's* sports pages focused on the skill of African American fighters. A sportswriter would point out, for example, "there was general prejudice against" them but also that "this was temporarily forgotten" in light of their boxing abilities.[96] Many of the African American amateur, semipro, and professional athletes of the late nineteenth and early twentieth century were the best at what they did, regardless of race, and their skill and professionalism attracted admirers across and in spite of racial boundaries. They, like Gans, made their "name and fame through sheer perseverance."[97] In doing so, they made the road a little less difficult for those African American athletes who came after them, although hatred and violence persisted.

Their work countered ingrained racism with skill and athleticism, which, in turn, created its own imperative. If white teams or white boxers wanted to proclaim themselves the best, they had to confront the reality of black athletes. African Americans were still segregated, but they could not be ignored. They countered segregation and Jim Crow with a social movement of their own: that of continued excellence in athletics, combined with a refusal to stop or to be silent. In doing so, they would demonstrate the moral bankruptcy of Jim Crowism in baseball and the ethical deficiencies of those men who promoted it.[98]

2

◇◇◇◇◇◇◇◇◇◇◇◇◇◇◇◇◇◇◇◇◇◇◇◇

The Foundations:
1905–12

On May 27, 1905, the *Sun* carried a short announcement, like many others placed in Baltimore's newspapers that spring, publicizing the formation of a new amateur baseball club. The opening sentence tells us, "The Weldon Club has organized." The short paragraph follows a similar announcement from "The Quaker Pleasure Club" and precedes the news that the "Port Covingtons defeated the South Baltimore Night Owls."[1] Within weeks, the Weldon Club would distinguish itself from those other amateur teams. Although the newspapers covered the team only intermittently and other primary source information is scarce, it is nonetheless possible to trace a history of the Weldons. They would eventually evolve into a semipro team and, even briefly, a member of the National Association of Colored Baseball Clubs. At their zenith, in 1909, the team, now called the Baltimore Giants, took the field against the best "colored" baseball clubs in the nation, including the perennial champions, Sol White's Philadelphia Giants. As the National Association lost momentum, so did the Baltimore Giants. A takeover by white ownership in 1912 coincided with the team's demise.[2] In 1913, it would reemerge, with the African American community's financial backing, and be christened the Black Sox.

The Smith Family

The May 27 announcement informed readers that Wallace L. Smith of 435 Druid Hill Avenue would serve as manager. His responsibilities included scheduling and personnel decisions; he was not a manager in the contemporary sense. Smith also played second base for the Weldons, at least for the first few games.[3] At 40, he likely could not keep up with players who were half his age.

Wallace Smith was born a slave in 1864, the property of the Kent family in Sunderlandville, Maryland.[4] His father had escaped slavery and enlisted in the Union Army but died at the siege of Petersburg five months before Wallace was born.[5] Little then is known about the Smith family until the turn of the century. In the early 1900s, available records tell us that Wallace was the owner of a successful business, the People's Coal, Wood, and Ice Company. He and his brothers William and Thomas also owned several saloons, in addition to The People's Coal Company, most notably, Tom's Place at 435 Druid Hill Avenue, which, after the acquisition of the Hotel Waldorf (437 Druid Hill Avenue), would become Smith's Hotel in 1913.[6] The Smith family's prominence within Baltimore's African American community and its financial resources enabled the Weldon Club to field what the *Baltimore American* called "one of the strongest teams in these parts."[7]

Calling Out Joe Gans

The May 27 announcement, like most others of the day, issued a general challenge to "all uniformed athletic clubs," but distinguished itself by declaring that the Weldons "preferred" a game against Joe Gans, the boxing champ and Baltimore native. It was an impudent move. Gans had been instrumental in building African American amateur and semiprofessional baseball in the city.[8] Joe Gans's team was also "made up of some of the best players of several different states" and had a regional if not national reputation.[9]

The Weldons' audacity paid off by getting the boxing champion's attention. In a letter to the *Sun*, published on May 30, 1905, he asked that the paper "Kindly state that I accept the challenge of the Weldon Baseball Club on behalf of my team."[10] Another letter from Gans, published on June 5, belied his initially polite response. It also gives some hints to the informal conversations in Baltimore's amateur/semipro baseball circles. Gans wrote, "The baseball team I have organized is, in my opinion, the best colored team in the state, notwithstanding what maybe the claims of other managers." That he meant Wallace Smith becomes immediately clear. Gans continued, "I have a match with the Weldon Athletic Club for next Wednesday [June 6] at the No. 1 diamond at Patterson Park. This game will be for the championship of the State and the winners will claim and defend it." Gans's statement demonstrates that he was willing to put his and his team's reputation on the line against a newly formed club. For that, Wallace Smith and the Weldons deserve enormous credit. More went into the debate than is present in the newspapers, and Smith, therefore, marshaled both formal and informal means to attract Gans's attention. However, his choice of an open field in Patterson Park sent a not-so-subtle message to the Weldons. Gans would schedule games in Baltimore's public fields, but only if he felt such games were not worth the rent of an enclosed ballpark. In other words, games against such teams were not worth the price of admission. Moreover, by playing in a public field, Gans ensured that the Weldons would not be able to profit from their game against him and thus from their public and private campaign to force him into a game.

As the teams and spectators gathered at the southwestern corner of Linwood and Eastern Avenues, the temperature reached into the upper 80s, and the forecast called for thunderstorms that afternoon and into the evening.[11] Wallace Smith started at second for the Weldons.[12] By the end of the fifth inning, both teams proved they could hit; the score was 5–5, and then the rain came.[13] The Weldons must have taken satisfaction in the result, playing Gans's team to a tie, but Gans was not pleased. On June 18 he wrote in the *Sun* that his "baseball team will play a game with the Weldon Club at Oriole Park on June 29. There will be a side bet of $100."[14] Gans's declaration of a side bet indicates his desire not just to project confidence, but also to defeat the Weldons and damage them financially. They, of course, would receive a portion of that game's gate receipts. If Gans's team won, their profit would take a considerable hit.

More importantly for the Weldons, they would be playing on Baltimore's largest baseball stage. Oriole Park, also known as American League Park, had been built for the inaugural season of the American League in 1901. The Weldons would be playing in a major-league venue.

The Weldons would lose that first game in Oriole Park, but the rivalry wasn't dead.[15] Gans scheduled a second game for July 17, and the *Baltimore American* reported that, in addition to spectators from the city, between 400 and 600 fans took the train in from Washington to see the rematch.[16] Both teams made money from the contests and from the publicity. However, news reports suggest that Gans was still irked by the Weldons profiting from the rivalry. He announced that the winner of an early September game between the two teams would claim 100 percent of the gate receipts. The Weldons "refused" Gans's "offer."[17] The competition between the two teams helped establish the Weldons, but by the end of that first season, they were no longer reliant on the rivalry to attract a crowd. The next several seasons would see them solidify their local reputation and begin to establish a regional following.

American League Park (Oriole Park) as it appeared in 1905. It was built for the Orioles, a charter member in the new American League. The franchise would eventually move to New York, becoming the Yankees. The ballpark would play host to community teams and the Orioles of the Eastern League and the International League. The city would realign the ballpark in 1909, moving home plate to what is, in this photograph, right field.

Regional Powerhouse

In 1906, the Weldons displaced Gans' Nine as Baltimore's premier "colored" team and started building a regional reputation. Wallace Smith stepped down as the team's manager, and Walter Langley assumed the role. That June, the Weldons attracted "large crowd[s]"[18] for a series of games at Brown's Grove. They were a premier draw for the resort that catered to Baltimore's African American community. Brown's Grove was the "only park in the State of Maryland run exclusively for Colored People and by Colored People."[19] As the summer progressed, the Weldons' reputation grew with their continued success on the field. They ended the season as the champions of Maryland's Colored State League and "added to their string of victories ... defeating the crack champion baseball team of the Pennsylvania Colored League."[20]

The Weldons also developed a distinctive style. They became known for playing a version of what John McGraw, the onetime Oriole manager, called "inside baseball." The Weldons' version, known in the papers as "fast ball," included a combination of smart baserunning, designed to put pressure on opposing teams; strong pitching; and solid defense. The team leader was their shortstop, June Matthews, who also served as the team's captain. Foulks was their ace, and Ed Wise, the catcher, was also a stand-out. The newspapers commented on the team's "clever base running," "clever pitching," and "sensational" fielding.[21] The language emphasizes both the ballplayers' physical skills but also their intellectual ability.

Starting in 1908, the Weldons played their games in an enclosed field on McComas and Light streets in South Baltimore. Built in 1906, as the Stadium Grounds, Union League Park was, at the time of its construction, the second-largest sports venue in the city, with a capacity of approximately 3,500. It was intended to be home to Baltimore's team in the Union

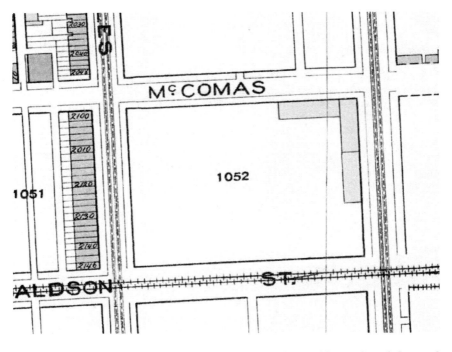

A map shows the South Baltimore field where the Weldons played, located at the corner of McComas and Light streets (Atlas of the City of Baltimore, Maryland Topographical Survey Commission, 1914).

League of Professional Baseball Clubs of America.[22] The league folded a few months into the 1908 season, but the Weldons quickly adopted the ballpark as their home field.

Union League Park was an intimate setting.[23] Families would watch games from the roofs of their row homes on Charles Street, just beyond the right field fence. Men would "would lower an empty bottle and six cents to the street, where a boy would take it to Hamberger's saloon to be filled and send it back up to the roof." Over the left-field fence sat the Pennsylvania and Western Rail Yards just to the south and east of Donaldson Street in Port Covington. At a time when segregation and racial tensions ran high in the city neighborhoods to the north, this area of South Baltimore was an integrated community, where people were treated with "respect and kindness" no matter where they came from or what they looked like. Lower Hanover Street was called "Checkerboard Road," because African American families, Chinese immigrants, and European immigrants lived together.[24]

The neighborhood community and the Weldons' large fan base from other parts of the city made the field their home, and the team developed a loyal and raucous following. A "brass band" was "in attendance" at their home games, and a "band of routers" would "accompany" them on the road, even travelling to games against all white clubs.[25] The *Baltimore Sun* advised its readers that "noise instruments of all kinds will be brought by the colored rooters" for a game against a white club to be played at Oriole Park.[26] The papers heralded the Weldons as the "Crack Colored Organization" who "snowed under" their opponents.[27] In September of 1908, they "won the pennant of the Colored League" before a sellout crowd at Union League Park.[28]

The Weldons had reached the apex of Baltimore's amateur and semi-professional teams.

In 1905, they were one of many clubs playing on the city's sandlots. By the end of the 1908 season, there was no better team in the state and, arguably, no better semiprofessional team in the region. Reflecting the same audacity and ambition that compelled the Weldons to call out Joe Gans in 1905, the newspapers announced in September of 1908 that they "would play the Cuban Giants.... The Giants are professional colored baseball players who are supported by white management. They tour the country and have a wide reputation."[29] The Giants were the "first all–African American professional team, organized in 1885 [and] bore the name Cuban Giants, perhaps to obscure the squad's true racial identity."[30] In 1908, they were a member of the National Association of Colored Baseball Clubs of the United States and Cuba and, in the summer of 1908, had toured the Midwest, playing games against, among others, Rube Foster's Giants.[31]

The Weldons were about to test themselves against an elite, professional African American team. The newspapers warned that the Weldons "will have to hustle if they expect to make a showing." Enthusiasm grew, and the papers announced that "a large crowd is expected."[32] Further rousing interest in the game, Joe Gans, the Weldons' old rival, would play for the Cuban Giants during the series. It was a warm and cloudy day, with the temperature in the low 80s. The rain would hold off until that evening, so the field at Union League Park was in excellent shape.[33] Foulks, the Weldons' ace, pitched the first game and allowed no earned runs; however, the Weldons, uncharacteristically, made six errors in the field and lost "a close and exciting game" 4–2.[34] In the second game, the "Weldons [were] snowed under," losing 11–1. Again, the Weldons did not play well defensively, committing three errors. They "used poor judgement at times, and it seemed as if they had an attack of stage fright."[35] However, for the first game, the Weldons proved to themselves at least that they could play competitive baseball against a professional team.

The Weldons' star players also made an impression on the Cuban Giants. Under the headline, "Weldons to lose Players," the *Baltimore Sun* announced that O. J. Barbour, the Weldons' center fielder; June Matthews, the team captain and shortstop; Foulks, the Weldons' star pitcher; and Ed Wise, their catcher "have signed contracts with the Cuban Giants, … and will leave shortly for the South where they are to play all winter."[36] At the end of the 1908 season, it appeared that the Weldons' audacity, a trait that had distinguished the team since its inception, had gutted it. The Weldons had demonstrated that they could play competitive baseball against one of the finest teams in the country; the games offered the Weldons' most talented players a showcase for their abilities, and it was that showcase that, ultimately, led to those players' departure.

The National Stage: The Baltimore Giants

The parade, signaling a reversal in fortune for the Weldons, started at 12:45 in North Baltimore, making its way down Druid Hill Avenue, home to the emerging "colored professional" class. A band escorted local politicians and dignitaries, together with the Washington Giants and Baltimore Weldons, through the heart of the city, including many predominantly white neighborhoods, crossing into South Baltimore along Light Street and then to Union League Park.[37] It was May 10, 1909, Opening Day for the Weldons. The weather was beautiful, sunny with the temperature in the low-to-mid 70s.[38]

Mayor J. Barry Mahool threw out the first pitch. The mayor's presence, let alone his featured role in a game between two African American professional teams, reflects how the game and coming baseball season had generated "much interest" in Baltimore, and that the team was motivated to reach across the city's racial divide.[39] By the end of his term, Mayor Mahool "earnestly proposed and enacted an apartheid statute as a progressive social reform."[40] The statute was presented as an "ordinance for preserving peace, preventing conflict and ill feeling between the white and colored races in Baltimore city, and promoting the

Mayor J. Barry Mahool signed the West Ordinance into law in late December 1920. He used two ceremonial pens, presenting one to Councilman West of the 13th Ward, who had it framed and placed on his office wall. Mayor Mahool's father had been an officer in the Confederate army.

general welfare of the city by providing, so far as practicable, for the use of separate blocks by white and colored people for residences, churches and schools."[41] The ordinance also sought to halt what letters to the *Sun* described as a "negro invasion" and to prevent "personal and social contact between the races."[42]

In a moment infused with irony, on the afternoon of May 10, Mayor Mahool stood in a ballpark alongside prominent African Americans, participating in the inaugural season of the Colored Professional Baseball Association, which included the Washington Giants, the Cuban Giants, the Cuban Stars, the Philadelphia Giants, the Brooklyn Royal Giants, the Saint Paul Gofers, the Chicago Leland Giants, the Chicago American Giants, the Harrisburg Giants, and the Weldons.[43]

Solidifying their team's role as representatives of the city, the Weldons announced shortly after Opening Day that they intend to change the name of the club to the "Baltimore Giants ... as the other clubs in the association are known by the names of their respective cities."[44] Reflecting their national profile, the Baltimore Giants were featured in newspapers in cities including Chicago, Philadelphia, New York, and Harrisburg. The *Baltimore Afro-American* began to cover the team, regularly, and the *Baltimore Sun* and the *Baltimore American* increased their coverage. The team was an ambassador of a city deeply troubled by racial conflict.

Once the game started, the Weldons' stars went to their accustomed positions. Foulks was the starting pitcher. Wise was his catcher. Barbour, the team's captain, was in center, and Matthews, now assistant manager, at short.[45] A week before, the Weldons signed the stars they had lost to the Cuban Giants.[46] The Weldons went on to win their first game, beating Washington 5–3.[47] It was a remarkable turn in fortune for the club, which just six months prior to Opening Day had lost their star players and whose future as an organization must have been much in doubt.

On the contrary, they were on a very firm financial footing. Two months before that opening game, in March 1909, the *Baltimore American* ran a story announcing that the "team will be the first colored club ever played in this city, under signed contracts."[48] They had an official headquarters, at 1305 Pennsylvania Avenue, and their business office was located at 1634 Thames Street.[49]

The newspapers stressed the leadership roles of those previously associated with the club. Not only was the team's former captain and shortstop, Matthews, now the assistant manager, Walter Williams, who had served as the Weldons' official scorer, would remain with the club.[50]

However, there was a shift in the team's ownership, which may explain the club's political connections and Mayor Mahool's willingness to throw out the first pitch. The *New York Age* listed the "officers of the Weldons: H.H. Lee, president; R.E. Hall, vice-president and manager."[51] The team's president came from a long-established and wealthy Baltimore family. H. H. Lee was a member of the 1812 Society, meaning he was a descendant of those Baltimoreans who fought the British in the War of 1812.[52] His wife was an active member of the Daughters of the Confederacy.[53] The team's vice president and manager was Robert E. Lee Hall, a prominent attorney who was mentioned as a mayoral candidate.[54] The team's officers quite likely saw their financial backing as an investment opportunity. Neither Hall nor Lee, nor any member of their families, is ever mentioned in connection with any other baseball club in Baltimore or the region. Because of their investment, they had a primary interest in the team's success and, it

Thames Street, ca. 1909. The Baltimore Giants' business office was located at 1634 Thames Street. In this photograph, the address housed a barbershop. The Broadway Market and the Port Mission can be seen in the background (*Baltimore Sun*).

seems, broadening the club's appeal to all of Baltimore's ethnic and racial communities. Keeping Walter Williams as scorer and re-signing and promoting June Matthews would have sent a message to the Weldons' core fans that the new ownership respected the work of the African American community in building the franchise. Locating the business office on Thames Street enabled the club to reach out directly to Baltimore's immigrant community; Fells Point was the home to the city's growing Eastern European population. An association between non–English speaking immigrants and African Americans would have reminded city residents of a similar alliance which defeated efforts to disenfranchise voters just a few years before. Literacy tests, written in English, threatened to take voting rights away from African Americans and those citizens for whom English was a second language.[55] The Weldons' new officers brought with them not only political connections but also considerable financial resources; there is an irony, however, in a team founded by a former slave now run by men with connections to the former Confederate States.

The team announced in early July that "all games will be played at Oriole Park ... until the season closes."[56] Oriole Park, the former American League Park where the Weldons played Joe Gans' Nine in 1905, was a larger venue, offering the Baltimore Giants more lucrative gate receipts but also a larger stage. Ownership promised that "[m]usic will be furnished" and initiated giveaways, with "a souvenir to the ladies."[57] The club's improved financial condition enabled them to be buyers. Whereas at the end of 1908, the Weldons lost their stars to the Cuban Giants, the Baltimore Giants signed the Cubans' starting shortstop, Moore, and a star pitcher from the Lafayettes, Green. Ownership hired a new manager, Lowry, to run the club's day-to-day operations, and he was ready to make some controversial moves: The team's assistant manager and one-time captain, June Matthews, would move to first to make room for the new shortstop. Matthews had "been playing phenomenal ball at short.... Manager Lowry's idea for making this change is because Matthews, being a fast man, will develop into a good first baseman as he covers a lot of ground and is sure death to ground balls."[58] The Giants also scouted regional semiprofessional teams, purchasing the contract of Doc Squarel from a club in Wilmington, Delaware.[59] The investments paid dividends. The newspapers noted that the "team has been greatly strengthened," and that they would play "before ... large crowds" at Oriole Park.[60] The highlight of that month was a game against the Philadelphia Giants, the league's elite club. Baltimore had lost badly to Philadelphia in May but defeated them in July.[61]

Later that season, the Baltimore Giants reached out to their old rival, Joe Gans, and invited him to umpire a game.[62] Gans was suffering from tuberculosis. After his last fight against Oscar "Battling" Nelson, in September of 1908, Gans appeared "ashen pale, his face terribly cut and his eyes glassy."[63] He would fight one last time, in March 1909, but "Gans was a shadow of his former self."[64] However, he seemed to want to heal "old wounds," reconciling with Maurice Herford, his former manager.[65] In August 1909, he even joined the Baltimore Giants as a player, saying "he has never felt better in his life."[66] He would die within the year at his mother's row home on Argyle Avenue, just three miles from Oriole Park, where he played his last baseball game.

After such a promising inaugural season, the Baltimore Giants and the Colored Professional Baseball Association would fade from the headlines. For two years, the Baltimore papers did not carry an announcement or news story about the team. During the 1910 season, a Washington, D.C., paper would record only a July series against the Washington Giants.[67] In 1911, the *Washington Herald* once again advertised a series between the Washington Giants and the Baltimore Giants.[68] The *New York Age* and the *Asbury Park Press* ran one story each, reporting on Baltimore's games.[69] Based on available evidence, the Baltimore Giants had returned to semi-pro status as a team, and ownership had stopped investing money in promoting the club.

However, 1912 would prove a newsworthy year. In May, the *Baltimore Sun* ran its first stories on the Giants in years. On May 20, the paper announced the "first game of a scheduled series between the reorganized Baltimore Giants, formerly the Weldons, and the Baltimore Yannigans, at Union League Park."[70] The story mentions Weldons and Giants stars O. J. Barbour, June Matthews, and Ed Wise, suggesting that the team's core of players had remained intact since 1909. The increased coverage was likely due to a change in ownership.

Three days earlier, the *Sun* ran a story detailing how "the Colored ball tossers have been taken over by a company formed by white ballplayers, who intend to run colored semi-professional baseball here during the coming season."[71] A month later, the *Sun* suggested that Giants players did not appreciate being "taken over" and "run" by the new ownership: "The Weldon Baseball Club has reorganized under new management."[72] The story goes on to list the familiar names of Wise, Matthews, and Barbour and includes other players associated with the old Weldon team and the Baltimore Giants: Charles Evans, Charles Thomas, and James Johnson, whose cousin was Jack Johnson, the heavyweight boxing champion.[73] The *Washington Herald* called the reorganized club "the Colored champions of Baltimore," and declared that "the Baltimore Weldon Giants ... played a peppery game, and Matthews did much to his credit."[74] The papers offer no further clues as to the outcome of the Weldon Giants season. However, the players and a new team, under the ownership of "colored professionals," to use the language of the day, would emerge in 1913.

Race and Ownership

It was not uncommon for "colored" professional or semiprofessional teams to have white ownership. The Weldons' rivals, the Cuban Giants, were owned and run by white men at that time. Based on what evidence remains, it seems that the style and attitudes of the white owners was crucial. Hall and Lee, for example, ran the club, at least for the 1909 season, with respect for the team, retaining business ownership, but leaving on-field decisions to the ballplayers or their representatives. Further, they treated the players with respect, naming June Matthews as assistant manager. In contrast, evidence indicates that the "company formed by white ballplayers" did not treat the team with respect. That would be a pattern for the team in the decades to come; Charles Spedden, a white man, would run the Black Sox with a respect for the ballplayers and for the African American community. George Rossiter, on the other hand, ran the club with less regard for the players and public relations. In the immediate future, however, other names familiar in the Weldons' history would re-emerge, notably the Smith family, and help to form the Baltimore Black Sox.

3

The Baltimore Black Sox: 1913–17

In early spring of 1913, the newly formed Baltimore Black Sox assembled for a photo. The team included many members of the Weldons and Giants. In fact, the players and the newspapers saw the Black Sox as the same franchise. Charles Thomas would tell his grandson that he "used to play baseball with the former Weldon Giants, later known as the Black Sox."[1] Likewise, the *Washington Herald* let its readers know that the "Baltimore Black Sox were formerly known as the Weldon Giants," and the *Afro-American* characterized the Black Sox as an "outgrowth" of both the Weldons and the Baltimore Giants.[2]

The new team also included some new faces, in addition to old faces in new roles and in new uniforms. New to the club, John R. Williams, the secretary and treasurer, stands on the left side of the photo, holding a Gladstone bag and wearing a tie and a driving coat. The Black Sox "manager," more of a general manager by contemporary standards, Walter Williams (no relation to John), stands on the photo's right side, wearing a bow tie. He had scored games for the Weldons and the Baltimore Giants. Charles Evans, kneeling, is to John Williams's right. His uniform carries a "C" on the left sleeve, indicating that he is the team's "captain" or on-field manager. He had played with both the Weldons and the Baltimore Giants and would play with the Black Sox through the 1921 season, starting as a third baseman but eventually moving to short, and then the outfield.[3]

Charles Thomas sits in the front row, to Walter Williams's left. Thomas would play with the Black Sox through the 1922 season. He was born in rural Elkridge, Maryland, and lived in a farmhouse on Montgomery Road with his parents, three brothers, and a sister. His father, William, had been born a free man in Washington, D.C., in 1862 and worked as a railroad porter. His mother, Mary, worked as a housekeeper and took in lodgers to support the growing family; Thomas's sister's family also lived in the house. All the children could read and write, and Charles was sent

45

The Baltimore Black Sox, 1913 (Cowans Auction House).

to Armstrong High School in Washington, D.C. He came to Baltimore in 1912 to play left field for the Weldon Baltimore Giants, working at a confectioner's shop to help support himself.[4]

We do not know, for certain, the identities of the other men in the photo; however, Joe Lewis may be kneeling next to Charles Evans. Lewis would have been 18 in the spring of 1913 and would play for the Black Sox into the 1920s. June Matthews is also likely in the photo. Matthews had been a fixture at short for the team since its inception, playing next to Wallace Smith for the Weldon Athletic Club.[5] Although there is no way to identify Matthews definitively, he may be the player standing directly behind Lewis. Records indicate that Matthews had "brown" skin and that he was "tall and slender."[6] It is likely that Ed Wise and O. J. Barbour, old teammates with the original Weldons, are also in the photo. Other members of that first Black Sox team include Booze Brown, Lush Waters, Walter Mitchener, and Blainey Hall.[7] No images of these men survive and there are no additional clues linking them to the men in the photo.

John R. Williams provides the key for dating the photo to the 1913

Some of the "Non-Coms" of 351st F. A.

Reading from left to right:—Back Row, Color Sgt. T.
C. Smith, Personnel Sgt. John R. Williams, Mail Sgt.W.
C. Anderson, 1st Sgt. Supply Co. Geo. R. Nokes, 1st Sgt.
L. L. Scott, Sgt. Cole; Front Row, 1st Sgt. Batry. B. Jack-
son, Sgt. Maj. V. Thompson, Sgt. Maj. Jos. Setters, 1st
Sgt. S. A. Trent B'try D.

Sgt. John R. Williams stands in the back row, second from the left (*Baltimore Afro-American*).

club. In addition to being the team's "secretary and treasurer,"[8] he also served in the 351st Field Artillery in the First World War. The *Baltimore Afro-American* ran a page one photo of the unit's non-commissioned officers on February 28, 1919.

Colored Professional

Who was John R. Williams? Why the "Black" Sox as the team's name? First, the man: Service records show that John R. Williams was born on July 1, 1892. Census records tell us that he grew up in a row house at 1627 Druid Hill Avenue. He lived there with his father, Jay Williams, his maternal grandmother, and four sisters.[9] His grandmother, Henrietta Brown, was still working as a housekeeper in her sixties to help support the family.

His father, a widower, worked as a waiter. Henrietta Brown could neither read nor write, but the 1910 census tells us that all five children, ages 13 through 19, attended school and were fully literate.[10] It must have been a tremendous sacrifice. At the turn of the last century in Baltimore, most teenage children, especially daughters, would have been working to help support the family.

John Williams graduated from Baltimore High School, which was an African American school for boys. The school was housed in a "proper building" and "fairly well equipped."[11] The "entire faculty [consisted] of able and efficient colored instructors [that had] ... been put in charge" of the school.[12] The faculty reminded students of the "obligation" that their education entails for every "member of the race." Graduates were told to see themselves as "no better than the masses who have not enjoyed such educational advantages" but instead to bring their "superior training and knowledge to bear on the practical matter of everyday life."[13] John R. Williams took that responsibility seriously, and, even though he was only associated with the Black Sox in 1913, his influence can be seen in the team's name and can be measured in the news stories and advertisements that appeared in the local papers during the Black Sox inaugural season.

His education and background suggest that he consciously used the words *colored professional* in advertisements for the club.[14] The phrase reflected the ideals Williams had learned at Baltimore High School, which in turn mirrored the philosophy of a "black elite circle" that was starting to rise in prominence. It was a belief system that advocated "merit-based recognition for every American of color," negating "a false line of reasoning that white supremacists gave against racial equality."[15] In an echo of the values taught at Baltimore High School, the "Black Elite" would:

> energetically ... [take] on the role of leaders of their race. They worked for the advancement of all people of color in the spirit of noblesse oblige, yes, but for other reasons too. Though they identified with all blacks according to race, there was another "consciousness of kind" operating, and that was class. So long as others lumped all African Americans together, those in the upper class were embarrassed by some of their unschooled, low-class counterparts, and that generated some of the energy they put into "uplift" activities.[16]

John R. Williams's formal clothing; Walter Williams's tie; and even the formal poses of the players in the photo could be read as a desire to "uplift." The ballplayers' facial expressions and somewhat stiff physicality betrays, perhaps, a dissatisfaction with being the subject of such an effort. Nonetheless, after the debacle of the previous year, when "white ballplayers" took control of the Baltimore Giants, such poses likely seemed a small price. The photo presents the team as a group of "colored professionals," equal to their white counterparts, and the baseball diamond offers them the opportunity to achieve a "merit-based recognition."

The "Black" Sox

An early notice, advertising the Black Sox and the upcoming season, also betrays those "elite" values. If not written by John R. Williams himself, it reflects his ideals.[17] The notice ran in the *Baltimore Sun*, declaring, "Baltimore is to witness for the first time professional colored baseball."[18] Williams most certainly knew of the Baltimore Giants and their status as the city's first professional team. The players who were on that team and played for the Black Sox would have likely brought it to his attention. Moreover, his childhood home on Druid Hill Avenue was on the Giants' parade route in 1909. The notice's exaggeration might represent a bit of salesmanship, but it also might be telling a white audience, the *Sun*'s readership, that not only the team's players but its ownership was African American. The Black Sox, therefore, would bear "witness" to what "professional colored baseball" meant for the city.

A notice that ran in the *Afro-American* two weeks earlier takes a different tone. That ad, intended for an African American audience, tells readers, "All games will be played at Oriole Park," not making note of the International League Orioles. Rather than open by mentioning "professional colored baseball," the *Afro-American* declares, "All lovers of the best there is in Negro baseball will rejoice."[19] The notice's tone is much more colloquial and familiar than that which appeared in the *Sun*. Significantly, it indicates, "This city will be represented by the Baltimore Black Sox." The words are a statement of pride. A "Negro" team will represent Baltimore.

The word *this* functions in the context of the *Afro-American* as a counterpart to the word *witness* that appeared in the *Sun*. Whereas in the *Sun* the word *witness* is used to show what the city (or what the white readership of the city) will be unable to deny: that given the opportunity, African Americans can perform at a level equal with other races. In the *Afro-American* the word *this* refers to what readers of the paper both would have known and were about to realize: that a city currently enacting laws to restrict housing and opportunities for its African American citizens will be represented by an African American team.

The separate notices subtly recognizes not only the different ways in which African Americans and whites would have experienced Baltimore;

the notices also demonstrate that there are two different Baltimores. The Black Sox, with their quality of play and play on the same field as the all-white professional Orioles, would demonstrate a professional caliber of play to those separate cities. Moreover, the Black Sox, in bringing "the best colored teams in the country" to Baltimore would embody the ideal of a "merit-based" playing field for African Americans.[20] It is in this spirit of racial "witness" to excellence, speaking to both the African American Baltimore and to the white-establishment Baltimore, that that team may have taken its name: The *Black* Sox.

Black Elites and "Lawless Negroes"

Early advertisements also offer clues about the financial backers for the 1913 Black Sox. The same ad that listed John R. Williams as secretary and treasurer lists Howard Young as president.[21] Young had spoken out against B&O Railroad's proposed segregation plans in 1912 and was one of the city's leading "Colored professionals."[22] He was a lifelong member of the Republican Party and "was never known to use a slang expression, raise his voice or curse."[23] Howard Young was one of fourteen children. His father, the Rev. Alfred Young, had been born a slave on the Lower Eastern Shore and moved to Baltimore after the Civil War, where he met and married Howard's mother, Emma Jane Carpenter Sorrell.[24] Howard's mother could neither read nor write and, most likely, had also been a slave in her home state of Virginia.[25]

Educated at Howard University in Washington, D.C., Dr. Young first worked there before moving to Baltimore in 1900 to open the city's first African American-owned pharmacy at 1140 Druid Hill Avenue, just a half-mile from John R. Williams's boyhood home.

The advertisements list the team's business address as Smith's Hotel, 435 Druid Hill Avenue, and the team and the hotel shared the same phone number, "Mount Vernon 4281."[26] Wallace Smith, founder of the Weldons in 1905, and his brother Thomas were once again a financial resource for the Black Sox. Smith's Hotel, moreover, was important not simply for its role in Negro League baseball history but also in African American history. The Smith brothers started the business simultaneous with the infamous "Segregation Ordinances," which Garret Power, a reporter for the *Sun*, describes as "Apartheid Baltimore Style" and which became the model for de-juro segregation throughout the South.[27] In May of 1913, shortly after the hotel opened, the *Afro-American* featured a guest column

Dr. Howard Young in his pharmacy on Druid Hill Avenue. In the first decades of the twentieth century, Druid Hill Avenue was the home to a rising African American middle class. The Druid Hill area also housed numerous African American businesses, including Smith's Hotel and the offices of the *Afro-American* (courtesy Maryland Historical Society).

that communicated the hotel's importance for the African American community nationwide: "I am stopping at a real hotel, one of the best in the country for my people. It is the Smith's Hotel on Druid Hill Avenue. It reminds me that when I was a boy [I] never dreamed of my people owning hotels, for I thought they were only for white folk."[28] The Smith brothers were on the front lines of the racial conflict, at the interface between African American self-assertion and legislative opposition to advancement. In 1903, the *Sun* labeled them "Lawless Negroes," libeling the family with accusations of voter fraud and of bribing public officials.[29]

The establishment of the Baltimore Black Sox occurred in the context of heightened racial tensions in the city. Simultaneously, the city began to enact laws designed to restrict opportunities for its African American citizens, and those African American citizens began to establish successful businesses in the city, creating opportunities for African Americans. Some

51

of those most prominent businessmen provided the team with financial security. They were Baltimore's "black cultural elite," and part of a larger, national movement to educate and empower African Americans in the early twentieth century. For these men, some of whom had been enslaved, empowerment was much more than an intellectual ideal: It was also an imperative. The Baltimore Black Sox, likewise, had been a franchise that a certain kind of "white ownership" had sought to "take over" and "run." The club's emergence, with a new name that embraced and proclaimed its racial makeup, taken together with the financial resources of the city's "colored" citizens, was ready to demonstrate not only the team's excellence but also what African Americans could achieve given the opportunity.

Colored Champions of the South

Opening Day was a celebration by and of Baltimore's African American community.

The newspapers described "large and enthusiastic crowds" at Oriole Park, marking the "opening games of the Colored Baseball League."[30] The League put on a showcase, sending the Brooklyn Royal Giants and the Cuban Giants to play a series of games against each other and against the Black Sox on May 8, 9, and 10. Unlike the Baltimore Giants' season opener in 1909, the mayor did not attend nor is there evidence to suggest he had been invited. Racial tensions were at a higher pitch in 1913 than they were in 1909.

James Preston was mayor of Baltimore from 1911 to 1919. He advocated segregation and enforced Baltimore's segregation laws.

3. *The Baltimore Black Sox: 1913–17*

Mayor Mahool may have been the architect of Baltimore's segregation ordinances, but mayor James Preston enforced them. Demonstrating his hatred of African Americans, the *Afro-American* published the details of his refusal to shake the hands of graduates of "The Colored High School" during their 1911 commencement. Rosa Linberry, a student at the school, would not accept the insult. She "slipped her right hand" into the mayor's limp hand. He then "gave a slight shake." The graduates roared their approval of their classmate's action.[31] A series of games by African American teams at Oriole Park, in a traditionally white neighborhood, could not have pleased such a man.

Nonetheless, the opening series of games was a success and a celebration of Baltimore's African American community's achievement. Not only did the best teams in the league come to the city, but city councilman Harry Cummings threw out the first pitch "from the grandstand."[32]

Cummings was the first African American elected to office in Maryland, and his campaign was a response to an effort to isolate and disenfranchise the city's "colored" population: "The Democratic legislature in 1890 gerrymandered the city, placing a majority of colored voters in the old eleventh ward."[33] Seeing a chance to have an African American elected to the city council, Harry Cummings seized the opportunity. Like John R. Williams and the Smith brothers, Cummings made his home on Druid Hill Avenue. His presence at the Colored Professional League's opening series of games emphasized the achievement of the city's African American community despite legislative efforts to limit opportunities.

The Black Sox played 40 games in the Colored Professional League in 1913 and would continue to play African American professional teams in 1914, 1915, and 1916.[34] Evidence also indicates that they played games against local and regional semipro and amateur clubs as well. The Black Sox played their home games not only at Oriole Park but also at Union League Park, their old home in South Baltimore, and at Back River Park, in Baltimore County. Jack Dunn, the Orioles' owner and manager, had built Back River Park to circumvent the city's restrictive Blue Laws, which prohibited paid admission to sporting events on Sundays. Back River Park was located just outside the city limits and was bordered by Eastern Avenue, Diamond Point Road, and Oriole Way. Demand for the venue was intense. That the Black Sox were a regular fixture on Sundays reveals their drawing power, and, indeed, "large crowds witnessed the games" the Black Sox played there.[35] The team's popularity, "with over three thousand" regularly attending, enabled them to give back to their community with regular charity games, benefiting local hospitals.[36] For games away from home, against semipro and amateur teams, the Black Sox were paid a "bonus," in the absence of gate receipts. They would refuse to play if the "promised bonus" was not paid.[37]

At the height of the team's popularity, during a series against the Lincoln Stars in July 1916, they "played before the largest crowds that ever saw two colored teams in" Baltimore. "The Elks convention being in session down there [South Baltimore], many white people were present at all the games."[38] The Black Sox had proven themselves on the playing field and proven that their appeal transcended racial boundaries, and, in 1916, they represented the best baseball Baltimore had to offer for a national audience. For the visiting Elks, the African Americans, and others who attended their games, the team bore "witness" to the abilities of African American professionals.

The club would achieve tremendous success on the field through the 1916 season, earning the Colored Championship of the South in 1913, 1914, and 1915.[39] In August 1915, the *Afro-American* began referring to them as "the famous Baltimore Black Sox."[40] A month later, "the manager of the Black Sox ... issued a challenge to any team in the state, white or colored."[41] Neither the Orioles nor the Baltimore Terrapins of the Federal League answered the challenge.

Evidence suggests that the Black Sox style of play was consistent with the "fast ball" played by the Weldons and Giants, characterized by strong pitching, solid if not stellar defense, and aggressive baserunning. Out-of-town papers commented on the team's skill. The *Indianapolis Freeman*, noted that the Black Sox "star third baseman ... made one of the greatest barehanded catches behind third base."[42] The *Baltimore Afro-American* describes another impressive play: "Johnson threw the ball from deep center catching" the runner "at the plate."[43]

What box scores survive reveal tantalizing clues regarding the club's on-field performance. Some record four double plays in a game.[44] Another offers evidence that four separate Black Sox stole a base in a single game.[45] The team's achievements were so impressive that it became news when they lost. The *Indianapolis Freeman* ran the headline "Black Sox Defeated" above the story of the team's "third defeat ... in thirty-one games."[46] In their inaugural season, they had bested "all the colored teams of Washington and Virginia" and "were eating everything up ... [that] summer."[47] They offered some of the best baseball in Baltimore, not simply the best semiprofessional or "colored" baseball in the city.

Despite their popularity and the quality of their play, the Black Sox showed signs of decline after a few years. In 1914, the team boasted "new uniforms" for the players, but, over the next couple of seasons, the team's finances deteriorated.[48] Whereas in 1913 ownership allocated funds to "strengthen" the club "by the addition of several out of town stars," in April 1916, the Dixie Giants "secured one of the greatest colored pitchers in the country,"[49] buying him from the Black Sox. A year earlier, management had let the team down. The Black Sox failed to appear at a home game at Union League Park, leaving fans "disappointed."[50] The team had to forfeit the box office receipts for that game. Quality of play on the field also began to decline. For the first time, the Black Sox did not win the Colored Championship of the South. However, the team retained its core players, including Matthews, Lewis, Thomas, and Evans. They were still a good draw; witness the games during the Elks Convention in July 1916.

However, by 1917, newspaper coverage and, therefore, information about the club becomes scarce. A notice placed in the *Afro-American* on April 7 indicates that the Black Sox "have grounds at East and Federal streets." The notice promises to "publish [updates] every week."[51] A box score, dated April 16, offers some details of what was likely the opening game of the season. It contains some familiar names, including June Matthews and Charles Thomas.[52] On April 28, an additional notice advertised a forthcoming doubleheader against a local semipro team but no additional notices would appear until October.[53] In 1917, H. L. Harris served as the team's business manager, and the club's offices were located at 521 Orchard Road.[54] There are no known records that offered clues as to Harris's identity.[55] However, it is likely the team was still under African American ownership, as the 500 block of Orchard Street was in an African American neighborhood and just a three-minute walk from Smith's Hotel and the offices of the *Afro-American*.

The Black Sox owners had started successful businesses outside of baseball, and they had achieved remarkable success in the private sector, especially considering public policy, which sought to limit opportunities for African Americans. By the end of the 1917 season, it was clear that the team, if it were to experience continued success, needed an owner with better knowledge of how to run a successful baseball business. In 1917, Howard Young and the Smith brothers would step away from the Black Sox, ending four years of African American ownership of the franchise.

4.

"Brains and Money": 1917–20

In October 1920, Rube Foster sat "smoking his pipe, in the stands of the Westport Baseball Grounds."[1] Foster spoke with confidence and authority on African American baseball. He also possessed a commanding physical presence. Harry Williams, writing for the *Los Angeles Times*, characterized Foster as a "human mastodon," weighing "something like a million pounds" and measuring "about seven feet across the shoulders."[2] A reporter for the *Baltimore Afro-American* described him as "the greatest baseball magnate the race has yet produced, and he not only looks it, but acts it."[3]

Foster had come east with his Chicago American Giants to play a best-of-nine series against the Atlantic City Bacharach Giants. The games would take place in Washington, D.C.; Baltimore; Wilmington, Delaware; Philadelphia; and New York. The series was advertised as "the World's Colored Championship."[4] It was a publicity tour, designed to market Foster's newly formed Negro National League.[5] For Foster, the series also provided an opportunity to judge the viability of a league on the East Coast, a possibility that did not escape the reporter for the *Afro-American* who noted that "what baseball needs in the East more than anything else is a League corresponding to the Western Circuit."[6] The anonymous reporter, admittedly intimidated by Foster, "ventured" to ask him a question.[7] The reporter's hesitancy is understandable; Henry Williams wrote that a batter "who will stand up to the plate with him [Foster] pitching deserves a medal for bravery."[8] The *Afro-American* reporter asked, "What are the necessary requisites for a championship baseball team?" Without hesitation, Foster replied, "Brains and Money.... You cannot keep good players without paying them good salaries, and the best team of individual players is not worth much, if there is not team work and team leadership."[9] Foster spoke in general terms, but he also described, perhaps knowingly, Charles P. Spedden, who had acquired the Black Sox in the fall of 1917. In three years, he would

56

put the team on a solid financial footing and build its on-field talent to a level commensurate with other professional "colored" teams.

In celebrating Spedden, it is important to note that Wallace Smith, his brother Thomas, and Howard Young were brilliant and successful businessmen. They had to have both determination and "brains," to borrow Foster's word, to build their business in the hostile racial climate that permeated the city in the first decades of the twentieth century. Robert Hall and H. H. Lee, the owners of the Baltimore Giants, were also intelligent and successful men. Foster was not speaking of just business acumen. Certainly, business sense comprised part of his definition. A key component in Foster's conception of intelligent ownership also involved an intimate understanding of baseball.[10] Charles Spedden had baseball intelligence and business acumen. He also had access to the financial resources to make the team a success.

"Black Sox Park"

On September 23, 1917, an announcement appeared in the *Baltimore Sun*: "The Mt Clare All-Stars will play the Black Sox two games today at Westport."[11] Weeks later, on October 14, the paper ran a short note, announcing the "first round of a series of games to be played at the Baltimore and Ohio Park, Westport, between the All-Stars of the Semi-Pro League and the champion Black Sox."[12] In retrospect, these stories offer the first clues that Charles Spedden and his partner, William Brauer, had taken over day-to-day operations of the team and also that the Black Sox' fortunes had been revived. The number of games they played began to increase with each passing year. The local press, including the *Baltimore Sun* and the *Baltimore American*, but most especially the *Afro-American*, began to cover the team with increasing frequency, and they, according to the papers, began to recruit more talented players and to cultivate a larger fan base.[13] After that October announcement, "Baltimore and Ohio" never appears on any notice, box score, article, or ad for the Black Sox. Further, by 1919, the local press begins to refer to the Westport Baseball Grounds as "Black Sox Park."[14] After four sometimes difficult seasons, the team had found a home.

Charles Spedden provided that home field for the Black Sox: In his words, he "took them off the lot and put them in an enclosed park."[15] He had a flair for promotion and an eye for on-field talent. Spedden was born on December 22, 1875, and grew up on Calhoun Street, a short walk from

B&O Railroad's Mt. Clare Station, where his father, Vincent, worked. Charles' mother, Mary, stayed home and looked after her father-in-law and tended to her four children, two boys and two girls.[16] Spedden would train as a clerk and work for various companies in the city before taking a job with the B&O Railroad in 1909, working in their coal and coke receipts office.[17] He also had a long history as a player, manager, and business manager with regional sandlot and semipro baseball teams, such as "The Acmes," the Gilbert Brothers Company team, the Armstrong Cork Company team, the court clerk's team, the Jefferson County Club, and the Coal and Coke division team of the B&O Railroad.[18] Clearly, Spedden had a passion for the game and possessed the type of baseball mind Rube Foster would have found essential for a successful team.

William Brauer, Spedden's partner with the Black Sox, was also his coworker at the railroad. Born on April 5, 1889, he was the son of German immigrants and grew up in neighborhoods near the Inner Harbor and Patterson Park.[19] Although he did not have experience playing for and managing local clubs, Brauer did enjoy baseball. He would participate in non-competitive games at B&O's family picnics.[20] His role with the team in those early days, was, most likely, more of a financial partner than a manager or business manager. The newspapers, when discussing the club's baseball operations, only mention Spedden.

In the winter of 1916–17, the B&O Railroad asked Charles Spedden to direct the business affairs of their semipro team and also of their new field, the Westport Baseball Grounds, which had been built the previous year as a showcase for competition in the "Semi-Professional Baseball League of Baltimore.... The grounds of the club are located at Clare Street and Maryland Avenue [now Annapolis Road].... Stands have been erected for the comfort of spectators [and] a fence completely encloses the grounds."[21]

Spedden saw the potential of the site. He "enlarged" the playing field "to nearly three times its original size" and supervised the construction of a "new grandstand seating 2,400."[22] Unlike Union League Park or even Oriole Park (Terrapin Park), Westport Park was not limited by a grid of surrounding streets and the resulting field was "the largest park in Baltimore."[23]

The location, along Maryland Avenue (now Annapolis Road) had been a recreational destination for Baltimore's African American community since December 1907. At a time of rising racial tensions in the city, Westport, a mix of white, working class neighborhoods and industry, would have been accustomed to African Americans in the largely industrial areas just south of the city line. Moreover, African Americans would

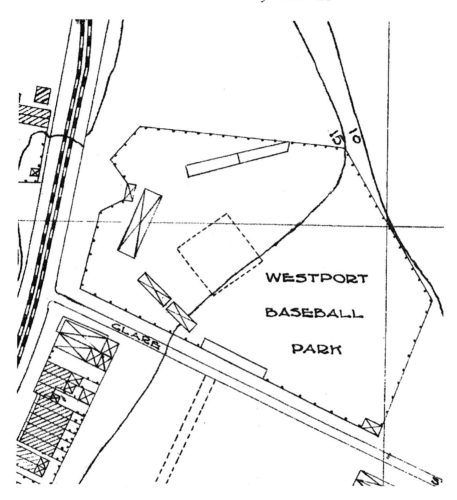

The detail from a topographical map shows how Westport Park would have looked in 1920, with three sections of covered grandstands and three open bleachers, giving it a capacity of about 5,000 (Maryland Topographical Survey Commission, 1920).

have felt comfortable traveling through those working-class neighborhoods to arrive in Westport.

In December 1907, John Kirby, who had purchased the Westport Skating Palace, announced the "Grand Opening" of the "Westport Colored Skating Rink."[24] A few months later, he opened the "Westport Rink Colored Theatre."[25]

SUCCESS

Westport Rink Colored Theatre

Every Evening at 9 o'clock.   10, 20 and 30 Cents.

Second glorious week, Starting *→* MONDAY, JUNE 29th

S. H. DUDLEY

And Swell Set Stock Company.

——In the Big Musical Frolic——

The Man From Bam

Everything New.   {FUN, MUSIC
A Carnival of....   {AND SONG.

The big Chorus of Dusky Damsels that drive ♪♪ away the Blues. ♪♪

EXTRA! ......Attractions on...... JULY 4th.
DONT MISS THE GALA DAY

Note—Special car service after Performance.

Direct wire from Gans-Nelson fight at Frisco.   Returns given out during Performance.

SUCCESS

The advertisement contains a border proclaiming "SUCCESS,"[26] part of an ad and print media campaign to generate interest in the theater. Articles appeared announcing that for "the first time in the history of the Afro-American in Baltimore a theatre has been opened where they can enjoy themselves to the fullest extent."[27]

For the next five years, the Westport Colored Skating Rink and Theatre drew large crowds for social and sporting events. The "Amazon Park" opened across the street and hosted African American community events such as picnics and church gatherings. Unfortunately, the establishment was unable to sustain its success as a recreational facility. By 1913, the former skating palace had fallen on hard times.

EXCURSIONS & PICNICS

HELP the Cadet Boys. A Grand Military Picnic, given by the Knights of Pythian Cadets, at Amazon Park, Westport, the new colored Park, opposite the skating rink, July 15th, 1909. Prof. Louis Gearing's Peerless Orchestra. Tickets 15 cents. Committee: Brig. Gen. George H. Carter, Major Charles E. Gladden, 510 Myrtle avenue; Major Wm. Haynes, Capt. Samuel Wright, Col. Samuel William, Chief Louis A. Williams, Col. Wm. Grayson.

Amazon Park opened in 1909 to cater to the African American community. The Westport Rink and the park helped to establish Westport as a recreational center for African Americans at a time of heightened racial tensions Baltimore. They also laid the foundation for the Black Sox in Westport (*Afro-American*).

It had become a center for illegal betting and gambling that exploited the African American community: "The men operating them [casino games] ... almost without exception were white men; almost without exception, the victims were Negroes."[28] Although Kirby sold the rink the following year, it could never regain its standing within the African American community. However, it had established Westport as a center for recreational activity.[29]

The Westport Baseball Grounds inherited the infrastructure that

Opposite: **Although the Palace Rink was originally built for a white middle-class clientele, by 1907 the Westport Rink catered almost exclusively to African Americans. The note at the bottom of the advertisement promises a "direct wire" on the Joe Gans-Battling Nelson fight. Gans would win that match, their second meeting (*Afro-American*).**

served the skating rink. A streetcar line (see topographical map) ran past the park along Annapolis Road; it was about a ten-minute ride from Baltimore and Liberty streets in center city.[30]

The Black Sox were also the beneficiaries of a convenient business arrangement. Charles Spedden, as Black Sox owner, leased the baseball grounds from himself, as the agent for the railroad. It was a classic case of conflict of interest but one that helped the Black Sox. It is likely that the railroad also profited from gate receipts. The Black Sox brought in more revenue for the baseball grounds than they would have otherwise generated. There is an irony, nonetheless, in B&O's association with the team in light of its recent segregation policies and forced relocation of African Americans.[31] Moreover, the Black Sox were no longer run by African Americans, but it becomes clear that Spedden had more than simply a financial interest in the club. Unlike the white ownership that purchased the Baltimore Giants in 1912, Spedden had no desire to "take over" African American baseball in the city. He wanted to develop a successful baseball team and no evidence suggests that he had a racial agenda. It will become clear that he came into ownership with certain prejudices; it will also become clear that he was able to grow as a person, perhaps because of his association with the team.

1918: "The team may be crippled somewhat"

When Charles Spedden took over the franchise, the club's success was by no means assured. The 1918 season would present two challenges for him and the Black Sox—one he would most surely have known and another that he likely could not have anticipated. He most certainly knew that the team had fallen on hard times; that was the first problem. Newspaper coverage had declined locally and almost disappeared nationally in 1917. The home field, the Simpson and Doeller Oval, was located on the east side of the city, far away from the team's base in the African American community and on a site not well served by public transit. With the Westport Grounds, Spedden was able to address a part of the problem. He would have to face the difficult task of reconnecting with the team's fans and of reestablishing the team's reputation in the city. He did have, however, one significant asset: the players. The core of the team had remained intact, even through recent struggles. He could count on men such as June Matthews, Charles Evans, Charles Thomas, and O. J. Barbour. That is, he thought he could count on them until the second problem arose. The United States entered the First World War, and, "as some of the best players of the Black Sox have been drafted, the team may be crippled somewhat."[32] The men who had been drafted also faced new challenges.

"Soldiers must not ask for legal rights"

The ballplayers who reported to Camp Meade for training had to confront racism, but, as they had in baseball, they also forced a racist society to confront the bankruptcy of its prejudices. Just as on the ball field, African American soldiers performed exceptionally well and were a source of pride for the African American community. The April 5, 1918, edition of the *Afro-American* would normally cover spring training. It carried no baseball stories. Instead, the paper's lead headline, immediately below its masthead, declared, "Colored troopers at Camp Meade drilling." The paper gave the soldiers a distinguished title. The term *trooper* was traditionally associated with a member of a cavalry unit and would have reminded readers of the Buffalo Soldier regiments formed just after the Civil War. That the troopers were "drilling" indicates that they were preparing for combat rather than for support positions as cooks or in maintenance.

THE AFRO-AMERICAN, BALTIMROE, MD. FRIDAY, APRIL 5th, 1918.

COLORED TROOPERS AT CAMP MEADE DRILLING

Members of the Baltimore Black Sox trained in Camp Meade for military service (*Baltimore Afro-American*).

They would be on the front lines, serving next to white soldiers. Below the headline, the *Afro* published a panoramic photo showing neat lines of troopers, in proper uniforms, well kept, and with rifles and bayonets.

African American non-commissioned officers (NCOs) took the troopers through their drills. The men looked and conducted themselves as soldiers.[33] A few months earlier, the *Afro-American* ran a story that stressed the significance of that achievement. The paper quoted Colonel James A. Moss, of the 367th Infantry, who stated that "colored" soldiers are "100% American," and not second-class citizens or 3/5th of a man. The paper added, "Our men are going to fight beside the white man," not in supporting roles.[34] The troopers demonstrated their equality and confronted a society with the reality that unequal treatment was inappropriate.

African American leadership took notice. Emmett Scott, who had been an advisor to Booker T. Washington and founded the National Negro Business League, served as a special advisor to president Woodrow Wilson's secretary of war. He wrote that a soldier developed "a keener and more sharply defined consciousness, not only of his duties as a citizen, but of his rights and privileges as a citizen."[35] Scott's observations were not an overt threat to a racist society, but the implications are clear. James Weldon Johnson, poet and author of "Lift Ev'ry Voice and Sing," known as the "Negro National Anthem," spoke of the potential benefits that the war would bring to the African American community. The Baltimore chapter of the NAACP, headed by former Black Sox owner Howard Young, sponsored a lecture by Weldon Johnson at the Metropolitan M. E. Church on

A Stirring Lecture
"What the War has done for the Negro"
By JAMES WELDON JOHNSON, of New York
Ex-Consul to Corinto, Nicataga
Sunday, April 7th, 1918, 8 p. m.
At Metropolitan M. E. Chrrch
Orchard Street near Druid Hill Ave.
Under Auspices of National Association of Advancement
For Colored People.

Many African American leaders saw the First World War as an opportunity to demonstrate the abilities of African Americans and to combat prejudice and racism (*Baltimore Afro-American*).

THE AFRO-AMERICAN, BALTIMROE, MD. FRIDAY, APRIL 12, 1918

Camp Meade Who Are in Training to Make the World Safe for Democracy. Batter

TAKES
RE BY STORM

SOLDIERS MUST
NOT ASK FOR
LEGAL RIGHTS

7th Annual Clinic of
Andrew Rankin Hospital

ORGANIC UNION
BY COLOR

Despite the equal treatment African Americans received during training, many soldiers faced discrimination and bigotry once their active service started (*Baltimore Afro-American*).

the corner of Orchard Street and Druid Hill Avenue, a short walk from Smith's Hotel.

Johnson declared that the war would lead to "greater freedom and fuller democracy for colored people." He hoped for an end to lynching, increased money for education, an end to police persecution, and an equal distribution of municipal benefits. He also warned that advancements would attract the attention of "forces opposed to the Negro."[36]

The *Afro-American* confronted part of that reality in its April 12, 1918, edition. Below the masthead, the *Afro* published a panoramic photo of the 351st.

White officers sit in the center of the photo, while African American troopers and their NCOs stand at the back and sit or kneel on the margins. A headline, whose irony could not have been unintentional, declares that African American men are "in training to make the world safe for democracy."[37] In the center of the page, just above the fold and just below the white officers, the center-lede announces, "Soldiers must not ask for legal rights." The story explains how a "Negro NCO" asserted his rights to sit in a theater while on leave. His white officer explained how while the NCO was legally corrected, he should have anticipated that his behavior would "provoke" a response. The officer goes on to explain that African American soldiers should "not go where" their "presence is not desired."[38] Forces in society and the army, as Weldon Johnson and Scott had intimated, would attempt to reassert control of African Americans and put them back in their place.

"The Big Noise of the Season"

Charles Spedden's focus had to be on fielding a competitive team and protecting his investment. He could not afford the prejudices asserting themselves in the military and in the culture at large. With his best players training for the war, Spedden would compensate in part by arranging for them to join the team when they were on leave; there is no doubt he "desired their presence." For an important game late in the season, Charles Thomas would "come up from Camp Meade to catch."[39] For another game, also late in the year, an article in the *Sun* noted that the Black Sox will be "strengthened by seven of their former players, who will come up from Camp Meade."[40] Spedden also embraced the public relations opportunities. In an advertisement, he asked that fans, "[c]ome out and show your appreciation for the boys over there." He had arranged for a "Patriotic Address" to proceed the raising of "service flag containing 12 stars ... in honor of the members of the Black Sox Base Ball Team who have heard the call of Uncle Sam."[41] In another stroke of marketing genius, Spedden arranged for games between the Black Sox and an "all-star team from Camp Meade," comprised of "several former Black Sox players."[42] Although his strategies might strengthen the ballclub for a game or two and would certainly draw fans to the ballpark, Spedden also took a long-term approach to keep the Black Sox competitive.

He scouted and recruited new players. *The Afro-American* reported that the Black Sox "lost a number of valuable men during the season on account of the draft, but have managed at all times to place men in their line-up to maintain their standard of playing."[43] The team's most valuable additions were pitchers: "Pastor" Pedro Morales, Ping Gardner, and Doc Sykes. No known records reveal where Spedden found Gardner, but he was an unmitigated success, "winning eight of his ... nine games." He was "an underhand curveball pitcher."[44] Frank "Doc" Sykes was born in Decatur, Alabama, and graduated from Howard University's School of Dentistry. He paid his way through school by working as a "red cap at Union Station" and pitching for the Lincoln Stars, an African American semiprofessional team based in New York.[45] Sykes was a "spitball pitcher who threw at three speeds—slow, slower and slowest."[46] The papers called Morales "the Cuban star."[47] He was a right-hander who had done well against major-league teams touring Cuba while pitching for Almendares.[48] He had also pitched for the Cuban Stars and for a semipro team in Altoona, Pennsylvania.[49] Morales would not play for the Black Sox after the 1918 season. Sykes and Gardner, however, would become fixtures on the team's staff. Spedden had shown an aptitude not only for scouting and recruiting but also for building a new team around pitching to compensate for the players lost to military service.

In addition to scouting and signing new players, Spedden reestablished the team's reputation in the Baltimore baseball community. He arranged a schedule made up almost exclusively of local amateur, corporate, and semipro clubs such as the Albrecht Athletic Association, the Country Lads, the Irvington Club, and the B&O Railroad's Baltimore division.[50] The Black Sox also made sure to schedule the Yannigans,[51] regarded by many as the best semipro team in the city. In hosting these clubs in Westport, Spedden ensured their good will, as the visitors would receive a portion of the gate receipts. Spedden had made the Black Sox and their home field the center of the city's semipro baseball community.

At the end of the season, Spedden staged the "Championship of Baltimore," to be held at the Westport Grounds. The Black Sox would play a series of games against an all-star team made up of "the amateur and semi-pro baseball clubs" in the city. The winning team would receive a silver cup and the players on that team would have a share in $25 in gold.[52] In an advertisement, he declared, "If you fail to witness these games [the championship series], you will … [lose] the opportunity of seeing some of the best exhibition of baseball ever given in this city."[53] In the space of a year, he not only resurrected the club but restored it to prominence.

Spedden also worked hard to win over and to renew the team's relationship with the African American community. In the first five years of the Black Sox history, the team had only taken out a single advertisement in the *Afro-American*—John R. Williams's announcement of the Black Sox as Baltimore's first colored professional team. In 1918, Charles Spedden took out nine "display ads." Just as Williams had used the team's first ad to assert the club's presence both in the city's baseball community and in the African American community, Spedden used the ads to create an image of the team as a source of pride for the community. The Black Sox were "the Big Noise of the Season," winners of "19 out of 20 games, and still going."[54] They were the "Colored Champions of the South."[55] In those advertisements, Spedden sought to show that the Black Sox were a part of the city's African American community; the ads spoke of "our record."[56] By extension then, the team's success meant the community's success.

The Black Sox finished 1918 with a record of 35–5, with three of "those losses by one run."[57] They defeated the all-stars of the Blue Ridge League, a Class D minor league made up of white professional ballplayers, by scores of "21 to 5 and 18 to 3."[58] Thousands came to see the team's games in Westport, so much so that Spedden built two new grandstands. The first expansion added 1,000 seats and the second added 500.[59] The Black Sox were poised to develop their reputation and fan base in subsequent seasons. The new year, 1919, boded well for the club. Many of their star players would return from military service. They were on a firm financial footing, and their home ballpark was one of the largest and best in the city.

1919: Black Sox "to test their strength"

As Opening Day approached, the newspapers declared that the Black Sox "players who were in France with Uncle Sam's boys have returned home,"[60] and the fans were ready to welcome the "Colored Troopers ... from overseas."[61] By mid–July, the team was complete: "Charles Thomas their hard-hitting catcher" was back from France, and the Black Sox were ready "to test their strength" not only against local clubs but also against regional teams from Pennsylvania, Delaware, and Virginia.[62] The team was not the same as it had been prior to the war. The Black Sox released O. J. Barbour and June Matthews, who had been with the club since its days as the Weldons.

The most notable addition was Scrappy Brown, who was "rated as the best colored infielder playing the national game."[63] Born Malcolm Elmore Brown on July 18, 1899, he grew up in Sparrows Point, home to Bethlehem Steel's shipbuilding and steelmaking headquarters.[64] His father, Andrew, worked as a rigger in the shipyards. Andrew's sister Carrie ran a boarding house and looked after Scrappy and his sister Bertha.[65] Brown was known not only for his fielding, but also for his speed and his ability to put the ball in play.[66] He would become a fixture in the Black Sox lineup and play for Negro League teams into the mid–1920s. William Nunn, writing for the *Pittsburgh Courier*, described Brown as "high above the average shortstop as a giraffe's head is above a turtle's." Nunn described Brown's trademark play: "Brown, running low, gracefully and at top speed scooped up a hard hit ball over second base with one hard, transferred it to the other in a split second, and whipped it true and hard to first without an instant's hesitation." Brown "could run, throw and field balls sensationally. He was a hawk for fly balls. And he had fire, dash, and personality."[67] He was a homegrown talent who would carry the Black Sox from a local power-house to a team with a national reputation. Other standouts on that 1919 team included Joe Lewis and Ping Gardner. Lewis continued to develop as a ballplayer, playing mostly third base. He was batting over .400 into September, and his defense "electrified" spectators.[68] Gardner emerged as the team's ace, winning 19 consecutive games.[69]

J. B. Hairstone was not a new addition, but he was essential to the team's success. He managed the club in 1918 and in 1919, also filling in for Charles Thomas as catcher until he returned from service. With a record of 83 wins and 11 losses, Hairstone deserved much of the credit for the team's success in the first two years under Spedden's ownership. Hairstone was born on April 6, 1891, in Martinsville, Virginia. His parents, Manual and Frances, could neither read nor write and were likely born into slavery in the 1850s.[70] He worked as a driver at the Sparrows Point shipyards and lived on J Street, a neighbor of Scrappy Brown[71]; Hairstone then likely deserves credit for drawing the young shortstop to Charles Spedden's attention. Hairstone described his managerial philosophy as making sure "every man on the club knows his position and what is expected of him," and that each player "works as a component part of the whole." He let his players know that as "manager [he] might see things in a different light and suggest plays that are diametrically opposed to the wishes of the men." Writing for the *Afro-American*, G. L. Mackay called Hairstone "the brainiest ball player to cavort around a diamond."[72] Hairstone coached the Black Sox without the benefit of many of the club's on-field leaders in 1918, integrating new players into the lineup and helping them form a cohesive unit. In 1919, he managed the return of veteran players and the transition to a younger team.

Unlike the 1918 season, when they played almost exclusively against local teams at the Westport Grounds, the Black Sox tested themselves against regional teams on the road. In August, they played teams in "Norfolk, Newport News, and Richmond."[73] They also booked home and away series against their old rival, the Philadelphia Giants, and the Wilmington Giants, "known as one of the best colored teams in and around the state of Pennsylvania."[74] The Wilmington team took the rivalry seriously, with a "large crowd" of their fans accompanying them to Westport.[75] The Black Sox were deliberately expanding their regional presence and cultivating relationships and rivalries with the best African American semiprofessional clubs in the Mid-Atlantic.

The Black Sox played their final game of the 1919 season against a reformed Weldon Giants team with June Matthews serving as manager and O. J. Barbour starting in center field.[76] It was a generous move on the part of the Black Sox and a gesture to the team's past and to the men who contributed much to the development of the franchise. Building on that base and under the leadership of Spedden and Hairstone, the Baltimore Black Sox had emerged as an elite semiprofessional club. Their pitching and their defense, particularly with Lewis and Brown at third and short, rivaled any professional African American team in the nation. The Black Sox finished the 1919 season with a record of 47–6.[77] The 1920 season would witness the growth of the franchise and lay the groundwork for a professional league in the east.

Simultaneously, the Black Sox and their home field in Westport became a fixture in Baltimore's and in the region's sporting geography. With expanded grandstands and additional seating capacity, the Westport Grounds that fall and winter played host to football games between clubs from Richmond to Philadelphia.[78] Of particular note, an ad in the *Afro-American* published in late October called the Westport Grounds "Black Sox Park."[79] The team and their home field had established themselves as an integral part of the city.

1920: "Coming like a house afire"

There were some notable departures after the 1919 season: Ping Gardner left to join the Brooklyn Royal Giants, and Scrappy Brown left to play with Hilldale for 13 games in September, only to return to Baltimore by the end of the season.[80] However, the core group of players that formed the 1919 Black Sox returned for the 1920 season. Charles Thomas was the Opening Day catcher and took over as the team's on-field manager.[81] The former manager, J. B. Hairstone, remained with the team and took over from Thomas as the starting catcher after he took a foul ball off his hand in July.[82] Both Hairstone and Thomas guided Joe Lewis's development as a catcher.[83] Lewis also continued to play third and second.

Doc Sykes stabilized the rotation. Other players developed into stars or were added to the team. Raymond Jasper "Jim" Hodges emerged as the team's ace, at one point winning 12 consecutive games.[84] Hodges was born in Hope Mills, North Carolina, and had pitched in one game for the Black Sox in 1918, allowing four runs but winning the game.[85] In 1919, he pitched the second game of a doubleheader, allowing one hit over five innings in a rain-shortened contest.[86] The following year was his breakthrough season. In midseason, the Black Sox added Darknight Smith to their rotation. Also known as "Midnight" and "Blacknight," he "pitched for Pittsburgh and several larger Northern teams."[87] His acquisition answered the club's need for a third starting pitcher as they began to compete against the elite African American teams. The newspapers described him as "the man with the 'fast' fast ball and 'slow' slow ball."[88] When he was on the mound, fans were told to "set back and gaze at a pitching treat."[89]

Harry Williams was the team's new starting third baseman. He had a strong arm but "demonstrated a little slowness at third at the beginning of the season, but [then] ... showed steady improvement."[90] Lefty Smith, the team's new left fielder, was a Baltimore native. He came from the Sandtown section of West Baltimore and grew up on Calhoun Street, not far from Spedden's childhood home. He was the youngest of six children. His father, Charles, was a coachman, and his mother, Sally, took in laundry to help support the family.[91] He was tall and slender. When he wasn't playing baseball, he took a job in the Baltimore Copper Works.[92] Blainey Hall, a member of the 1913 team, was also a local prospect. He was the youngest of three children, born in Ellicott City, Maryland.[93] His father, Caleb, was a farm laborer, and his mother did laundry for a "private family."[94] The 1920 census lists his occupation as a "salaried" and a "baseball player."[95] Randolph "Buck" Ridgely, the second baseman and leadoff hitter,[96] came to the Black Sox from the Brooklyn Royal Giants.[97] In mid–July, the *Afro-American* assessed the team: "all of the team's victories have been due to the pitching of Sykes and Hodges and the batting of Thomas and Hall. The latter is a natural slugger [and] bats either right or left handed.... In the outfield, the Black Sox have in Smith, Hall, and Evans a trio of performers who have not been beaten in covering ground ... and all of them are good batters."[98] The team's scouting and player development deserve special recognition. It's impossible to know the details, but it is likely that a trio of current and former catchers (Spedden, Thomas, and Hairstone) deserve the bulk of the credit.

The 1920 season demonstrated that the Black Sox outclassed and outplayed every amateur and semiprofessional team in the city, state, and region. The *Washington Evening Star* called the Black Sox "the strongest Colored baseball aggregation in the South."[99] They started the year by winning 24 of their first 27 games.[100] By midsummer, they had "hung up a string of victories a yard long" and were "coming like a house afire."[101] At the end of the season, the *Baltimore American* noted that the "Black Sox had not lost a series to a local team in three years."[102] Charles Spedden had rebuilt the Black Sox into the most dominant semiprofessional baseball club, African American or otherwise, in the region. But he had greater ambitions.

Although the Black Sox would continue to play local clubs throughout the season, starting in late June, they began to play the bulk of their games against the strongest African American teams on the East Coast, traveling as far south as Fayetteville, North Carolina, and as far north as Buffalo, New York. The Black Sox managed to split the series against the Pittsburgh Colored Stars of Buffalo on the strength of pitching and defense: "a triple play that checked a Pittsburgh rally in the fourth inning materially aided the Baltimore Black Sox in winning."[103] The Colored Stars had defeated the Toronto Maple Leafs of the International League, 7–0, in an exhibition game. The Maple Leafs would go on to win 108 games that season, finishing second to the Baltimore Orioles, who won 110. The Colored Stars' victory in that game had marked them as a premier African American team in the East, and, that the Black Sox played the Stars to a series tie, demonstrated that the Black Sox were also a premier club. They were somewhat less successful in the three games played in Fayetteville, North Carolina; they won only one game.[104] In those games, the Black Sox pitching and defense performed well. They lost the third game of the series, 1–0, on a controversial balk call in the ninth inning that gave the Fayetteville Red Sox the game and the series.[105] Games against clubs like the Colored Stars, the Fayetteville Red Sox, and other teams such as the Pennsylvania Red Caps, the Cuban Stars, and the Manhattan Giants showed that, in the words of the *Afro-American*, "Manager Thomas has one of the strongest semi-professional teams in the East."[106]

The Black Sox also played four of the teams that would in 1923 comprise the Eastern Colored League. The Black Sox experienced little success. They won only one game against the Brooklyn Royal Giants.[107] A headline in the *Afro-American* tells the story of their games against the New York Lincoln Giants: "New York Makes Clean Sweep."[108] For a Baltimore team that was accustomed to dominating their opponents, those games must have come as a shock. The newspapers were quick to offer advice: "Manager Thomas must relieve the pitchers more frequently," advised a sportswriter for the *Afro-American*.[109] Another story may have stuck at the heart of the Black Sox problems: "Man for man the Lincoln

Giants [are] not as strong a team as the Black Sox, but the Giants had team work and this counted."[110] The Black Sox would go on to lose two games to the Bacharach Giants in September when Baltimore's pitching and defense broke down.[111] Later in the season, they played well against Hilldale, winning the season series.[112] The games were an important test for the Black Sox. Certainly, as the papers noted, they had the personnel to compete, but they lacked experience. In the years leading up to the formation of the Eastern Colored League, the Black Sox would cultivate rivalries against these clubs, and, in the process, grow and develop as a team.

In addition, the Black Sox were able to establish themselves not simply as a regional powerhouse but also cultivate a regional fan base. They played games against other leading African American clubs in Washington, D.C., and attracted "a large and appreciative audience of colored and white citizens ... at the American League Park."[113] They also began to play games at Harlan Field in Wilmington, Delaware. The Harlan baseball grounds were comparable in size and seating capacity to Westport Park. Harlan Park opened on June 23, 1917, as the "new athletic park of the Harlan and Hollingsworth Corporation."[114]

In 1918, with the infusion of major-league players who were avoiding military service, the shipyard upgraded and expanded the ballpark to accommodate anticipated large crowds. The fans came and saw "Shoeless Joe" Jackson win the Shipyard League's batting title and lead Harlan and Hollingsworth to a championship. When the star players returned to the major leagues, Wilmington's appetite for baseball lingered and was satisfied by the Black Sox and other African American teams who came to Delaware, lured by the promise of large gate receipts. They were not disappointed. A game between the Black Sox and Hilldale attracted more than 5,000 fans: "Every available seat in the park was filled and the overflow extended in left and right fields."[115] The teams scheduled two additional games in Wilmington that season, attracting comparable crowds.[116] Although the fans came in part to satisfy a craving for high-quality baseball, as they also did in Washington, Delaware fans also came to delight in the success or failure of the Black Sox specifically.

They had nurtured a relationship with a team in Wilmington that shared their name and, consequently, had become players in a local heated rivalry between the Wilmington Black Sox and the Harlan Giants. In response to the Harlan Giants "padding" their roster with players from nearby Chester, Pennsylvania, the Wilmington Black Sox recruited six players from Baltimore, including Scrappy Brown, to play in their games against their rival. The Black Sox won that game and a few weeks later, the Baltimore Black Sox came to Wilmington for a previously scheduled game against the Harlan Giants, winning 9–0.[117] The Wilmington Black Sox took to the papers to publicly taunt Sammy "Chippy" Johnson, Harlan's manager: "Why don't you say something Chippy? You howled like a stuck pig while you were buried by the Wilmington Black Sox.... We know such a (fast?) team as the Harlan Giants must have an excellent alibi, when they even padded and went down to an ignominious defeat.... If you would only come out of your hole."[118] The Harlan Giants responded, also in the newspapers, by telling the Wilmington Black Sox to "put up or shut up," and challenged them to a series of games, involving only "local players." The winning team would also win a side bet of $500.[119] The rivalry made for good copy and roused the passions of Wilmington fans. It also enabled the Black Sox to generate interest in games played in Delaware, with fans channeling local loyalties into rooting interests for Baltimore or their opponents at Harlan Field.[120]

The Black Sox' record was 66–29 in 1920.[121] They had dominated the portion of their schedule devoted to local and regional teams and had played about even with the stronger African American clubs on the East Coast. For the first time, the team also published the season's batting records for Westport Park, making note of their new official scorer S. E. Cohen's diligence in tracking records for home games, as records for road games were unavailable. The press release notes that the Black Sox "batting averages were high considering the batting averages of players in the National and American Leagues due to the fact that professional players are up against stiffer pitching. Off the brand of pitching the Sox have been up against, every regular batter has been able to hit above .300." Blainey Hall led the team with a .587 average, collecting 128 hits in 218 at-bats. Harry Williams hit .579, and Charlie Thomas batted .437. Joe Lewis hit .400 and Lefty Smith batted .415. Charlie Evans led the team with 316 at-bats and his average was .376. Buck Ridgley hit 406.[122] Because of the club's success, its popularity, and the quality of its players, the Black Sox and Charles Spedden can rightly take credit for Rube Foster scheduling stops on his championship tour in Baltimore and in Wilmington. The Black Sox were "on the map" for African American baseball in the East.

They "shook the overcrowded stands"

Rube Foster attended one of the last games played at the Westport Baseball Grounds, the first field in Baltimore to go by the name "Black

Sox Park." From his vantage point in the stands, he would have seen, just to the north and across the Gwynns Falls, the Black Sox' new park, which had been under construction since February.[123] Baltimore, then, must have occupied a central place in his conception of a professional African American baseball league in the East.

Foster would put a premium on a club leasing or preferably owning their own ballpark. At the meetings that established the Negro National League in February of 1920, Foster insisted that the "circuit [the NNL] will not officially operate until each city has a park, either leased or owned."[124] Baltimore, in his view, almost certainly had the "brains and money" to support a successful franchise.

Rube Foster may have hinted as much in his interview with the *Afro-American*, and it was no secret that the Negro National League had filed articles of incorporation in Maryland.[125] That anonymous reporter who "ventured" to ask Rube Foster a question wrote a story markedly different than news coverage from the other cities on the American Giants championship tour of the East. That coverage sought to create excitement for a game and for the series, unlike the story in the *Afro-American*, which focused on the future of "colored" professional baseball. The *Washington Post* played up a local angle, letting its readers know "Tom Johnson, the District boy" would pitch for Foster's team.[126] Coverage in the *Evening Journal* (Wilmington, Delaware) insisted that it was "a game everybody should see."[127] Likewise, the *Courier News* (Bridgewater, New Jersey) pointed out "a crowd of 22,000" came to the American Giants' game against the Detroit Stars for the Western championship, suggesting that tickets for the "World Championship" would be at a premium.[128] The *New York Tribune* also engaged in a bit of salesmanship, announcing "[t]here will be a World Series game at Ebbets Field to-day, even though the Dodgers and Indians are playing out in Cleveland."[129] The *Washington Herald* opted for selling the game as a "legitimate" championship, letting its readers know, "The American Giants have defeated every colored aggregation west of Pittsburgh, and the Bacharachs have cleaned up all the crack colored teams east of that point."[130] The *Afro-American* did not have to market the game to generate enthusiasm, nor did it have to inform its readership about the American Giants or the Bacharach Giants.

Instead, the story in the *Afro-American* betrays a confidence that a new league would be formed but also Baltimore's central role in a professional league for African American players in the East. Such confidence reflects on Charles Spedden's leadership in building the Black Sox franchise and on the professionalism the club's players demonstrated in creating a winning team. The Black Sox' future was secure as was Baltimore's future in what would become the Eastern Colored League. In fact, as the *Afro-American*'s story suggests, a professional league in the East would need Baltimore and the Black Sox to thrive. The Baltimore community's response to the game between Foster's club and the Bacharach Giants validates such an interpretation. Not needing to be sold on coming to the game, "one of the largest crowds that ever packed Black Sox Park" went to Westport and "shook the overcrowded stands" with their cheers.[131] Baltimore was a "baseball town," and its fans were well informed, knowledgeable, and enthusiastic. They could also look forward to a new ballpark and continuing rivalries against the teams that would eventually comprise the Eastern Colored League.

5

"We have kept our
promise to you":
1921–22

In 1921 Rube Foster's Chicago American Giants would win their second of three consecutive Negro National League championships. They were masters of the "inside game," led by their star center fielder, Cristobal Torriente. The Negro National League was a success, and teams in Kansas City, St. Louis, Indianapolis, Columbus, Dayton, Detroit, and Cincinnati gave a financial boost to and were a source of pride for African American communities in these cities. Fans in the east were growing increasingly impatient for a league of their own.[1] They, too, had strong teams in the Black Sox, the Bacharachs, Hilldale, the Royal Giants, and the Cuban Stars. They, too, had thriving municipal economies that could support professional, "Colored" teams that played baseball at a high level. In the white professional baseball world, Baltimore native Babe Ruth led the Yankees to their first American League pennant. The Yankees lost the World Series to the New York Giants, managed by former Oriole John McGraw. In Baltimore, Jack Dunn's International League Orioles would earn their third of seven consecutive pennants. Western Maryland native Lefty Grove would win 25 games and pitch to an ERA of 2.56. In Westport, the Baltimore Black Sox, the dominant semipro team in the region, would move into their new home, Maryland Park.

Once completed, Maryland Park would rival any Negro League ballpark in the nation. At the start of the 1921 season, it could seat only about 2,500 in uncovered bleachers. Nonetheless, a "big crowd" of about 4,000 fans (many of them standing) came to see the first regular-season game, on Sunday, May 15, 1921.[2] Charles Spedden, who had supervised construction, promised "plenty [of] room," "good car service," and "good baseball."[3] The team split a doubleheader that afternoon against the Rex Athletic Club of Washington, D.C., committing seven

77

errors in the first game.[4] They would go on to play better baseball that season.

Playing a "first-rate grade of ball"

The Black Sox had retained almost all its stars. Jim Hodges left to manage his hometown team in Fayetteville, North Carolina, and Charlie Evans would see his role on the club and his playing time diminish as the season progressed.[5] Even without Evans, the outfield of Smith, Hall, and Hairstone, the *Afro-American* observed, were "fleet of foot, have fine throwing arms and [are] dangerous swatters."[6] Hairstone, in fact, would steal "second, third, and home" in one inning that season.[7] In "Joe Lewis and Manager Thomas, the catching department is well taken care of." The infield was anchored by Scrappy Brown who "is playing a sensational game at short."[8] He was "rated among the best in the country," having "no equal this side of the big show."[9] Midnight Smith remained "one of the best colored pitchers in the business," striking out as many as 17 batters in a single game.[10] His home record was 10–4.[11] Doc Sykes "toyed with" opposing teams and "administered the visitors a brand of 'gas' that had them gasping for breath."[12] He finished the year with a 13–3 record at Maryland Park.[13] The Black Sox would recruit new players as well. Joe Wheeler and Nick Logan would round out the pitching staff, and Chick Meade would play third base.

Nicholas "Nick" Logan was born in Marshall, Virginia, in 1896 and moved to Baltimore with his family by 1910.[14] He had pitched a few games for the Black Sox in 1920, but 1921 was a breakthrough year.[15] The highlights of his season were a no-hitter against the Pittsburgh Stars in May and another against Cumberland in August.[16] His best game would be a one-hitter against a semipro team from Philadelphia. In that game, he struck out 15 and only three balls left the infield.[17] Logan would lead the Black Sox in wins at home with 18 against seven losses.[18]

Joe Wheeler joined the Black Sox in July after pitching for two local Washington, D.C., semipro teams (the Washington Braves and the LeDroit Tigers).[19] Wheeler proved "well-nigh invincible" in Baltimore, winning 11 games and losing only one at Maryland Park.[20] The highlight of his season was a one-hit shutout against an all-star team of white semipro and minor-league ballplayers.[21] Joe Wheeler was born in Washington, D.C., in 1896 and, when he wasn't pitching, worked as a laborer to help support his widowed mother.[22]

Chick Meade: "Generally known as white"

In late May 1921, "after a great deal of dickering," the Black Sox signed Chick Meade to play third base.[23] He "made a favorable impression."[24] His "throws from third to first go like a shot, and he is swinging the war club viciously."[25] Meade would not remain with the team after the 1921 season, and he would not merit any more than a passing mention if it were not for his behavior off the field. In the mid–1920s and early 1930s, he was repeatedly arrested, convicted, and served "four terms for forging checks."[26] Upon his release from prison, the *Afro-American* disclosed an additional fraud that Meade had committed against the Black Sox, African American professional baseball, its fans, and the historical legacy of the men who played the game. The paper reported that Chick Meade was "generally known as white." Larry Lester, cofounder of the Negro Leagues Museum, sums up the man, describing him as a "habitual criminal" who "sought refuge as a light-skin Negro to avoid discovery by the authorities."[27]

Chick Meade was born in Fairmont, West Virginia, and grew up on Jefferson Street, near the banks of the Monongahela River. He lived with his extended family: his parents, Fred and Mary; his younger brother and sister; his paternal grandfather, and two uncles.[28] His family was well known in Fairmont, and Meade's father was a barber and "a leading member" of the community.[29] Chick Meade was well educated and "highly intelligent."[30] When he left Fairmont for Cumberland, Maryland, he, too, became a barber. He also started to play organized baseball with John Brown's Cumberland Colts and was recognized as the "brains of the club."[31] John Brown's Colts were known as a "classy Black ball club," and were distinct from the Cumberland Colts, a white professional team that played in the Class D Blue Ridge League.[32] In 1915, Meade's name appears in the Cuban Giants lineup, and he would go on to play for the Pittsburgh Stars, Taylor's A.B.C.'s, and the Brooklyn All Stars before joining the Black Sox in 1921.[33]

Census records add an important and exculpatory note to Chick Meade's life and reveal the damage done to his reputation and, by association, the historical legacy of African American professional baseball. In 1900, the census taker recorded the family's race with the letter "C," meaning "colored."[34] Census records from 1880 list both his paternal and maternal grandparents as "M," designating "mulatto."[35] The 1930 census lists Chick Meade's father as a "Negro."[36] Chick Meade was not a white man passing as a "light-skin" black man to play ball; he was a light-skin, mixed-race African American and, as such, would not have been able to play for a white professional team. Meade did commit fraud and served his time, but he did not misrepresent his race to play for the Black Sox or any other African American club.

"Get the habit"

Charles Spedden worked hard to cultivate enthusiasm for the team. Advertisements told fans to "Be a Sport. Come out and support your Ball Club. Others do it. Why not you? Get the habit. Boost." The Black Sox did their part, reaching out to new fans while simultaneously cultivating a relationship with their fan base. Spedden made efforts to improve attendance with women, offering "special arrangements for ladies" and a guarantee that "ladies will be admitted free to the Monday games."[37] He even hired "two young lady ushers" and had specially designated seating areas reserved for women and "their escorts."[38] Certainly, the lady ushers were as likely to attract the attention of single male patrons as to reassure the ladies with escorts, but the atmosphere in the park was convivial and even celebratory. The Black Sox began to develop a reputation as a "combination of baseball and comedy artists." They would "mix their diamond efforts with well-nigh stunts that approach[ed] the theatrical."[39] J. B. Hairstone, the team's former manager and star outfielder, was known as the "funniest player in colored baseball,"[40] and, writing in 1970, Ralph Matthews recalls how Scrappy Brown would "hit a homerun and then run through the grandstand waving his cap collecting from $50 to $100."[41] The efforts of management and the players did not immediately create enthusiasm for the team.

Attendance at Maryland Park had become a serious problem: "The Sox are playing some of the best baseball ever seen here and only a handful of spectators are giving them support."[42] The team might attract a "big crowd" for a Sunday game, but weekday attendance was abysmal.[43] For the opening exhibition game, and first game at Maryland Park, 200 fans saw the Black Sox beat a semipro club from Catonsville.[44] Once the regular season started, apart from Opening Day, attendance did not improve. A crowd of 400 saw the Black Sox defeat a semipro team from Norfolk.[45] Only 100 saw Nick Logan pitch his first no-hitter of the season.[46]

Exacerbating the problem, one of the few fans in attendance at a game in July was knocked unconscious by a foul ball.[47] The *Afro-American* admonished the fans, letting them know that the "city is represented by the best team it has ever had" and warning "it must be supported in order that the players may be retained. The weekday crowds are way below the standard, hardly paying the expenses of the visiting club, while on Sunday crowds with a star attraction scarcely draw 2000. Any other city with such a classy team as the Sox would draw from 8,000 to 12,000 persons on a Sunday."[48] The *Afro-American* was not simply offering a hypothetical comparison. At Harlan Field in Delaware, the Black Sox would draw up to 5,000 for a weekday game and almost twice that for a Sunday game: The Delaware papers noted that the "Black Sox are favorites of Wilmington fans."[49]

Lack of attendance at Maryland Park remains a perplexing issue. Part of the problem probably was the team's success. Fans had become accustomed to the Black Sox dominating local and regional clubs so much so that the games were no longer sufficiently entertaining. In October, the *Baltimore American* reported that the Black Sox had "not lost a game to a local team" all season, and the *Afro-American* noted that they were "playing in such a fashion as would have put the fastest big leaguers to the test."[50] Out-of-town papers also took notice. The *Harrisburg Telegraph* reported that the Black Sox are "one of the strongest aggregations of colored players in the United States."[51] Fans may have taken the Black Sox for granted, but Maryland Park itself may have contributed to the problem. Attendance had been much stronger at the Westport Base Ball Grounds, which had covered bleachers and a seating capacity nearly double that of Maryland Park. It would take major improvements to Maryland Park to reestablish a relationship between the fans and their ballpark, and by extension, their team.

Certain games did generate considerable enthusiasm. In October, the Black Sox played a doubleheader against a team from Brooklyn for the city championship; Brooklyn, in this case, is an area in Baltimore County on the south bank of the Patapsco River about three miles from Maryland Park. The *Afro-American* described "the partisanship on both sides [as] unusually pronounced." The Brooklyn club, called "the white boys" in newspaper coverage, "came reinforced by several hundred white rooters who let the Sox rooters know they were there." They "kicked on every decision that was rendered." The Black Sox "crushed the visitors completely," but the animosity was so great that the *Afro-American* inverted Brooklyn's half of the box score.[52] The enthusiasm for the games against Brooklyn's white semipro team, and the carryover into the news coverage, highlights one of the contributing problems, together with the condition of Maryland Park, that affected team attendance.

The Black Sox had no natural rivals. They beat every semipro team in the region, finishing with an overall record of 82 wins and 23 losses.[53] Although they did play competitive African American clubs, such as the Hilldale Giants and the Bacharachs, these clubs were not rivals in the traditional sense. Because there was no comparable league (to the Negro National League) in the east, there was no pennant race, no resultant rivalries, and no consequent fan enthusiasm. Newspaper coverage reflected the situation. Stories about the Black Sox and their antecedents, the Weldons and the Giants, traced an upward trajectory for the clubs. In 1921, the Black Sox reached the apex of what they could become outside of a league format.

Consequently, compelling narratives, just the kind that generate fan enthusiasm, were in short supply. Instead, the papers focused on an accomplishment or a remarkable performance of a player rather than on coverage of the team in general.

"A ball club in every sense of the word"

Perhaps understanding the problem, Charles Spedden began to lay the groundwork for a professional team that would strengthen the case for not only an Eastern League but Baltimore's place in it. In July, Spedden filed articles of incorporation for the "Black Sox Baseball and Exhibition Club," issuing $20,000 in stocks. William Brauer and Charles Spedden purchased shares, as did Doc Sykes.[54] In November, the team announced that players would be under contract for the 1922 season. They would earn salaries "ranging from $125 to $200 dollars a month,"[55] rather than a percentage of the gate receipts. The *Afro-American* speculated that the contracts would also incentivize teamwork over individual performance. The *Afro* was also careful to point out that it "had no criticism to offer against the individuals who composed the Sox team this season, each one of whom has shown a high degree of team work." Nonetheless, the paper raised an issue that would surface in 1922. At the close of 1921, fans had great cause to be optimistic, and the newspapers credited Spedden as the one "responsible for the present state of development of the Sox and the first-rate grade of ball" enjoyed by the fans.[56]

In January 1922, the team installed "officers," each with specific duties. William Brauer would be the treasurer. Spedden would continue his work but now with the title of "General Manager." Marion Watkins would serve as "Chairman."[57] Watkins, an African American, owned a print shop and the New Deal Nite Club,[58] which featured performers such as Mamie Smith and later Cab Calloway. Watkins was also "believed to be an official of the M & S Syndicate," a numbers-running operation.[59] Ernest Weeks would be the secretary.[60] Weeks had a job as a compositor in a printing office, perhaps working for Marion Watkins.[61] George Rossiter would be "president," reflecting his financial stake in the team. Rossiter owned businesses in South Baltimore.[62] His most successful was a seafood restaurant on South Hanover Street.

Rossiter was a Baltimore native, born in September 1884. He was the son of Irish immigrants from County Wexford who came to Baltimore just after the

Matchbox cover from George Rossiter's Famous Seafood Restaurant. Rossiter owned several businesses in the South Baltimore area (Sanborn).

Civil War. George was one of seven children. His father was a grocer, and his younger brother, Edward, was a newspaper reporter. The family lived in a two-story row house, No. 7 Randall Street, in a community that was a mix of native Marylanders and immigrants, largely Irish and German. As a young man, George Rossiter worked as a clerk for his father's grocery store.[63] The family also lived less than a half-mile from Union League Park where the Black Sox, Weldons, and Giants played ball. It does not strain credulity to imagine him going to games there and seeing the team he would later serve as president and, ultimately, as principal owner.

During its first meeting, the newly organized board of directors established a "Building Committee," to oversee improvements to Maryland Park. There would be an "extension of the grandstand seats," the "bleachers [would] be covered," and seating capacity would be expanded.[64]

On June 23, 1922, a display ad ran in the *Afro-American,* telling "colored baseball fans" that "we have kept our promise to you. Our park has been extensively improved to a point that the colored citizens of Baltimore

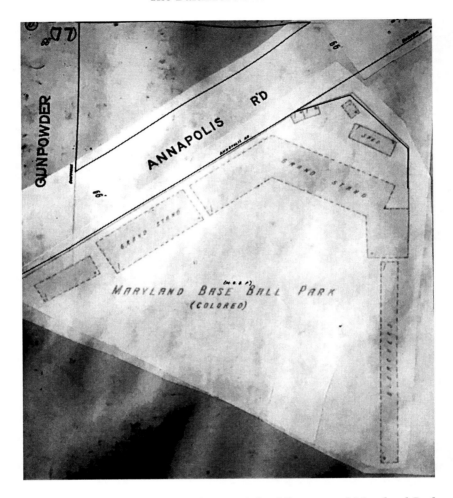

Detail from the Sanborn Map. The map is backlit to reveal Maryland Park. Sanborn would send subscribers updates to their maps. Consequently, almost all the extant editions of this map have a blank overlay covering Maryland Park. Sanborn would have instructed that the overlay be placed on top of the Maryland Park image because the ballpark was no longer in use and had been razed.

can boast that they have a park that compares with any colored baseball park in the United States."[65] By all accounts, the field was in fine condition as well: "the grass has grown and the diamond presents a beautiful appearance."[66] The board of directors had addressed one of the contributing issues to poor attendance.

The ownership group also made efforts to stabilize the roster and to increase the competitiveness of games at Maryland Park. The Black Sox became members of the Philadelphia Baseball Association, which included dozens of white and African American semipro teams in the Mid-Atlantic region.[67] The Philadelphia Association was "organized as a club protection. No player under contract with any of the clubs can jump to any other organization in the association, and notices of changes [trades] must first be approved by the association."[68]

The ownership also announced "Big League colored teams and semi-pro white teams" would "play here."[69] This meant that the Black Sox would be competing against not just the local and regional teams, which they had dominated, but top-caliber clubs from across the country. The weekends would feature "big colored attractions" (i.e., teams from the Negro National League and teams that would comprise the Eastern Colored League) in line "with the policy inaugurated at Maryland Baseball Park."[70] Clubs such as the Brooklyn Royal Giants, Richmond, Tate's All Stars, and the Bacharachs had been playing sporadically in Baltimore for years, but the new policy meant more regular games and games with these teams on Saturday and Sunday in anticipation of large crowds. The frequency of the games even generated some excitement about an informal "colored championship of the East," with stories in the *Baltimore American* noting that the "Black Sox stepped a notch higher in their drive to win" or "stepped another notch toward" the so-called championship.[71] It was not an actual pennant race but it did help to increase attendance and to generate rivalries with teams like Hilldale and the Bacharachs. The ownership group made an announcement just before the season started: "Messrs Rossiter and Spedden have taken this [these] steps with the belief that the colored fans of Baltimore will support a colored ball club if it is a ball club in every sense of the word."[72] The improvements to the ballpark, the desire to stabilize the roster, the efforts to sign players to contracts, and the steps taken to improve competition all contributed to the professionalization of the team, laying the groundwork for membership in the Eastern Colored League.

1922: *"Look Out! Here it comes!"*

The Black Sox started the 1922 season "brilliantly." The papers heralded the arrival of "the 'new' Black Sox," who were "bigger and greater than ever." To celebrate the start of the season, Henry Bloom published a

Black Sox Started Season Sunday

The caricature expresses fan anxiety and hopes for a new season (*Baltimore Afro-American*).

cartoon in the *Afro-American* that channeled fans' speculations about the coming season.[73]

In the cartoon, Doc Sykes delivers a pitch to Charlie Thomas; the caption warns opposing teams to "Look Out!" Other newspaper articles called Thomas "one of the shrewdest colored baseball leaders in the country."[74] Another part of the drawing asks if J. B. Hairstone will bat for a higher average than last year; he had led the team in batting in 1921 with an average of .445 at Maryland Park (101 hits in 227 at-bats).[75] Red Miller is at the center of the illustration, with caricatures of fans asking, "Yer think he equals Chick Meade?" The cartoon mirrored the print coverage. Articles and advertisements trumpeted "an all-star professional club, including Peirce, Blainey Hall, Scrappy Brown, Reds Miller [sic], and other professional men." Fans' questions about the new third baseman seemed to resolve themselves at once: "Miller took his position at third and soon had the thousand or more fans ... in an uproar of favorable comments."[76] The excitement about the season and even the speculations reflected in the cartoon focus primarily on the players rather than the team.

The question of the Black Sox playing as a team would embroil the new manager in controversy. Spedden had hired Bill Pierce to take over from Charlie Thomas. Like Thomas (and Spedden), "Big Bill" was a catcher and had played for the Philadelphia Giants, the Lincoln Stars, Pennsylvania Red Caps, and the Lincoln Giants.[77] Pierce's emphasis on "strict discipline" in order to "play as a team" caused problems in the clubhouse.[78] In early May, just after Henry Bloom published his cartoon, two of the men depicted "quit" the team: Charlie Thomas and J. B. Hairstone.[79] Two weeks later, George Ford, a backup infielder, left the club.[80] Facing mutiny, management yielded to player demands and fired Bill Pierce in June, replacing him with his predecessor, Charlie Thomas.[81] The *Afro-American* drew a portrait of a deeply dysfunctional club. "The management says that they dropped Pierce much against their will, but in order to hold the club together and give the spectators a run for their money, as the present organization almost to a man refused to do his best as long as Pierce was managing the team." The paper reflected that "this throws the team right back into the rut" of "arguing among themselves, battling with men on, as best suited to their judgment and pouting with each other when things just did not suit one or the other's fancy."[82] Charlie Thomas faced significant challenges in reassuming control.

He responded confidently and he and Spedden began to shape the team, persuading George Ford to return. Hairstone was content to remain with the Bacharachs, and George Greyer, the team's Opening Day first baseman, found a new home with Harrisburg.[83] In June, the Black Sox also dropped two of their stars from the roster: "[N]either [Scrappy Brown nor Midnight Smith] seemed capable of delivering the brand of ball that the club's owners desire to have the team serve up this season."[84] Brown would not return to the Black Sox that season.

A refocused Midnight Smith did come back, pitching a no-hitter in August.[85] Also in August, the Black Sox once again dropped George Ford, citing his "indifferent play" and because he "refused to run out" a hit ball.[86]

He would come back to the team in 1923. Charlie Thomas, perhaps because of Bill Pierce's heavy hand, was able to successfully discipline his players and urge them to play as a team. His discipline would have come across as less severe than Pierce's. In addition, Thomas had a history with the players and took a stand, with them, against Pierce.

Charlie Thomas's new term as manager was not simply about discipline and control. Under Thomas, the Black Sox had big years from their new and old stars. Doc Sykes won 30 games, losing just 5. He had benefited the most from the contract system, earning a team-high $300 a month.[87] In September, he pitched a perfect game against the Bacharach Giants and a lineup that included Ghost Marcell, Robert Hudspeth, and John Henry Lloyd.[88] At the end of the year, the *Afro-American* noted that Sykes "had the best season he has had since coming to this city."[89] It could be argued that no pitcher in baseball had a better season in 1922 than Sykes. A team of white major-league players, in fact, "could not fathom the pitching of Sykes."[90] Nick Logan also performed well, pitching another a no-hitter.[91] He also won a game he pitched with a ninth-inning, walk-off home run.[92] The Black Sox acquired another pitcher to complement Sykes, Logan, and Midnight Smith. Submarine Lee, "a new Hurler from Chappie Johnson's Philadelphia Royal Stars," put "fans in a fever of excitement by his sensational submarine delivery."[93] Acquired late in the year, Lee "won 5 out of 6 games," defeating the Bacharach Giants on consecutive days.[94] He also pitched a no-hitter against the Richmond Giants.[95] Charles Spedden had given Thomas a talented group of players, and Thomas had brought them together as a team.

"Boojum"

Spedden's most important contribution to the Black Sox that season was signing Ernest "Jud" Wilson in late June. In his debut, he hit two, three-run home runs, one in each game of a doubleheader. A reporter described how he watched "a little white pill rise up, up into the air and sail over the right field fence way beyond the confines of the park and the crowd went wild."[96] Wilson would have six hits in nine at-bats that afternoon.

In his first 13 games (47 at-bats), he hit .425, with four home runs, two triples, four doubles, and even stole a base.[97] He was the perfect team player as well, starting wherever needed. He played right field, second, first, and even started a game at short.[98] His defensive versatility did not hurt his hitting. After 21 games (67 at-bats), he was hitting .522.[99] He

Hall of Famer Jud "Boojum" Wilson starred for the Black Sox teams of the 1920s (courtesy Larry Lester).

would finish the season with a .470 average in 119 at-bats. He had a "muscular, bull-shouldered torso cast on contradictivly small but wiry legs." He played with "raw, unmitigated fury."[100] Satchel Paige would later give Wilson his nickname, saying that the ball coming off his bat "made a sound all its own": "Boojum"; the papers called him "Babe."[101] Jud Wilson played for Baltimore through the 1930 season and was Satchel Paige's teammate that year.

Wilson's life off the field is not well known. He was born, depending upon the record consulted, in 1893, 1894, or 1897.[102] What is known, with a fair degree of certainty, is that Wilson played sandlot and semipro ball in Washington, D.C., for the Georgetown Athletics and Montrose A.C. before joining the Black Sox at the suggestion of Scrappy Brown.[103] Wilson was born in Remington (Lee District), Fauquier County, Virginia. He was the eldest of five children. When he was in his teens, his father died. Wilson's mother, Eliza, took in laundry to support the family, and Wilson left school to work as a laborer; he might have been as young as 13.[104] Wilson's brothers and mother subsequently disappear from government records, and there is no later census that lists his sisters.

Military draft registration forms do mention them and indicate that Wilson was their sole support. They also offer a clue as to mysteries surrounding his age. He told the draft board that he was 22 and that he was born in 1894. He also told them that he worked as a "telephone helper" for "American Telephone and Telegraph." A "telephone helper," sometimes called a "groundman" as opposed to a "lineman," was nonetheless a skilled position.[105] Some advertisements required applicants to be 21.[106] If he was his younger sister's sole support, he may have lied about his age to get work as a groundman and then told the draft board what he had told AT& T. Despite being his sister's sole support, he was drafted and served in the 417th Service Battalion, a "Motor Supply Train," under the Quartermaster Corps.[107] His unit was demobilized in September 1919. Wilson then disappears from the public record for three years, only reemerging to play his first game for the Black Sox in 1922.

"Black Sox Had Great Season"

The Black Sox finished the season with a "long string of home victories."[108] Since Charlie Thomas had taken over as manager, they had played better, finishing with a home record of 52 wins, 19 losses, two ties, and one forfeit. They also "played strong teams." They split the season series against Hilldale. The Black Sox had won series against the Bacharachs, Tate's All Stars, and "all white clubs that played real baseball."[109] The season culminated with a game against an "All Star team of players from American and National" League clubs. In setting up the game, Charles Spedden made it clear that he was giving the fans what they had desired. He wrote that he was "complying with numerous requests made by the patrons of Maryland Baseball Park for a big league baseball club to play the Black Sox."[110] Spedden doubtlessly saw the opportunity for a large payday, but it should not be overlooked that he listened and responded to fan requests and made it clear that he had. He did not attempt to take credit for the idea. Rather, he vested credit in the fans and in doing so demonstrated that he saw their value and appreciated their contributions to the team's success. More than 7,000 saw the Black Sox and Doc Sykes shut out the All Stars, 4–0. Jud Wilson had three hits, and Sykes contributed a double. The papers pointed out the contributions of individual players but also noted that it was a "team" victory.[111] The Black Sox had become a team, and both the team and their home, Maryland Park, were becoming an even stronger part of the city's African American community.

"Every one of them refused"

Baltimore's African American community was also making advances. As Sherry Olson notes in *Baltimore: The Building of an American City*, "Compared to the complete neglect of the Progressive period before the war, the planning of the 20s did begin to create and invest in spaces for blacks."[112] The city's school board established an "investment quota" of 10 percent for "Colored Schools," matching the percentage of the city that was African American.[113] The city built "ten new [school] buildings ... with several playgrounds, cafeterias, gyms, and showers," and "a third of graduates went onto college or normal school."[114]

Advances did not mean equality. The new funding for schools did nothing to rectify the decades of unequal treatment and neglect. Vocational education for African Americans was also limited. Baltimore's white schools offered graduates the skills and training to join burgeoning industries in electronics, radio, and automotive repair. African Americans were barred from taking that sort of vocational training. Girls were taught to be cooks and cafeteria workers, and the boys who did not go on to college became manual laborers.[115]

Moreover, the "new spaces" created for African Americans were "always restricted and overwhelmed by numbers. When a swimming pool was created for whites in Druid Hill Park, a smaller space was built for blacks."[116] It was a step forward, but it was not equality. Racism persisted even in the pool's celebratory opening.

J. Cookman Boyd, president of the park board, declared that it was "the only one of its kind [a public pool for African Americans] ... within the confines of this broad land of the United States." It was built with

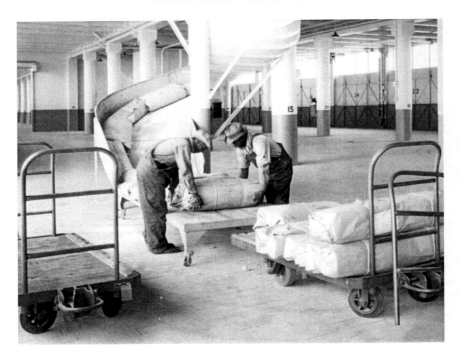

Two African American men work as laborers in a new Western Maryland warehouse in Port Covington. The railroad offered ample employment opportunities for electrical workers and machine operators, but the city's schools offered vocational training only for white students. African Americans, although they did reap the benefits of Baltimore's rapid postwar growth, were restricted to lower-skill, lower-wage positions (Hughes Company, ca. 1921).

reinforced concrete and had bathhouses, laundry facilities, and modern lighting. "Pastors of colored churches from all over the city" and a "children's choir" joined in the opening celebrations. The reporter for the *Sun* referenced a joke to commemorate the event, writing that "all the prayers in the prayer book couldn't have got some of the colored folks into the water after what Gen. Felix Agnus said about an alligator."[117]

Despite the virulent racism of the *Sun* and of certain city officials, Baltimore's African American community was becoming more prosperous, and that prosperity reflected itself in support for their team.

Opposite, bottom: The Druid Hill pool was half the size of the public pool built for the white community, and the *Baltimore Sun* and city officials engaged in racially offensive jokes at its opening (*Baltimore Sun*).

Young men and women enjoy the first day of Druid Hill's public swimming pool. It was the first municipal pool built in the United States for African Americans (*Baltimore Sun*).

For 1922 at least, the Black Sox drew well. The strategy to pay a premium for strong competition on weekends, coupled with expanded and more comfortable seating at the ballpark, worked. Six thousand fans turned out for a doubleheader against the Bacharachs in May.[118] A game against the Harrisburg Giants drew 8,000.[119] Games against Hilldale in July and September recorded attendance at 7,000 and 7,500.[120] In total, more than 150,000 fans came to Maryland Park for 74 games.[121] To put those numbers in perspective, in 1922, the Boston Braves drew 167,000 fans at Braves Field for 76 games.[122]

The team's success also gave birth to frustration for two reasons: First, as stated in the *Afro-American*, "Baltimore ought to be in the Negro National League: Indianapolis, Cleveland, St. Louis, Kansas City, Detroit, all have teams in the league, and not one ... has a population anywhere near the 108,000 [African Americans] which the latest census gives Baltimore." Second, the *Afro* pointed out that "the management of the Black Sox ... approached any number of colored men of the city who are known to be men of means ... and laid before them the plans in contemplation and invited them to come in and help finance the club, but practically every one of them refused."[123] For the *Afro-American*, the city should have received greater respect on a national level because of its African American population, its support of the team, and the club's on-field excellence. In addition, the team should have received greater respect from the African American business community. The spirit that inspired men like Howard Young and John R. Williams to invest their time and talent in the club was now noticeably lacking in the paper's view. In 1923, the first issue would be resolved with the formation of the Eastern Colored League, the long-anticipated counterpart to the Negro National League.

The second issue was not resolved. In Charles Spedden, the African American community had a man who listened to them and who, as will become evident, grew to recognize and then overcome his prejudices. Nonetheless, the memory of a "white ownership" who wanted to "take over" African American baseball in the city was still strong. It was a testament to the players on that Baltimore Giants team, men like Charlie Thomas and Charles Evans, that the club survived to become the Black Sox. The African American community did not know George Rossiter well. The *Afro-American* consistently referred to him as "white," while referring to Charles Spedden as "white" only once and in connection with Rossiter. The paper was justifiably suspicious. Spedden had proved sympathetic, but the African American community needed more than sympathy for reassurance. They needed ownership and men with the financial means to support the club. Excitement generated by the new "colored" league and the tension of the pennant race would put the issue of African American ownership in abeyance for a few years, but it would inevitably resurface.

6

"On the map for colored baseball": 1923–26

After the 1922 season, Charlie Thomas chose to leave the team and focus on a new career with the American Sugar Company. The Black Sox would feel his loss that first season in the Eastern Colored League. He was the team's last direct link to its days as the Weldons and the Baltimore Giants. His leadership helped to hold the club together through many difficult times. If it were not for him and Charles Evans, it is likely that the team would have folded after its takeover by hostile "white ownership" in 1912. He was also instrumental in the formation of the ballplayers that would comprise the Baltimore Black Sox. He tutored J. B. Hairstone and Joe Lewis, both of whom went on to long careers with the Black Sox and in the Negro Leagues. Most recently, in 1922, he once again pulled the team together after Pierce's short managerial tenure. Thomas also nurtured a young pitching staff, helping Doc Sykes, Nick Logan, and Midnight Smith mature and develop. It is significant that none of those men achieved without Charlie Thomas what they had achieved with him behind the plate or as their manager. He was also an exceptional ballplayer in his own right, consistently hitting well above .300. Thomas's departure was not the only change for the club. On April 7, 1923, Charles Spedden resigned from his post at the Baltimore and Ohio Railroad.[1] He was now working exclusively for the Black Sox as their general manager and supporting his wife and three children solely on that income.[2] The team would need and indeed would benefit from his "baseball intelligence" as they established themselves in the Eastern Colored League.

The Mutual Association of Colored Baseball Clubs

On December 22, 1922, the Baltimore Black Sox, their fans, and baseball received a Christmas gift. The *Afro-American* ran the headline,

"Eastern Clubs Organize."[3] At long last, there was a professional African American baseball league in the East to serve as a counterpart to Rube Foster's Negro National League. Foster's vision, as he sat in the stands at the old Westport Baseball Grounds, had come to fruition. The league's official name was "The Mutual Association of Colored Baseball Clubs," but it was known almost immediately more as the Eastern Colored League or the ECL. There were six charter members and they were organized under a "commission" with each team having one representative. At their inaugural meeting, William Tucker represented the Bacharach Giants; Nat Strong stood for the Brooklyn Royal Giants; James Keenan represented the Lincoln Giants; Edward Bolden spoke on behalf of Hilldale; Alex Pompez stood for the Cuban Stars, and Charles Spedden represented Baltimore. The commission established an initial 45-game schedule but permitted teams to exceed that number if "patronage warrants." The clubs also established a fund to "purchase" a pennant to be awarded to the league's winning team.[4]

On the local level, Charles Spedden put a considerable amount of money into upgrading Maryland Park. To mark the start of the new Eastern Colored League, he made it the "most complete colored baseball park in the country." The *Afro-American* offers details: "The entrance will be changed so that those who purchase tickets for the grandstand will go through one gate while those who buy for the bleachers will enter another, thus there will be no congestion at the entrances. The outfield has been re-seeded, the ground leveled, and if the ground can be secured the right field fence will be moved back about 35 feet;

Maryland Park, ca. 1926 (Maryland Port Authority).

... another new grandstand in that field will be rebuilt.... [H]ot and cold showers have been put in the clubhouses and also individual lockers."[5]

Aerial photos taken by the Maryland Port Authority offer visual evidence of these changes, including the grandstand in right field and the separate entrances. The improvements increased the park's value to an estimated $35,000, which the team had paid in full.[6]

Ownership also upgraded the team's roster. The Black Sox of the Eastern Colored League would be comprised of old and new faces. Jud Wilson would play first base. Joe Lewis would catch, but the team had also acquired Julio Rojo, a native of Cuba, to help behind the plate. Rojo was known for his expertise in handling pitchers and had better defensive skills than Lewis.

Cleo Smith would be at second. Rags Roberts, Lefty Smith, and Blainey

Julio Rojo would be a fixture in the Black Sox lineup from 1923 through 1926. In 1925, fans voted him the team's MVP over more acclaimed teammates Jud Wilson and John Beckwith. Born in Sagua la Grande, Cuba, in 1894, Rojo is pictured playing for La Habana. The umpire standing behind Rojo is Valentin "Sirique" Gonzalez, a fellow member of the Cuban Baseball Hall of Fame.

Hall, part of the original 1913 team, would be in the outfield. Red Miller would remain at third. Wyman Smith was scheduled to be the everyday shortstop, although Ed Poles and Charles Lindsay would also see time at short. Doc Sykes would anchor the pitching staff and be joined by Nick

Logan, Mac Mahoney, and Jodie Wheeler. George "Chippy" Britton, now going by Britt, would be a super utility man, including serving as a regular member of the pitching staff. Rojo would be the on-field manager, but in-game decisions would be up to a game captain, which rotated among the team's members. All the players were under contract, with the top salary at about $350 a month. The team's total payroll would vary from month to month but would generally fall between $3,500 and $3,700. There was a roster limit of 15 players.[7]

1923: "And all was blackness"

On Sunday May 27, 10,000 people crowded into Maryland Park to see the Black Sox battle the Hilldale Giants for first place in the Eastern Colored League. The games were the second and third in a four-game series. In the first game, Hilldale had "successfully defended first place," on their home grounds in Darby, winning 6–1.[8] Nip Winters pitched a one-hitter for the Giants. Nonetheless, the fans that poured into the stands in Maryland Park that Sunday had reason to be optimistic. The Black Sox had played very well at home through the first month of the season, winning six of nine games.

They had swept the Cuban Stars in an Opening Day doubleheader and won a three-games series from both the Brooklyn Royal Giants and the Bacharach Giants.[9] The team's stars had performed exceptionally well. Against the Bacharachs, Anthony "Mac" Mahoney "pitched a heady brand of ball. His mixture of fast ones, hooks, and tantalizing drifters kept the Giants popping or rolling easy grounders to the infield."[10] Against Brooklyn, Arnett "Hooks" Mitchell hit a game-winning sacrifice fly. Chippy Britt, the runner on third, "went dashing for the plate after the catch and was on his way to the dressing room when the ball got to the plate."[11] Mitchell pitched the next day's game against Brooklyn, winning 5–2, striking out five, and walking one.[12] Julio Rojo, known as a star defensive catcher, was batting .315. Jud Wilson, batting an uncharacteristic .273, nonetheless led the team in homers with two; he was also the only Black Sox to hit a home run, but six of his teammates had stolen at least one base. The Black Sox were playing their own brand of inside baseball. The second baseman, Cleo Smith, was batting .423. Blainey Hall was hitting .393. Rags Roberts, the center fielder, was hitting .423. The left fielder, Wyman Smith, led the team with a .454 average.[13] Defensively, the Black Sox were "brilliant."[14]

On the field, the Black Sox thrived, but off the field, they faced racism. Just after the Black Sox started their season in the newly formed Eastern Colored League, the *Baltimore Sun* published a caricature of Doc Sykes.

The cartoon depicted a figure in blackface, reported to be a likeness of Sykes, with the caption, "very dark," describing both the cloud cover and the pitcher. The accompanying story carried forward the motif, telling readers that "things look dark for locals in Colored League," and that "things grew blacker and blacker for the Black Sox."[15]

Undaunted by the overt racial bias in the *Sun*, the fans responded very well. A doubleheader against the Bacharach Giants on May 6 attracted "more than 9,000 paid.... All the boxes were filled to overflowing, while the grandstand seats were also packed. The new stands ... were filled."[16] Five thousand came to see the Brooklyn Giants the following weekend.[17] Opening Day was also likely a sellout, although there are no surviv-

In 1923, the *Baltimore Sun* published a racist caricature of Baltimore pitcher Doc Sykes (*Baltimore Sun*).

ing records or accounts of those games. The 10,000 fans that came to see the Black Sox battle Hilldale for first place in the Eastern Colored League on May 27 were "in a high state of excitement" and the atmosphere was "electric." Hooks Mitchell and Mac Mahoney pitched for the Black Sox. In the first game, Mitchell held Hilldale to a pair of runs, winning, 8–2. The offense played inside ball, scoring six runs in the first five innings on 12 singles, frustrating Hilldale's pitcher, Red Ryan, as none of the balls were hit hard. The second game was much closer. The Black Sox once again played inside ball. The highlight of the game, and the decisive run, came when Cleo Smith stole home in the sixth. The Black Sox won, 4–3.[18] They led the ECL with a record of 8–4; Hilldale had fallen out of first with a record of 5–3.

Hilldale regained first place the next day, beating the Black Sox, 9–8. The Black Sox had nearly won the game in the ninth. There were two runners on with two out and Hooks Mitchell due up.[19] Thus far that season, Mitchell had two game-winning hits as a pinch-hitter in the ninth. For those games, Red Miller was the team's captain. For this game, Mac Mahoney was serving as captain. He chose to pinch-hit himself for Mitchell. The *Afro-American* explained his reasoning: "Mahoney's decision was right according to the 'dope,' … a right handed batter stands a better chance of hitting a left-handed pitcher."[20] For the new captain, the "fate of the game and the leadership of the Eastern league was now hanging in the balance, and it was up to Mahoney to 'save the day.' It was equally up to Winters [Hilldale's pitcher] to turn that day into night. Mahoney swung at three that wasn't and all was blackness."[21] The fan reaction was predictable, but the *Afro-American* reported that Mitchell too was upset.[22] The team would never recover. They would go on to win only 11 more games that season, while losing 26.

The collapse was of biblical proportions. After starting the season 8–4, and sitting in first place, they would finish last with a 19–30 record.[23] Running with the biblical theme, the *Baltimore Sun* called them "as meek as lambs" on the basepaths, which was not a good strategy for a team that had played inside baseball so well to start the season.[24] The *Afro-American* speculated that the Black Sox "had been hobnobbing with some of the religious sects … and had been overcome with a spirit of brotherly love, thereby deciding henceforth to do unto all men as they wished to be done unto."[25] The out-of-town papers were less kind. The *Philadelphia Inquirer* declared, "Hilldale again is Baltimore's master."[26]

Scriptural hyperbole aside, the Black Sox "lost games by failure to keep awake on the diamond and come through in the pinches."[27] They practiced "poor base running" and committed "several bad errors" in a series against the Cuban Giants in June.[28] In a July series against the Lincoln Giants, "Bad errors helped to spell ruin for the Sox."[29] At the end of July, the *Afro-American* reported that "the Black Sox can't knock the ball out … because it takes all of their time to knock out half pints and pints" and this during Prohibition.[30] For all intents and purposes, the Black Sox' season ended on May 28, with Mac Mahoney's decision to pinch-hit for Mitchell. The collapse was immediate and absolute. A week later, the *Afro-American* reported that their play "doesn't leave a very good taste in the mouths of fans, and especially when during the ... games there were a number of good chances thrown away."[31]

At the end of the season, Charles Spedden decided to "junk" the team, keeping only George Britt, Jud Wilson, Julio Rojo, and Clarence Lindsay. Spedden could not help but notice that "attendance dropped Sunday after Sunday." He was sympathetic with the fans and blamed "too much 'moonshine,'[and] too many games lost" for the "poor attendance." Pitching was also a problem. Doc Sykes, who had anchored the staff for years, found that he was suddenly "unable to pitch winning ball."[32]

In September, Sykes took out an ad in a local paper, letting his "patients and friends" know that he was "no longer connected with the Baltimore Black Sox," and that he would now give his "entire time to my dental practice."[33] His retirement would not be absolute, but he would never again pitch to the level and with the consistency of previous years.

Team batting was a bright spot. Blainey Hall led the club with a .360 average. Jud Wilson hit .352 and Rags Roberts finished with a .356 average.[34] Lack of team leadership had also been a clear problem and it is debatable if Charlie Thomas would have made a difference. His skill at handling pitchers and his even greater skill at handling players would doubtlessly have been an asset.

Needing stronger on-field leadership going into the next season, Spedden named Pete Hill the new manager in November 1923, at the same time announcing his decision to "junk" most of the team.[35] His decisiveness sent a signal to fans that things would change immediately, that management took the team's problems seriously and was willing to take action to solve them. For the players and potential players, Spedden's choice of Hill also sent a clear message. He had played with Sol White and the Cuban X Giants, had been an assistant to Rube Foster in Chicago for years, and had most recently managed teams in Detroit and Milwaukee.[36] Hill was a well-respected baseball man and brought with him the experience and skill to manage in Baltimore.

1924: "One of the most valuable players in organized baseball"

At the end of the 1923 season, the Eastern Colored League added two additional franchises, in Washington and Harrisburg.[37] Competition between the clubs in the now eight-team league would be even more intense than it had been in 1923. Talented players would be at a premium.

Frank Sykes earned his nickname, "Doc," because he was a practicing dentist, earning his degree from Howard University. He was born in Decatur, Alabama, and attended Morehouse College as an undergraduate. He advocated for civil rights, most notably testifying on behalf of the nine teenaged African American men accused of raping a white woman in the "Scottsboro Case." In retaliation, the Ku Klux Klan burned a cross on his lawn. He died in Baltimore in 1986, at the age of 94. His ashes were spread over his alma mater (illustration courtesy Gary Joseph Cieradkowski, StudioGaryC.com).

Fans could be forgiven if they were curious then and perhaps even a bit skeptical as the Black Sox gathered at Maryland Park on April 1, 1924, for spring training. Most of the team had never played with one other, and, with two or so exceptions, they had not met Pete Hill. Before starting their workouts, they assembled for a portrait.

The team was not complete; Julio Rojo had not yet arrived from

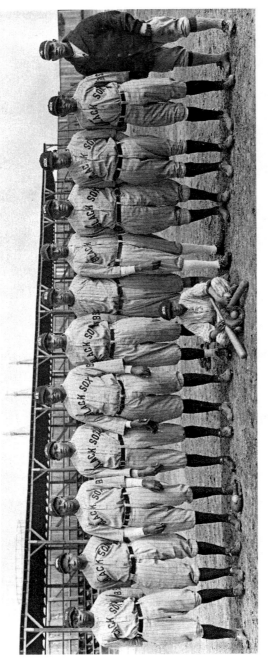

Cuba, and there would be personnel changes before Opening Day. Moreover, Pete Hill had not yet been fitted for his Baltimore uniform. Nonetheless, Charles Spedden declared that "his authority over the players will be absolute ... provided he brings Baltimore a winning club."[38]

His training regimen and professionalism had immediate effect. The *Afro-American* noted that he had "increased the efficiency of the Sox,"[39] observing that "each man works in splendid harmony."[40]

Spedden had scoured the country to give Hill the players he needed to make a winning team. The notable additions included Kid Mason, a left-handed pitcher from the Norfolk

1924 Black Sox. From left: Ed Poles, Wade Johnston, Bill Force, Charlie Mason, Neal Pullen, Crush Holloway, Carr, Connie Day, Jud Wilson, Kid Strong, Pete Wilson, Pete Hill. The team's mascot, Marsell, is sitting in front (courtesy Hughes Glass Negatives Collection, the Photography Collections, University of Maryland, Baltimore County).

Black Sox manager Pete Hill, 1924 (courtesy Hughes Glass Negatives Collection, the Photography Collections, University of Maryland, Baltimore County).

All-Stars.[41] Bill Force was a right-handed pitcher who had played with the Detroit Stars under Pete Hill and "wanted to do so again." Bob McClure was also a right-handed pitcher who got his start in the Texas League before playing with Tate's All-Stars.[42] Joe Lewis had been let go, and Bill Pullen had been acquired to help Rojo with the catching duties. Pullen had played in the Pacific Coast League.[43] The new left fielder was Wade Johnston. In 1923, he played for the Kansas City Monarchs, stealing 26 bases.[44] Crush Holloway would play center. He, too, had played for Pete Hill in Detroit.[45] Connie Day, who had played for the Indianapolis ABCs, was the new second baseman. He stood 5-foot-8 and weighed less than 160 lbs.[46] He was "a 'natural' ball player. Blessed with a very large pair of hands, very few grounders pass him." He also, the *Afro-American* observed, had "the uncanny ability to sense where the batter intends to hit."[47] Just as the season started, the Black Sox found a new third baseman. George Rossiter made the trip to Indianapolis to sign Henry Blackmon, who had been Day's teammate with the ABCs.[48] Fans had cause to be not just optimistic but enthusiastic about 1924. Ownership had assembled an all-star team. As spring training ended, there was a buzz about the Black Sox.

On April 26, 1924, the sun was shining. The temperature, in the mid-to-high 50s, might have been a little cool, but with thousands expected at Maryland Park for Opening Day, it would be warm enough.[49] There was excitement in the stands as the Baltimore Black Sox and Bacharach Giants "marched" onto the field, to the sounds of "The Battle Hymn of the Republic." Frank Kelley, the Democratic boss of the 18th Ward, conducted the ceremonies. Although part of the city's Irish Democratic machine, the 18th Ward included many African Americans. As such, he was far more sympathetic to their concerns than was the mayor's office. William Everett, a protégé of Kelley's, threw out the first pitch. A young child stepped forward and presented "beautiful bouquets of flowers to George Rossiter, Charles Spedden, and Pete Hill."[50]

The crowd was "enthusiastic," even as they saw the Black Sox commit six errors and lose the game, 7–2.[51] The next day, the fans responded by filling "the grandstands, bleachers, and [they] climbed up on the roof" only "to see the Sox drop Sunday's doubleheader," as well, making nine errors.[52] The 1924 season had started the way the 1923 season had ended. The fans could be forgiven for thinking that, despite offseason changes, the on-field results were likely to be the same.

In truth, the 1924 Black Sox were a far stronger club than they appeared during the opening weekend, and, to their credit, the fans continued to support the team. At the end of May, they were just one game under .500 and due to play a doubleheader against their archrival, Hilldale. Five thousand fans crowded into Maryland Park. The Black Sox won the first game. The team was at .500, despite a horrible start, and had gained a game on Hilldale, the league's best team. The second game was a slugfest. Hilldale was leading, 12–9, going into the ninth, with the heart of the

Black Sox order due up. The way both teams had been hitting, the crowd could sense a comeback, but, suddenly, the umpire "awarded" the game to "the visitors by forfeit."[53] The umpire later defended his decision by citing impending darkness. The Black Sox responded by pointing out that he had let a game continue earlier in the year under worse conditions. Caught up in the moment, the fans erupted onto the field. The newspapers reported that all "5,000 rush[ed] to mob Aubrey," the umpire. The police had to rescue him.[54] The team proved resilient. After splitting another doubleheader against Hilldale in late June, the Black Sox were 11–10 and in third place in the Eastern Colored League. They were, nevertheless, only a half-game ahead of both Harrisburg and the Bacharachs. The Black Sox were a competitive club, but poor pitching and "hits lacking at opportune moments" plagued them.[55]

An unexpected meeting between Cum Posey of the Homestead Grays and Charles Spedden at the train station in Philadelphia changed everything. The Black Sox were not supposed to travel by train, but their bus proved so uncomfortable the players begged Spedden to finish the trip by rail. Spedden relented.[56] He found himself at the station then quite by chance. The week before, Cum Posey and John Beckwith, "one of the most valuable players in organized baseball," had an on-field confrontation.[57] Posey had called for a pinch-hitter, but "Beckwith waved him back." For Posey, it was "the climax" of a season-long power struggle: "Beckwith," said Posey, "was unable to fit into our organization … and we felt that we either had to let him go or ruin the morale of the club."[58] When word of Beckwith's availability leaked, teams from the ECL and the NNL reached out to him, but Spedden had the jump on them all. Without hesitation, "he immediately hopped aboard the first train to Pittsburgh," discovering he had just missed

After his arrival, John Beckwith sat for a formal photographic portrait at the Penn Studio (Huggins and Scott).

Beckwith, who had taken a train to Chicago earlier in the day. Spedden wired ahead to Beckwith's Chicago home and then "boarded a flyer" from Pittsburgh in pursuit of the star shortstop. Shortly after his arrival, Spedden met with Beckwith. Later that day, he wired the team in Baltimore: "On my way East with Beckwith."[59]

Charles Spedden had engineered a coup. The acquisition of Beckwith had turned a competitive Black Sox team into the best club in the Eastern Colored League. He transformed the Sox from a .500 club into one that challenged Hilldale for the pennant. Sitting at 11–10 before Beckwith, the Black Sox played .700 ball with him in the lineup, winning 22 of 31 games.

The papers raved about Spedden's acquisition, writing that "Beckwith fills up a bad hole," and that the "Sox have one of the greatest performers" in the game. The fans were equally excited.[60] In his first game as a Black Sox, he went 3-for-4, hitting a triple. In his first 21 games, he hit .432.[61] The team played at an electrifying level, sweeping the Cuban Stars and the Washington Potomacs.[62] By mid–August, Baltimore was in second place, just four games behind Hilldale.[63] John Beckwith had earned the title of "team captain."[64]

The euphoria was tempered by the sudden death of Black Sox star third baseman Henry Blackmon. On an off-day in August, he decided to go to the doctor, complaining of a "throat ailment." Within days, he would pass away. It was a devastating moment for the team and the city. The "members of the club attended the funeral in a body," and "thousands of fans blocked traffic" on Pennsylvania Avenue. John Beckwith, who had played with Blackmon for only a few weeks, was heartbroken and helped to carry his coffin.[65] Ben Taylor observed, "Blackmon was one of the three great third basemen in the East." More importantly, he "was one of the best natured men in baseball," and his death dealt a "severe blow to the Sox and baseball in general."[66] His passing also galvanized the team.

Fate and the Eastern Colored League seemed arrayed against Baltimore. In late August, the *Afro-American* ran the headline, "Black Sox have fighting chance to win the 1924 Pennant."[67] The Black Sox most certainly could out play Hilldale in the final month of the season, as they had in July and August. In mid–September, the papers carried the news that the "Hilldale club has been given the 1924 pennant." As a team, the Black Sox were "dissatisfied." The fans were "disgusted." Hilldale had "lost more games than the Sox," but they had also played more games, so they had a higher winning percentage. The Black Sox' remaining games were either cancelled or played as exhibition games.[68] Their final record was 33–19, for a .635 winning percentage. Hilldale finished 47–22, for a .681 percentage. The Black Sox would go on to sweep a scheduled doubleheader from the Lincoln Giants. If those games had counted, Baltimore's winning percentage would have been .648, but fans and the newspapers pointed to the umpire Aubrey's decision to forfeit a game to Hilldale earlier in the season as the difference. Even taken into consideration, those three games against Lincoln and Hilldale would have made for a closer finish, but Hilldale would still have a higher winning percentage. The real issue was an unbalanced schedule, which saw Hilldale play more games than Baltimore. Nonetheless, the season ended on a bitter note. The tragedy of Henry Blackmon's untimely death, taken together with the ECL's decision to end the season early, left Black Sox fans bitter and dissatisfied.

They could find some recompense in individual performances. John Beckwith finished the season batting .371, with a .431 OBP (on-base percentage) and a 1.035 OPS (on-base percentage plus slugging percentage). Jud Wilson batted .385, with a .431 OBP and a .934 OPS. Crush Holloway led the team with 18 stolen bases and batted .324.

Writing of the 1924 season, Ben Taylor characterized John Beckwith as a "sensational" fielder, a "demon at bat," and "one of the most feared men in the league." Taylor called Wilson "a really great ballplayer," and "one of the hardest hitters in the game." Taylor thought that the club's weakness was its pitching staff, but that Blackmon's untimely death "helped keep them from winning the pennant."[69] Fans could look forward then with some optimism for the 1925 season, hoping that Charlie Spedden could somehow find better pitching to back up a great hitting and fielding team.

"Baltimore on the map for Colored baseball": The Colored World Series

The apex of Spedden's leadership and of Maryland Baseball Park came when Baltimore hosted two games in the 1924 Colored World Series. The choice of Maryland Park was an acknowledgment of Baltimore's prominent role in the newly formed Eastern Colored League, of Spedden's status within the league, and of the city's importance: "Baltimore was seen as a major Black capital, geographically and economically well placed."[70]

Baltimore did not disappoint. Excitement was intense prior to the first series game.

As early as seven o'clock Sunday morning crowds could be seen making their way to the Maryland ballpark to see the World Series between Hilldale and Kansas City. Every available means of transportation was taxed to capacity and the jitneys, taxis and busses did a land office business. The ticket windows were opened at 9 o'clock and it took six expert sellers to handle the monster crowd which lined the park for blocks.

One of the busiest men in captivity was Charles Spedden. He couldn't turn around unless a hundred fans were at his heels.[71]

Newspapers reported that "every hotel and lodging house in the city was packed and many visitors were seeking sleeping quarters." Accounts put the attendance at a minimum of 10,000 but perhaps as large as 12,000.[72] The fences between the playing field and the seats had been removed, and at least two additional rows of seating had been added. Fans stood in the aisles. There were a few ladies present, and whites and blacks sat together in the integrated grandstands. Their clothing (hats, ties, and dresses) attests to the occasion's prestige. The *Baltimore Sun* and national papers covered the game, which lasted twelve innings before being called because of darkness. The teams played the next day, but, because it was a Monday afternoon game, it was not well attended. Nonetheless, Baltimore had made an impression.

1925: "Late hours and bad booze, mixed with wild women"

The 1925 season began with hope and anticipation. The pitching staff had improved somewhat. Charles Spedden had signed Bob Clark from the Richmond Giants and Nick Logan, who had previously pitched for the Black Sox.[73] Spedden had also scouted the Pacific Coast League, signing John Mungin, a right-handed pitcher.[74] However, John Beckwith was the real game changer. Beckwith would be the new on-field manager, with Pete Hill running the club's "business end."[75] With Beckwith running the club, batting in front of Wilson for the entire season, and holding down shortstop, fans had every reason to believe that the Black Sox could play at the same level in 1925 that they had played from July to September in 1924.

The Black Sox, on paper, had improved during the offseason. Their lineup could now boast the "Four Horsemen" that included Wilson, Beckwith, Crush Holloway, and Heavy Johnson; Johnson, the former Kansas City Monarch, signed in early April.[76] Together, they were the "heaviest hitters in baseball."[77] Fans anticipated that the club would then have its revenge against Hilldale, for outplaying Baltimore over the course of an entire season in 1924, and against the Eastern Colored League, for not giving the Black Sox their fair shot at the pennant.

6. "On the map for colored baseball": 1923–26

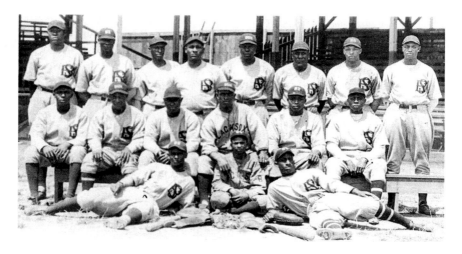

The Baltimore Black Sox team photograph from 1925. Back row, from left: Harry Jeffries, unknown, Connie Day, Heavy Johnson, John Beckwith, Jud Wilson, Julio Rojo, Crush Holloway; second row, from left: Bill Force, Bob Clarke, George Britt, Pete Hill, Kid Strong, unknown; front: unknown (Huggins and Scott).

The Black Sox responded with some truly outstanding individual performances to start the year. In a doubleheader against the Brooklyn Royal Giants in May, Jud Wilson had four hits and a stolen base. Against the Cuban Stars, John Beckwith "won the second game [of a doubleheader] with a homerun over the center-field fence." In the first game, the Cuban Giants were playing "small ball," and successfully. Their leadoff hitter lined a weak single past second. The next man up bunted safely. The next hitter, with runners in motion, "hit a hot drive to Britt who made a perfect catch, threw to Beckwith, who caught [the lead runner] before he could get back to second. Beckwith threw to Day who covered first." It was a triple play. The "10,000 fans" who had "packed in Maryland Park and overflowed to the outfield"[78] had gotten their money's worth, even though the Black Sox dropped the first game. By mid–June, the Black Sox had three players among the league leaders in hitting. Wilson was batting .448; Beckwith, .375; and Day, .375. Three other Black Sox starters were hitting above .300.[79] Baltimore had three of the ECL's leading basestealers: Holloway and Johnson had four each, and Wilson had three.[80] In addition, Beckwith was leading the ECL in home runs. Despite impressive individual achievements, the Black Sox "were hanging out in third place" behind both Harrisburg and Hilldale.[81]

G. L. Mackay, the *Afro-American*'s sports editor, wrote that the club has "not shown the brand of baseball they are capable of." He admitted that the "pitching staff ... hasn't shown any exceptional ability," but that was not the real problem. In his analysis, the team had a split personality. At times, they "will bring the fans to their feet with superb plays that equal anything in the big circuits, and, just as suddenly, these same players will deliberately throw away a game with some of the most stupid backlot baseball imaginable." The "fans," Mackay observed, were "frankly disappointed" and had a right to be because, it was "rumored, that the gay white lights are also responsible for the condition or rather the lack of condition of several of the players."[82] Mackay did not name names, but he didn't have to. The players had been put on notice that their off-the-field behavior had negatively affected their on-field performance. Baltimore in general, and the African American community in particular, was akin to a small town. The *Afro-American*'s office was across the street from Smith's Hotel, where many of the Black Sox players lived. The reporters would dine at Smith's or gather in the bar. With Mackay's article, they had been warned that there would be no "gentleman's agreements" about silence. The papers would call the players out if necessary.

There were, subsequently, signs of hope. More than 8,000 fans saw Kid Strong, who had been with the team in 1924 but who had come into his own in 1925, win "both ends of a double-header from Hilldale."[83] Strong's new "jump steady" pitch was suspected of being the result of a doctoring, and "games [were] held up to examine the ball."[84] The umpires never found evidence of tampering, and Strong and the team were on a roll. The Black Sox swept the Wilmington Potomacs, with Strong both pitching the second game and getting the game-winning hit.[85] By the end of July, Baltimore was tied with Harrisburg for second place, with a record of 22–11, but then they imploded.

On July 30, the *Baltimore Sun* broke the news that "two Black Sox players" had done "battle with Umpire" W. H. Shewell in Harrisburg. Jud Wilson had been "arrested," and a "warrant was issued" for Beckwith who "left the city before the warrant could be served."[86] The *Afro-American* sorted fact from fiction, determining that "Wilson's arrest was a frame up" and that he "had nothing at all to do with the fight."[87] Shewell, G. L. Mackay asserted, was "one of the most incompetent umpires we have ever seen work a game."[88] His "one-sided decisions" had infuriated the Black Sox. Regardless, Beckwith's behavior was inexcusable. He attacked Shewell not in the heat of the moment but "after the game." The team had already boarded their bus when Beckwith "got out ... and gave the umpire a severe beating."[89] The Eastern Colored League suspended Beckwith, and "Charlie Spedden" announced that "Pete Hill will handle the reigns."[90] Beckwith would remain with the team but was no longer manager.

In August, the Black Sox won four games and lost seven.[91] The *Afro-American* characterized their play as "almost quitting." They dropped doubleheaders to both Harrisburg[92] and the Cuban Stars, with Kid Strong losing three of the four games.[93] The *Afro-American* called out the team, quoting Charles Spedden, who warned that "the whole outfit is due for a general house cleaning." The paper declared that "what started out looking like a winning combination turned into a lot of highly temperamental, disgruntled players that have the fans disgusted." Most damning of all, the *Afro* noted, was the "late hours and bad booze, with wild women" that "have the Sox shot to pieces."[94] It is a testament to the club's raw talent that they were in third place.

Perhaps responding to the *Afro-American's* article, to Charlie Spedden's public statement, or to Pete Hill's steadying hand, the Black Sox won four of their final five games, finishing with a record of 30–19.[95] Statistically, the team's stars had very good years.

Beckwith finished the season with a league-leading .419 average, losing the home-run title to Oscar Charleston by one. Jud Wilson also batted .400, and six other Black Sox finished the season hitting .300 or higher.[96] Nonetheless, 1925 was a season of bitter disillusionment for Black Sox supporters. In a telling vote, Julio Rojo, the team's catcher and regarded as a good team player, won a reader's poll for most valuable Black Sox player, beating out the Four Horsemen and the club's other, more prominent stars. Rojo received 6,328 votes. A total of 750 fans voted for Beckwith.[97] Perhaps fittingly, the Black Sox' final day of 1925 saw them losing in 12 innings to Hilldale in the first game of a doubleheader. Kid Strong had allowed two runs for the first twelve innings, striking out seven, but gave up three runs in the 13th. The second game, and the last game of the year, was called for darkness.

1926: "Morale breaks"

In January, Charles Spedden and George Rossiter announced that Ben Taylor would be the team's new manager. Taylor asked the press to "tell people they will see a different ball club from the one they have been seeing." As the roster, "outside of a few changes in the outfield," would be "the same as last year," Taylor's meaning was clear. He would provide a change in leadership that the Black Sox needed. He was the son of a Methodist minister and had played for the St. Louis Stars, the Lincoln Giants, Rube's Foster's Chicago American Giants, and the Indianapolis ABCs. In 1922, he became manager of the Bacharachs and, in 1924, of the Washington Potomacs.[98] He had experience playing and managing in the Eastern Colored League. His Hall of Fame plaque in Cooperstown describes him as a "soft spoken and modest team leader" who was also a "top flight defensive first baseman and clutch hitter." He was confident and the fans were hopeful that he would indeed be the difference. For the first few weeks of the season, Taylor appeared prophetic.

Opening weekend, 1926, was the Ben Taylor and Crush Holloway show. Holloway "brought down the stands [more than 10,000 paid] with his scintillating catches." He also "walked, stole second and third, and scored a run on a sacrifice." Taylor homered "over the left-field fence."[99] The new manager was seen as "one of the few great veterans left in the game." He had done "as much or more to promote the sport than anyone else in colored baseball."[100] At the end of the first week, Taylor was hitting .400 with a double to go along with his home run.

Crush Holloway was batting .358 with a triple. Wilson and Beckwith were just hitting their stride and batting .312 and .307 respectively.[101] The team record was two wins and two losses, but there was cause for hope: The first-place Hilldale Giants, with a record of 3–0, were coming to Maryland Park to play a doubleheader.[102]

The excitement was palpable and had an epic quality, literally. The center-lede article in the *Afro-American* began, "Hark, hark, how the dogs bark/The Hilldales are coming to town:/With bats and balls, gloves 'n' all./To battle the Sox from the mound." It was to be a "great battle" for first in the Eastern Colored League. The fans had never forgiven Hilldale for their legitimate success, for their lack of Black Sox-like dysfunction, and for what was perceived in Baltimore as their illegitimate 1924 Eastern Colored League pennant. It was a mixture of jealousy and bitterness that made for a supreme rivalry. There was also nervousness: "The Sox have a powerful hitting team, but the pitchers are causing Manager Ben serious concern." Kid Strong had held out for a higher salary, but a new hero had emerged. Sixteen-year-old Norman "Lefty" Bowers could "make a ball do everything except talk." In a game against the Cubans, it "did somersaults at the plate, hesitated and stopped awhile.... Once, it looked like the ball had decided to return back to the pitcher." It seemed as if fate, for once, favored the Black Sox.

For the doubleheader, "an estimated throng of over 10,000 ran over the outfield and on top of the grandstand." The Black Sox, as it turned out, need not utilize their teenaged magician. Kid Strong surprised the fans by starting the first game and it was "masterly." He struck out seven, walking only two. "His support was flawless." John Beckwith had a homer and two doubles. Jud Wilson had three hits. In the second game, John Mungin and George Britt held Hilldale to two runs. Judy Johnson, Hilldale's Hall of Fame third baseman, went 3-for-4, but otherwise, the Black Sox stars ruled the day. Beckwith and Wilson had multiple hits as did Holloway, who tripled and stole a base. The Black Sox had realized their "ambition," sweeping Hilldale and securing first place in the ECL standings.[103]

All was well in Baltimore, and the papers gave credit to the new manager: "Ben Taylor has the respect of every man on the club and is conducting himself in a way that has gained the confidence of fans and players." The *Afro-American* pointed to "a spirit of cooperation that has never existed before. On and off the field there is a cordial relationship and good feeling among the team members."[104] In early June, the Black Sox, at 8–4, had a game and a half edge on second-place Hilldale. Jud Wilson was batting .500. Beckwith was hitting .433, and Holloway's average was .419.

Over the next month, however, the team suffered an epic collapse. Their play was "disastrous." They lost four straight league games.[105] By mid–June, they had dropped from first to fifth place.[106] The team's poor pitching, lack of hitting with runners in scoring position, and "mistakes in the field" proved "devastating." The *Afro* identified the moment the collapse began with the headline, "Sox morale breaks in seventh when Oms hits homer over right-field fence." Kid Strong had pitched around the Cubans' star center fielder in two previous at-bats, but Strong "accidentally got one in the neighborhood of the plate."[107] Baltimore would lose the first game, 7–1, and the second game, 5–1. Wilson, Beckwith, and Holloway combined for three hits in the two games. The team's woes continued. Hilldale not only beat but "smothered" the Black Sox in a rematch.[108] Baltimore's pitchers surrendered 19 walks in a 17–5 loss.[109]

Ben Taylor took the blame. The *Afro-American* defended him, writing that he was "handicapped by men not being in condition to play." Nonetheless, the fans gave Taylor "some of the worst abuse ever given a ballplayer," and Taylor commented that he had never "come into contact with or played before a crowd of people that are as unjust as the people of Baltimore."[110] The fans were in a state of panic. They were witnessing another season slip away, and their response was visceral.

Management reacted with a sense of urgency. The papers reported, "Spedden has been scouring the country" for pitching talent, and then a shocking headline greeted fans.[111] "John Beckwith is traded to Harrisburg." In return for Beckwith, the Black Sox received $1,000 and three players: Mack Eggleston, a third baseman; Wilbert Pritchett, a left-handed pitcher; and Darltie Cooper, a right-handed pitcher.[112] Ben Taylor thought he had "the best of the deal" as the team "sorely" needed pitching help.[113] The trade did not work out as planned. A week later, Cooper left. The official story was that he had a "sore arm," but in reality, he "quit baseball rather than play on the Baltimore team."[114] Before the trade, the Black Sox, despite their recent collapse, were somewhat competitive, with a 14–15 record.[115] After the trade, they would win only 4 of 18 games.[116] In their first four seasons in the Eastern Colored League, with John Beckwith on the team, the Black Sox would win 66 games and lose 43, a .606 winning percentage. Without him, the team went 15–24, a winning percentage of .385.

After his departure, the Black Sox exhibited signs of increasing frustration and desperation. A week after the trade, Jud Wilson was thrown out of a game for arguing with an umpire. In that same game, Ben Taylor was "reprimanded for rough tactics." They lost three straight to the Lincoln Giants.[117] After losing a doubleheader to Hilldale in August, Taylor benched Jud Wilson. He didn't make a road trip with the team.[118] Taylor himself had trouble holding it together. In a game in August, he "ran from the dugout and started to argue with the umpire. After finding it useless to convince the umpire he was wrong, the manager grew threatening." The Black Sox were forced to forfeit the game because of Taylor's behavior.[119] To make matters worse, Kid Strong showed up for a scheduled start against the Bacharachs "so intoxicated" that "he couldn't play."[120] Before the season ended, management traded Connie Day and gave Heavy Johnson his unconditional release.[121]

"History was made"

The Black Sox' 1926 season ended in disappointment, but Baltimore fans could look forward to championship baseball at Maryland Park that October. The Eastern League chose the city to host the third game in the 1926 Negro World Series between the Atlantic City Bacharachs and the Chicago American Giants; Spedden served as the league's commissioner for the series.

Fans witnessed one of the most significant games in baseball history.[122] Red Grier pitched a no-hitter, the first in the postseason, predating Don Larsen's perfect game by thirty-one years. After the 1924 Series, the *Afro-American* wrote that "history was made.... A brand of ball was played that was not excelled by any of the Major Leagues."[123] Maryland Baseball Park proved itself to be a part of that history, a part of the development of the Negro Leagues, and a part of the corresponding history of baseball.

"Baseball in Baltimore is hanging by a slender thread"

Despite the success of the World Series and the relative success of the team at the box office, the Black Sox were experiencing financial problems. The team had a payroll of $3,000 to $3,500 a month. The cost of paying visiting teams had risen from $350 in 1923 to $400 in 1926. Simply put, "the club has not cleared expenses."[124] Add to these basic costs, Maryland Park itself required $6,000 a year in maintenance.[125] The team also had to cover the salaries of the ballpark's staff and front office personnel, which included Spedden's salary as general manager but also the salaries of people such as Bill Lewis, the park's announcer; the team's umpires; Cliff Thompson, who handled drinks and concessions; and Uncle Henry, the groundskeeper.[126] The club also had to pay for equipment. In 1926, the Black Sox purchased $1,150 of gloves, bats, balls, and protective gear from the Spalding Company, which, in January 1927, had not been paid in full.[127] As Charles Spedden told the *Afro-American*, "Baseball in Baltimore is hanging by a slender thread."[128] The Black Sox were not alone. Eastern League franchises in Washington and Wilmington had already folded, and the Brooklyn Royal Giants were in serious financial trouble.

In early 1927, the team's fiscal situation reached a breaking point. The Spalding Company filed a lawsuit against the Black Sox, George Rossiter, and Charles Spedden for the $350 balance owed on their account.[129] The team settled the balance and avoided court, but the source of the money for the settlement caused further problems. In February, the Eastern Colored League announced Charles Spedden's "enforced retirement ... from the affairs of the Baltimore Black Sox."[130] It accused him of shorting the Eastern League of its share of commissions for the 1926 World Series. The amount of the shortage was $385. The *Afro-American* announced that "Charles Spedden is no longer manager and generalissimo of the Black Sox."[131]

"A darn good guy"

Charles Spedden took pride in his work for the Black Sox, boasting about it in a political advertisement: "Vote for the man who put Baltimore on the map for Colored baseball."[132] There is little doubt that he had saved the Black Sox in 1917 and had rebuilt the franchise into a regional power-house and, subsequently, a team with a national reputation. As members of the Eastern Colored League, with Spedden as GM, the Black Sox were a winning club, with a 100–97 record. He helped organize the Eastern Colored League and was instrumental in the organization and manage-ment of World Series games between the ECL champions and the Negro National League champions. His legacy has been largely forgotten.

In Baltimore, Spedden worked to make going to the game an enjoy-able experience, reaching out into the community, sponsoring excursions so fans could meet and socialize with the players and management. In August of 1923, the team rented "Wonderland Park," an African Amer-ican amusement park in Baltimore. He hired Cliff Jackson's Krazy Kats and invited fans to "dance" with the team's stars.[133] After the 1923 season, he established the Black Sox Café on West Saratoga Street, in an Afri-can American neighborhood. Advertisements invited fans to "stop in" for "news about your ball club" and to "talk it over."[134] His efforts built com-munity support that crossed racial boundaries. He brought a large per-centage of white fans to the ballgames while maintaining a strong black fan base. Advertisements ran in the *Baltimore Sun* telling its readers that "white patronage [is] solicited."[135] In 1923, the *Afro-American* reported that "about 20 per cent of the attendance is white," and that by 1925 that ratio had grown to about 50 percent.[136] White fans were an important revenue source for the team, but their attendance at the games also focused on race relations in the city. The language used by the *Afro-American* is particu-larly instructive. In October of 1923, the paper noted a "good sprinkling" of "white" fans and, in 1925, observed that "Baltimore has a large Colored population and mixed with a large following of white fans."[137] The words "sprinkling" and "mixed" are not so subtle references to integrated seating at Maryland Park; Oriole Park had segregated seating.[138] Moreover, the *Afro-American* told readers that they "will find the races evenly divided when the Black Sox play at home,"[139] creating a verbal play on words with notions of separate but equal but also affirming the equality of blacks at the baseball team's "home."

Charles Spedden, for all the good he did for the team, initially man-ifested a latent prejudice in hiring at Maryland Baseball Park. In 1923, almost all the workers were black, except for the ticket office. In response to questions raised by the *Afro-American*, Spedden indicated that "he has tried the experiment of using Colored men in the box office but has not found them satisfactory in the rapid handling of change and furthermore that they are most always short when the count is made."[140] Spedden's remarks would prove ironic in light of the scandal that compelled him to leave the team in February of 1927. Despite his manifest flaws, Spedden, in effect if not in intent, did much for race relations in the Baltimore.

Maryland Baseball Park and the Westport Baseball Grounds were in a nonresidential area on the city's borders. They were adjacent to segregated white neighborhoods, and, during the time he ran the team, there were no reports of racial tensions from black or white fans, travelling to the park or from within the park. It was a remarkable state of affairs given that racial tensions plagued the city in this period and that the *Baltimore Sun* had a reputation for manufacturing racial incidents.[141] Although Spedden cannot take credit for the fans' good behavior or for the *Sun's* restraint, it is appropriate to give him credit for, perhaps unintentionally, demonstrating that blacks and whites can mix without violence and that a large black presence in a white neighborhood does not lead to violence.[142] Such was the discourse that led to Baltimore's segregation laws and kept many of the neighborhoods racially divided long after a Supreme Court ruling meant that those laws could not be enforced.[143] Spedden also never tried to segregate seating at Maryland Baseball Park, even though, in doing so, he may have attracted more white fans to Black Sox games. Significantly, in January of 1924, the *Afro-American* reported that "the entire working force from ticket takers to umpire will be colored. This will be the first time in the history of the city and the move is bound to meet with favor."[144] Charles Spedden knew how to market the team, could recognize his shortcomings, and was willing to change.

Spedden also hired black umpires. At the time, teams hired their own umpires, and each crew had two members rather than the four that is customary today. Rube Foster and the Negro National League made a concerted effort in 1923 to hire and train black umpires, but the Black Sox had led the way years before Foster's push.[145] The Baltimore *Afro-American*, under the headline "Best in the League" reported their names.[146] Spedden lured Henry "Spike" Spencer away from Washington, D.C. The team's other umpire was Charley "Square Deal" Cromwell whose service dates back to at least the 1920 season at Westport and probably earlier.[147]

In 1923, Rube Foster tried to hire him away from the Black Sox, and Spedden offered Cromwell "inducements" to stay in Baltimore.[148] For this and for his reconsideration in hiring for the ticket office, Spedden deserves credit. Maryland Baseball Park and the Black Sox welcomed and ultimately nurtured "colored professionals" in baseball.

BALTIMORE

Charles Cromwell
UMPIRE

Charlie "Square Deal" Cromwell's umpiring career spanned four decades, starting with the Black Sox at the Westport Baseball Grounds and ending with the Elite Giants at Bugle Field. Charles Spedden persuaded him to stay in Baltimore even though Rube Foster was determined to have him in Chicago. When George Rossiter became the team's principal owner, he fired Cromwell for what was likely reasons related to race. Cromwell found work easily, such was his reputation, and he finished his career working in the Negro National League (illustration courtesy Gary Joseph Cieradkowski, StudioGaryC.com).

In relaying the news of his departure to its readers, the *Afro-American* called it "the passing of one of the colorful figures in baseball,"[149] using an expression whose double meaning is indeed high praise for a white owner-general manager of a professional African American team. Robert Wilson, the sports editor for the *Pittsburgh Courier*, wrote that Spedden "was a darn good guy and always decent to me, which is rather more than I can say for some of the league's executives."[150] Evidence also suggests another motive in the ECL's action against Spedden. He had been mentioned as a candidate for league commissioner, but because "bitter feelings" would "result from his selection" he was passed over. Rivals in the ECL office may have engineered his departure. In truth, each host club underreported attendance at World Series games. Spedden may have simply made enemies which catalyzed his dismissal.[151] Nonetheless, with his departure, George Rossiter assumed the duties as general manager, while maintaining his role as business manager.

6. "On the map for colored baseball": 1923–26

He had skill in scouting and recruiting talented players, but he would also prove to be tone deaf to the concerns of the Black Sox' core fans in the African American community. He also placed less emphasis on maintaining Maryland Park. The next five seasons would showcase Rossiter's skills but also his shortcomings.

7

$\diamond$

Building a Champion:
1927–31

Bill Gibson, writing in the *Afro-American*, characterized George Rossiter as "a hard man to find."[1] When Rossiter did reach out to the press, he came across as irritable, misunderstood, or even racist. In response to questions about ticket prices increasing as the crowd grew larger for a particular game, Rossiter responded by saying the charge was a "lie," but he added, in an apparent non sequitur, that "if race men [i.e., blacks] would put up the cash he would be glad to sell out and retire." He added that white patrons make up 60 to 70 percent of ticket sales, and that he would have to increase the police presence at games.[2] Despite his assurances, a year later he backed out of a proposed sale of the Black Sox to a consortium of black businessmen.[3] He also fired the team's umpires, Spencer and Cromwell, determined to "insist on the use of white umpires" until "Negro umpires ... prove competent."[4] In 1930, he faced charges of segregation at Maryland Baseball Park, when his plans to have seating reserved for white patrons became known. His comments and behavior eroded support in the African American community. Reflecting the tense relations between ownership and that community, the *Afro-American* almost always identifies Rossiter as "white," which was not unusual for the time. The paper only once identifies Spedden as white, and that was its first story about his partnership with Rossiter.[5] Certainly, Rossiter did not have the same relationship with the press in particular, and the African American community in general, that the "colorful" Charles Spedden enjoyed.

The deteriorating condition of Maryland Baseball Park did not help Rossiter's cause. A year after Spedden's departure, stories began to appear noting that the team would have to invest between "$15,000 and $18,000" to get the field and stands "in proper condition for the coming season."[6] By June, the repairs had not been made.[7] The stories also revealed that the Black Sox no longer owned Maryland Baseball Park. It had become the property of the B&O Railroad at the end of the 1927 season, and the Black

122

Sox were responsible for $2,400 in rent for a facility they once owned but were still responsible for maintaining.[8] In 1929, the *Afro-American* noted, "improvements have been PROMISED."[9] They were not forthcoming, and, by 1930, the press called for a new ballpark owned by the team and in a new location.[10]

To be fair, George Rossiter did attempt to introduce some improvements to Maryland Park, such as electric lights. An advertisement published on August 18, 1928, announced that the "Maryland Baseball Park has been beautifully electrified and can be used for outings and night carnivals."[11] Rossiter had opened a potential new revenue stream for his club. Less than two years later, the Black Sox scheduled their first night game, which was to take place on June 23, 1930. The subsequent game would serve as a metaphor for Rossiter's relationship with the fans. He possessed an eye for publicity and innovation, but his efforts fell flat because he would not invest enough to make his ideas a success.

The press enthusiastically embraced the then revolutionary concept of baseball under the lights. The *Baltimore Sun* reported that "night baseball will make its bow to Baltimore."[12] It was to be an historic event, coming only six weeks after the first professional baseball night game was played in Des Moines, Iowa; the Orioles would not play their first night game until September 4.[13] Rossiter's experiment did not go well. On June 24, the *Baltimore Sun* reported, "Baseball enthusiasts who gathered at the Maryland Baseball Park, Westport, last night to see what was to have been the first night game in Baltimore got their money back." The lighting was so poor that Frank Warfield, the Black Sox manager, would not let his players take the field, fearing injury.[14] Rossiter would install a new lighting system but not for another year; the historic moment had passed. George Rossiter did invest in players for his team, and the Black Sox, over the next five years, would eventually become his team. Initially, he deferred to more experienced baseball men.

1927: "Ben Taylor's team"

Ben Taylor's first season as Black Sox manager had been in 1926. That year, the team was a model of dysfunction both on and off the field. In his defense, the "Black Sox owners brought Ben Taylor here and gave him charge of a team that they had picked out themselves." In 1927, the papers reported that he "has been given wider latitude" and has responded with a willingness "to risk his reputation."[15] He "searched the country for talent" and demanded a greater discipline from his players. At the end of spring training, his efforts seem to have borne fruit. The team finished the exhibition season with a 6–2 record. On the field, "men are hustling at all times." Off the field, there "seems to be perfect harmony and every man seems to be rallying to Manager Taylor."[16] In 1927, the Black Sox were "Ben Taylor's team."[17]

The Opening Day lineup would feature some familiar faces. Jud Wilson started at third and Taylor was at first. Crush Holloway was in left field and Mack Eggleston was the catcher; Rossiter traded Julio Rojo to Harrisburg. Scrappy Brown returned to the Black Sox and was the starting shortstop. Pete Washington was the new center fielder. Born in Albany, Georgia, Washington had played for the Potomacs and the Lincoln Giants. He was known as an outstanding defensive player.[18] Dick Jackson was the new second baseman. He had played for Harrisburg in 1926 and was a native of Greenville, South Carolina. Pete Johnson was the new right fielder. He was known for his speed and ability to get on base: He "can draw more walks from good hurlers than any man in baseball. This is because of his shifty position at the plate."[19] The pitching staff included Black Sox veterans Bob McClure, Bill Force, and Kid Strong, who "did very well after his suspension" for reporting to a game under the influence.[20]

Laymon Yokely would also join the staff as a regular. He had pitched for the Black Sox in 1926. Ben Taylor had seen him play for Livingston College, "had a word with" him, and "told him how impressive he looked." Yokely, a Salisbury, North Carolina, native, was just 19. "Under the guidance" of the Black Sox catchers, he "rounded into a fairly good relief hurler."[21]

More specifically, he "learned control ... as well as a change of pace" to go with "what one might call an assortment of curves."[22] Ben Taylor had put together a better team than the Black Sox fielded in 1926, although the '26 club, with Heavy Johnson and John Beckwith, had more individual stars.

As the 1927 campaign approached, the Eastern Colored League announced a few changes. The season would be split, with the first- and second-half winners playing a series to determine the pennant winner. Teams would also play games in neutral cities such as Richmond; Mt. Holly, New Jersey; and Wilmington, Delaware.[23] The intent was to widen the audience for the league but also to make sure not to dilute the product for local fans. With the increased number of games, owners were concerned that fan enthusiasm might drop. Indeed, fan support had stagnated in 1926. The Black Sox were not the only team to experience financial difficulties, although they were the only club that did not cut players' salaries in response.[24]

Laymon Yokely, the legend goes, tossed seven no-hitters over his career. He played for both the Baltimore Black Sox and the Baltimore Elite Giants. At his peak, in the 1928–29 seasons, he compiled a combined record of 28–14 (illustration courtesy Gary Joseph Cieradkowski, StudioGaryC.com).

Fan support would be a lingering theme of newspaper coverage throughout the 1927 season. Opening Day attracted just 4,000 fans, compared to the 9,000 to 12,000 that had come to previous openers. Nonetheless, it was a raucous crowd that enjoyed the "glorious sunshiny day." Coverage in the *Afro-American* reflected the convivial spirit. Commenting on the Black Sox "new uniforms," the paper said the team "looked like flaming gold" and, "Evidentially, the Prince of Wales gave them some instructions on how to dress." Unfortunately, there are no extant photos of the uniforms and no other available descriptions. Thomas Smith, Weldons founder Wallace Smith's brother, and William Curran, the future Maryland attorney general, threw out the first pitch. "Evidently," wrote the *Afro*, Curran "has not played ball recently. On his toss-in ... the ball fell halfway between the plate and the pitcher's box. Tom Smith merely smiled."[25] The doubleheader "furnished innumerable thrills." The Black Sox would split the games against Harrisburg, but Crush Holloway and Jud Wilson gave the fans reasons to celebrate. Holloway went 3-for-8, with a home run over both games, and Jud Wilson had four hits in eight at-bats, including two doubles. He also stole a base and executed an unassisted double play.[26]

The first weeks of the season would showcase the team and its players. In a game in mid–May, the Black Sox "smothered" the Cuban Stars. Kid Strong allowed one run and three hits, while the Black Sox scored 15 runs. Jud Wilson had five hits, including a home run.[27] Earlier that week, Laymon Yokely pitched a two-hit shutout against Hilldale. Yokely would also beat the Lincoln Giants in late May to win his third straight. In that game, Pete Johnson had three walks, a hit, and four stolen bases. Bob McClure won seven consecutive games. In a matchup against Hilldale, the Black Sox stole nine bases, with Pete Johnson accounting for three. On June 25, the Black Sox were in first, with an 18–10 record.[28] McClure and Yokely were first and second in the ECL with seven and six wins respectively.[29] Wilson was batting .373, and Jackson led the league with a .442 average.[30] An early July slump cost the team the first-half title. They finished second to the Bacharachs.

Nonetheless, there was reason to be optimistic about the second half of the season. The Black Sox were playing competitive baseball and, for the first time in years, were playing as a team. Fan support still was wanting. The *Afro-American* noted that "attendance ought to be 5,000 and 6,000 instead of 3,500 and 4,000." The paper blamed the length of the games, most running for more than two and a half hours: "Things are too slow," wrote the sports editor. Fans "want to see snappy action and not a funeral."[31] Although the length of the games was doubtlessly a factor in poor attendance, the Black Sox had also alienated a large part of their fan base with their behavior on and off the field in previous years. Families were unlikely to come if it meant seeing drunken players taking, or attempting to take, the field. Fights between players and umpires, and subsequent arrests, made the situation worse. Moreover, the team's lack of conditioning, which had squandered leads in the previous two seasons, likely spoiled the fans' view of the club. Ben Taylor had gotten off to a good start in rebuilding the club's reputation and the team's conditioning and competitiveness. The second part of the season held considerable promise.

Until bad luck hit, the Black Sox were on the way towards fulfilling that promise. On July 23, they were in first place, with five wins in six games. But then, Pete Johnson, the "league-leading base stealer and free pass king, was injured stealing second base."[32] He broke a bone in his foot. Without Johnson, the Sox were "left … without a first-string outfielder," and without the team's catalyst.[33] Absent Johnson, the Sox played just under .500 ball. On August 13, they were in third place at 8–7, but they were just three and a half games behind the Bacharachs.[34] Baltimore's pitching carried the team. Kid Strong threw an 11-inning no-hitter against Hilldale in late July. If the pitching could hold up, they might just keep pace and have a chance at the second-half title when Johnson returned. Then, on August 13, the Black Sox' team bus crashed outside of Aberdeen, and "several of the players were cut by flying glass."[35] The Black Sox were heading north to play a game in Wilmington against the Cuban Stars when a concrete truck sideswiped their bus, which slammed into a telephone pole. Ben Taylor was "painfully injured about the head and arms. More than 20 stiches were required to close a wound on his left arm." Kid Strong, Dick Jackson, Pete Washington, and Jud Wilson were also injured.[36] Although only Taylor would miss more than a few games, the accident derailed the chances at the second-half title. The papers reported on a "team in patches," who "plucked" Bill Monroe from Howard University and William Craddock from North Carolina State to compensate for injuries.[37] The team's efforts proved fruitless. News reports indicated that the "injured Sox are slipping badly."[38]

There were a few bright moments in September when the injured players returned. In a game against the Bacharachs, the Black Sox trailed, 7–3, in the ninth. They managed to push a run over and then loaded the bases. Jud Wilson, who had hit two home runs already that day (and had stolen a base), came to the plate. He hit a grand slam to give the Black Sox a walk-off win. The spectators at Maryland Park "rushed onto the field" and showered "Wilson with dollar bills."[39] On the last day of the season, with all their regulars in the lineup, the Black Sox beat the Cubans, 9–0. Yokely pitched a two-hit shutout, and Jud Wilson had two home runs and a stolen base.[40] The Black Sox showed what they could do if healthy.

They finished the second half in fifth place with a 12–16 record. The team's stars had performed well. Ben Taylor, despite injuries, finished the season with a .347 average, good for ninth in the ECL. Mack Eggleston was fourth with a .393 average, and Jud Wilson led the league in hitting, batting .495. He had 105 hits in 212 at-bats. If it had not been for his injury, he would have likely batted over .500. It was his most remarkable season in his 20-year, Hall of Fame career. It was also, arguably, the most impressive batting performance in professional baseball history.

Despite the team's remarkable first half and the considerable accomplishments of its stars, fan support dwindled as the season progressed. Ralph Matthews, the *Afro's* sports editor, called Baltimore the "Hickest of Hicks towns." He wrote that he was "a Baltimorean, which may or may not be anything to brag about," and "when Baltimore does something to be ashamed of," he "naturally feel[s] ashamed too." He wrote that when the Black Sox had put a winning team on the field in the first half of the season, "Baltimoreans ... stayed home and read the funny papers on Sunday or motored to aristocratic Highland Beach." He wrote that there is "something wrong with Baltimore" and that he is "ashamed of Baltimore."[41] The Black Sox reported that they had been "losing money for several years" and that they were "trying to keep baseball in Baltimore."[42] They had to cut expenses. Rather than allot less to players' salaries, the team began to neglect Maryland Park.

1928: "Guerrilla warfare"

Black Sox fans could not have written a better script for the start of the 1928 season, which began with a doubleheader against the Cuban Stars. A large crowd gathered for festive pregame celebrations. Al Smith, the soon-to-be Democratic candidate for president, threw out the first pitch to Walter Emerson, an African American who would win election to the city council's 4th District seat. Theodore McKeldin, the future Republican mayor and governor, served as master of ceremonies. McKeldin advocated for civil rights and for an end to segregation.[43] As for the games themselves, the *Philadelphia Tribune* summed them up: The "Cubans" offered "stiff opposition before losing."[44] The star of the first game was Jud Wilson who hit a home run, a double, and stole a base.[45] In the second game, Pete Washington hit a game-winning double.[46] Writing for the *Pittsburgh Courier*, W. Rollo Wilson christened the Black Sox "the class" of the Eastern Colored League, adding, "Crush Holloway, Pete Washington, and Rap Dixon are a defensive trio which cannot be matched."[47] Dixon, who had played with Harrisburg in 1927, was an invaluable addition to the 1928 team who "converted the Baltimore Black Sox from a good club to a top notch outfit."[48] The *Philadelphia Tribune* heaped praise on the Sox outfield, writing that "each" is "a heavy stickman, each possessed of a rifle arm, and each a defensive expert," adding that they "work together with much precision. They are young, clever, alert, fast, and they think." Robert Ball went on to observe that Clark and Eggleston, the Black Sox catchers, were also standouts, catching six of seven Hilldale players trying to steal in a single game.[49] Laymon Yokely anchored the pitching staff, starting his year with a two-hit shutout against the Bacharach Giants.[50] Hall of Famers Ben Taylor and Jud Wilson started at third and first. George Rossiter even provided the team with new uniforms, which offered a stylized "B" on the right sleeve and a stylized "Sox" on the left sleeve.[51] The front of the grey uniforms contained red trim.[52]

At the start of June, the Black Sox were in first, having lost just two games. The "Fan-Sees" column of the *Afro-American* summed up the season in evaluating a doubleheader against Hilldale: "The Sox were poison on extra-base hits ... clouting eight doubles, two triples, and a homerun." Defensively, they turned "four double plays." At the plate, Rap Dixon made a "hobby of three-base blows." Jud Wilson "ripped out five hits in seven times at bat, two big doubles, a homerun, and scored six runs." Pitching the first game, "Big Jess" Hubbard allowed only one runner to reach third. In the second game, Laymon Yokely pitched brilliantly, striking out Oscar Charleston twice. The column closes by telling readers to "Put that in your pipe and smoke it."[53] The Sox were indeed off to an "auspicious" start.[54]

Nothing could stop them from winning the Eastern Colored League pennant except the demise of the Eastern League. The same day that the *Afro-American* published the "Fan-Sees" column praising the Black Sox, the paper also carried the story of the Cuban Stars and the Lincoln Giants leaving the ECL. There had been rumblings in the spring about the ECL's viability. In April, the papers reported that ownership had "voted to disband the Eastern League and play independent baseball," but by the end of that month, owners announced that the "Eastern League will continue."[55] Isaac Nutter, the league president, tried to put a positive spin on the news that hit the papers in early June. He told the press that "the Eastern League will continue to operate," and, "All games played between league members ... will count in the first-half standings." He had plans to entice two new franchises into the league, but nothing came of those efforts. There were no more standings. There was no first-half, let alone a second-half title. Instead, there was "guerrilla warfare" for the players now freed from their contracts.[56] The teams in the former ECL were now independent clubs.

The fans' response was predictable. The *Afro-American* wrote, "Sports lovers demand league baseball where something more than the result of the game is at stake."[57] Later in the summer, Bill Gibson observed, "Some of the Eastern clubs have been making money in the absence of any organized body of baseball in the East," adding, "They are in the minority." He reasoned, "Before the league had been organized there had been no real criteria. But now that is has been born and has gone we have a comparison."[58] The *Afro-American* editorialized, "now games are just games."[59] The Black Sox' season continued, and they continued to play games against the former members of the Eastern League.

The newspapers covered those games as if they were an informal pennant race. Going into September, the Black Sox' overall record, against all teams, was 51–15. Jud Wilson was hitting .495, Rap Dixon was hitting 424, and Crush Holloway was batting .355.[60] The papers looked ahead to a "crucial test" against the Homestead Grays in which "Eastern supremacy will be at stake."[61] Laymon Yokely pitched the first game of the series against the Grays. He won the game and had seven strikeouts, with two against John Beckwith. The *Afro-American* proclaimed that "Yokely is master," and the *Pittsburgh Courier*, the Grays' hometown paper, wrote that "Yokely is one of the most sensational pitchers in colored baseball."[62] Unfortunately, he was injured in that game and unavailable to pitch the rest of the series. Using three different pitchers, the Black Sox lost the second game of the opening doubleheader 11–2.[63] Their pitching depleted by injury, they would lose the three remaining games in the series.[64] In the unofficial race for the championship of the former Eastern Colored League, the Black Sox lost to the Homestead Grays. There is some consolation, however, in knowing that the Black Sox fielded one of the most talented teams in the country that year. Their lineup included two future Hall of Famers, Ben Taylor and Jud Wilson, and two men who are mentioned as Hall of Fame candidates, Rap Dixon and Laymon Yokely. In addition, in the last official standings of the Eastern Colored League, the Black Sox were in first place. Furthermore, to George Rossiter's credit, the Black Sox' roster remained stable and intact during a period of "guerrilla warfare" between the clubs in the former ECL.

1929: "Woe be unto those who stand in their way"

After the debacle of the 1928 season, club owners in what had been the Eastern Colored League faced a daunting challenge. In early July, Bill Gibson, in his weekly column for the *Afro*-American, wrote, "Smoke is still rising from the smoldering heap once called the Eastern League and it is hoped that 1929 will see a real league come into being."[65] In order to retain fans and quality ballplayers, they had to play within a strong, league structure. In response, they formed the American Negro League, which included the Black Sox, Hilldale, the Homestead Grays, the Bacharachs, the Cuban Stars and the Lincoln Giants.[66] Ed Bolden, president of the Hilldale club, became the commissioner. The teams agreed to a first- and second-half schedule, with a playoff between each half's champion to determine the pennant. The season would start in early May, with the first half extending into July. The second half would begin after the July 4 holiday and extend into September.

At the same time discussions were underway to form a new league, George Rossiter engineered a series of trades, reshaping the Black Sox. In late January, he announced that manager Ben Taylor, who had transformed a dysfunctional team into a perennial contender, would go to the Bacharachs for Dick Lundy, their manager and shortstop.[67] In early February, the Black Sox traded Crush Holloway and Dick Jackson to Hilldale for Red Ryan, a pitcher, and Frank Warfield, their manager and second baseman.[68] In March, the Black Sox acquired Pud Flournoy, a left-handed pitcher who had played for the Brooklyn Royal Giants.[69] In early April, Rossiter engineered a trade with the Bacharachs. Starting catcher Mack Eggleston would go to Atlantic City in return for John Cason, a catcher, and third baseman Oliver "Ghost" Marcell. The decision to trade away men who had successful track records in Baltimore was a risky move. Rossiter's reputation as a baseball executive was clearly on the line. When partnered with Charles Spedden, Rossiter deferred to the former catcher for personnel decisions. Pete Hill and Ben Taylor also were more prominent figures than Rossiter regarding trades and player development. The 1929 team was now the club that Rossiter had assembled. The responsibility was his alone.

The new team was met with a mixture of optimism and skepticism. There was no doubt the team had star power. In assessing the outfield, Bill Gibson, writing for the *Afro-American*, noted, "Mason, Hubbard, and Dixon ... present plenty of beef and we hope they will field as well as they hit. Of Dixon, we have no doubt, for already we class him the best in baseball."[70] Flournoy, Yokely, Red Ryan, and Submarine Lee would anchor the staff.

Lee had pitched for the Black Sox in 1922 and had gone to Hilldale, where he played for Dick Lundy. Bob "Kiki" Clarke would become the starting catcher, and Harry Gomez, who had played for Harrisburg and the Havana Red Sox, would serve as his backup.[71] But it was the infield that set the Black Sox apart. Gibson wrote that they "showed up in great form."[72] The team's new shortstop, Dick Lundy, known as Sir Richard, was "the best in the world." He possessed a "powerful right arm." He also had a mind for the game, having managed the Bacharachs for three seasons.[73]

Jud Wilson would return to first, the position most suited to his skills. The new third baseman, Ghost Marcell, has been called "a veritable Brooks Robinson in the field," and the best third baseman in pre-integration baseball.[74]

The team's new manager, Frank Warfield, was known as "one of the most consistent and brainy second basemen in the game."[75]

The *Afro-American* christened the four the "Million Dollar Infield."[76] The appellation became the Black Sox' calling card and featured in advertisements. Looking back on the team in the mid–'70s, John Holway, author of numerous books on professional African American baseball, called the Black Sox infield "the best the game has ever seen." Notably, Holway had witnessed the great Orioles infields of the 1960s and '70s with Boog Powell, Dave Johnson/Bobby Grich, Luis Aparicio/Mark Belanger, and Brooks Robinson.

There was no doubt the 1929 Black Sox had the

Oliver "Ghost" Marcell played for only a year with the Black Sox but was part of the 1929 championship team. He was a member of the "Million Dollar Infield," the nickname given to Marcell, Frank Warfield, Dick Lundy, and Jud Wilson because it would have cost a major-league team a million dollars to pay them all (illustration courtesy Gary Joseph Cieradkowski, StudioGaryC.com).

talent to win the pennant in the American Negro League, but Bill Gibson cautioned his readers that a championship, "Twill be no cinch."[77] Frank Warfield told fans that the team does "look fine on paper but it will take a lot of effort to whip them into shape as a team. Teamwork is what wins pennants and not individual stars."[78] The fans would know this, of course. The immensely talented Baltimore teams that included Jud Wilson, Pete Hill, and John Beckwith failed to win a championship, due in large part to their failure to play as a team. Ben Taylor had changed the culture in Baltimore, and there were lingering doubts that what had been the Black Sox characteristic dysfunction might return. Bill Gibson was "particularly concerned about how Warfield and Lundy" would "relate to one another, both having been managers."[79] Jud Wilson and Ghost Marcell had reputations for carrying their tempers onto the field. It would not be an easy thing to bring the club together. Frank Warfield would manage to not only bring them together but to have them play ball at a competitive level throughout the season.

The first half started well for the Black Sox. They "lustily lambasted Alejandro Pompez's Cuban Stars to the tune of 10–2" in the home opener. Submarine Lee allowed two runs on six hits. Jud Wilson went 3-for-5 with a home run and a walk. The *Afro-American* observed, "It was simply a case of too much Black Sox."[80] The team would win their first two games on the road as well. Red Ryan won both games against Hilldale, allowing just five runs over 18 innings. Ghost Marcell collected four hits in four at-bats in the first game of the series.[81] They went on to sweep the Bacharachs with Yokely and Ryan winning games. In the first game, both Frank Warfield and Rap Dixon would get three hits. Dixon's three-run home run made the difference in a 6–4 win. Red Ryan held the Bacharachs to just three hits and no runs in the second game and went 2-for-3 at the plate.[82] The Black Sox would not lose a game until late May, when they dropped a 10–1 decision to the Lincoln Giants.[83]

Rossiter's offseason maneuvers were paying off, but it was the team's familiar faces that emerged as stars: "The big bats of Jud Wilson and Rap Dixon have begun their thunder for the Baltimore Black Sox."[84] Dixon would carry the team in late summer after Wilson had carried them through the spring. The highlight of the season's first half came against Hilldale in early June. The game was tied in the first game of a double-header, when, in the bottom of the 10th, Jud Wilson came to the plate. He

waited out the first two offerings of Darltie Cooper, when the third one came whizzing and curving in over the plate, the Black Sox first baseman, steadying himself, took a lusty clout at the ball, and at the sound of wood and horsehide meeting [that "Boojum" sound], the stands rose as a man. Oscar Charleston, playing deep centerfield began a trot for the fence, and as the ball, only a white speck, high in the air, came riding out, he stopped and watched it as it cleared the fence with several feet to spare. So overjoyed were the supporters of the locals, that when Wilson trotted across home plate, the crowd surged onto the field and a purse of almost thirty dollars was soon collected.[85]

Wilson had been among the most consistent and one of the most feared hitters in professional baseball in the 1920s. His skill and achievement had rivaled Babe Ruth and Rogers Hornsby. Wilson's longevity with the team meant that many fans had grown up with him. His walk-off home run, with Oscar Charleston watching it as it sailed over the fence and towards the Patapsco River, may well have been the highlight of his remarkable career.

The Black Sox were unstoppable, until mid–June. They lost six of seven games on the road[86] and four straight to the Homestead Grays. Frank Warfield benched Jud Wilson. The Black Sox dropped from first and were now tied with the Grays for second place.[87] It was a familiar position for the Black Sox, who had repeatedly started off well only to fade in June, but there was something different about this team. Bill Gibson sensed it, writing that the "Sox are out to regain their lost laurels and woe be unto those who stand in their way."[88] Gibson's words were prophetic. Laymon Yokely proved to be the stopper, pitching a three-hitter against Homestead.[89] The Sox would go on to win six of their final eight games to finish the first half with a record of 21–10. As Bill Gibson had foreseen, Baltimore surged past the Homestead Grays and the Lincoln Giants to guarantee a spot in postseason play, at the very least. If the Black Sox could also win the second-half championship, they would win the pennant outright. Bill Gibson wrote that there "is rejoicing, yes, there is the sound of the lute and the trumpet in Baltimore."[90]

The team played competitive baseball in the first weeks of the second half, led by Laymon Yokely, who stuck out seven on the way to an eight-hit shutout against Hilldale.[91] However, the Black Sox did not dominate the start of the second half the way they had started and finished the first half. At the end of July, they were in first, but tied with Homestead, "with Hilldale and the Lincoln Giants a half game behind."[92] In late July, at Forbes Field in Pittsburgh, the team's star center fielder, Rap Dixon, was struck by a pitch. In the fourth inning, a ball hit him "on the right temple and eye nerves were thought to have been bruised." His teammates carried him off the field, accompanied by a doctor, who "advised him not to play" the next day.[93] Dixon not only played on Sunday, the next day, he returned to the field on Saturday.

When Dixon returned, he achieved one of the most extraordinary records in baseball history. At the plate, he "shattered the air like a volcanic eruption," going 6-for-6, with three doubles. On the basepaths, he showed his remarkable speed, scoring from first on Dick Lundy's single to right field.[94] In the next games, a doubleheader against Hilldale, "Dixon blasted out hits like a charge of TNT." He went 8-for-8. He had reached base 16 consecutive times and had 14 straight hits, including three hits off Hall of Famer Smokey Joe Williams. Of those 14 hits, four were doubles and one was a home run. In 1893, Piggy Ward, playing for Cincinnati, reached base 17 consecutive times. In 1957, Ted Williams would reach base 16 consecutive times. Dixon achieved his record against the best pitchers in the Negro American League, men whose ability matched those of major-league pitchers in 1929. Darltie Cooper, the same man who had surrendered Jud Wilson's walk-off home run in June, stopped Dixon's streak.[95] The achievement stands as a testament to his exceptional talent, made even more remarkable because Dixon had been struck in the head. He was widely known as having an exceptional arm and range in the outfield and as "one of the cleanest players in the game."[96] He played with and against men who are in Cooperstown and demonstrated on the field that he was at the very least their equal.

Dixon's streak also catalyzed the team, stirring it from its midsummer doldrums. On the day Dixon was hit, the Black Sox were 7–4. They would finish the second half with a record of 25–10, winning 18 of their final 24 games. Nonetheless, as Daniel Nathan points out, "It was certainly a hard-fought championship, as four of the league's top clubs were very competitive."[97] There was some disappointment that the Black Sox would not play the Kansas City Monarchs for a Negro League championship. As James Bready, author of *Baseball in Baltimore*, observes, "It was not to be, not when the two leagues were raiding each other's rosters." Bready does note, "What did happen was a postseason series against barnstorming big-league all stars.... The Black Sox won handily, six games to two."[98] Laymon Yokely dominated the all-stars. The *Sun* called him "Master," an exceptional appellation with all its racial implications.[99] Indeed, he was masterly, beating a Lefty Grove-led all-star team twice. In 1929, Yokely won 17 games, including throwing a no-hitter. On two occasions he pitched both ends of a doubleheader.[100]

The 1929 pennant was a triumph for the city and for its African American population. Baltimore was accustomed to baseball titles. A generation earlier, the Orioles dominated the National League with three consecutive championships in the 1890s. The Eastern and then International League Orioles won eight titles, seven of them consecutively (1919–25). The 1929 Negro American League title was particularly sweet. It was the first professional title for the team since the semipro and amateur championships a decade earlier. The fans had endured temperamental stars, truncated seasons, and controversial finishes since then. Indeed, as W. Rollo Wilson wrote in the *Pittsburgh Courier*, the Homestead Grays' local paper, the "Baltimore Black Sox deserved to win the pennant." Moreover, they fielded a team with talent to rival any major-league club.

In that sense, the pennant also vindicated George Rossiter. His choices during the offseason had paid dividends. Frank Warfield was a "highly effective leader ... who proved his leadership by making a half dozen temperamental stars give him sound teamwork." Rossiter "had to give up the best runner and lead-off man in the East and a second baseman whose past record had been brilliant indeed to get Warfield but he was worth the price."[101] His other deals brought in Ghost Marcell and Dick Lundy, giving Baltimore the best defensive infield in baseball. Offensively, Rap Dixon finished the season batting .432, with 16 home runs and 25 stolen bases. He shared the league's MVP honors. Jud Wilson batted .405 with 11 home runs and 22 stolen bases.[102] "There was plenty of comment in the press over the trades and changes" made prior to the season, but Rossiter and the Black Sox had the last word. No one could have known it then, but 1929 was to be the zenith of the franchise.[103]

1930: "The equal of many Major Leaguers."

In April, columnist Paul Menton, writing in the *Baltimore Evening Sun*, wondered, "What has become of baseball's colored champions of 1929, the Baltimore Black Sox? ... Was George Rossiter, the jovial Irish owner of the Sox, still gathering strength for his nine, or was he satisfied with the team as it carried through last summer?"[104] Readers of the *Afro-American* could have answered Menton's questions. Frank Warfield would return as the club's manager. He had a reputation as "aggressive" and "brilliant."[105] Ghost Marcell, the team's third baseman and a member of the Million Dollar Infield, would not return. He was involved in an altercation with Warfield in Cuba, where they were playing winter ball: "Warfield and Marcell ... were engaged in a game of cards with several other players here. Marcell is said to have been losing heavily, and asked Warfield for some money he claimed the manager owed him from last summer. Upon the latter's denial of the debt, Marcell is said to have made a lunge at Warfield, and in the ensuing scuffle, Marcell's nose was badly bitten." Marcell "obtained a warrant for Warfield's arrest." The *Afro-American* explained that, during the 1929 season, the two often clashed: "Warfield is said to have removed Marcell from the game because he was not in condition or not up to form."[106] After the incident in Cuba, either Marcell or Warfield had to go.

With Marcell gone, Bill Gibson speculated that Jud Wilson would return to third base and that the team would need a first baseman, an outfielder, and help in the rotation.[107]

To cover first, Rossiter persuaded Mule Suttles to leave the St. Louis Stars. He was "the homerun king of the Negro League" in 1929.[108] Warfield and Dick Lundy would play second and short, and Fats Jenkins would join Rap Dixon and Pete Washington in the outfield. Jenkins, who Rossiter had lured from the Bacharach Giants, was "as fast as lightning" and "a great hitter."[109] To round out the pitching staff, Rossiter acquired Satchel Paige from the Birmingham Black Barons. He would join Script Lee, Willis Flournoy, and Laymon Yokely in the rotation. The *Evening Sun* reported that Paige "is said to be a sensation."[110] The *Afro-American* sources suggested that his fast ball and curve were better than Yokely's.

Satchel Paige gave Jud Wilson his iconic nickname, "Boojum," when they were teammates with the 1930 Black Sox. In the 1920s, the newspapers would often call him "the Colored Babe Ruth," although his batting style resembled Rogers Hornsby more than Ruth. Wilson played for 24 years, with a career batting average of .361 (illustration courtesy Gary Joseph Cieradkowski, Studio GaryC.com).

As the team took shape, Bill Gibson rated the 1930 Black Sox "the best ... of either race in this area of the United States," which included the Yankees, of course, but also Connie Mack's world champion Philadelphia Athletics.[111]

THE BLACK SOX BIG GUNS ARE READY TO BOOM—The big five Black Sox stars as they appeared Sunday at the Maryland Park. Left to right, Page, Dixon, Suttles, Flournoy, and Manager Warfield, who will not play in the first few games on account of minor ailments.

(Baltimore Afro-American).

Fan excitement was tempered by the failure of eastern owners to form a league. In January, George Rossiter declared "we must have organized baseball in the East at any cost." He added, "No one with any sense is going to try to buck up against the problems which arise in trying to play independent baseball."[112] Meeting in February, with their backs against the wall and in spite of the desperate pleas of Rossiter and Jim Keenan, owner of the Lincoln Giants, "Club owners in the American Negro Baseball League voted to disband the organization," citing high salaries, lack of discipline, poor umpiring, and poor schedules as reasons.[113] The Black Sox would, in spite of Rossiter's warnings, play independent baseball in 1930.

An optimist might have vested faith in the quality of the Black Sox roster to draw fans. If the club played well and the fans responded, George Rossiter would be able to keep his team intact. He even made long-delayed improvements to Maryland Park, including adding 1,000 reserve seats where there had been bleacher boards.[114] The team and its new stars played up to expectations. In an early exhibition game, the "Sox celebrate[d] Easter by lambasting" their opponent in a doubleheader. Mule Suttles hit four home runs, and Satchel Paige pitched a shutout, striking out eight.[115] On Opening Day, the Black Sox drew a large crowd for a doubleheader against their old rival, the Hilldale Daisies. Herbert O'Connor, state's attorney of Baltimore and future Maryland governor, threw out the first pitch. Laymon Yokely started the first game, and it was a disaster. The team lost, 19–5. In the second game, the Black Sox bounced back, winning 8–2, behind Satchel Paige, who scattered five hits and went 1-for-3 at the plate.[116] In his next start, Paige allowed four hits and struck out 11 as the Black Sox beat the Lincoln Giants, 11–1. Mule Suttles also homered in the game. At the end of June, the Black Sox' record was 37 wins, six losses, and two ties. The team and its new stars had delivered a quality product, but, as Bill Gibson lamented, "crowds have been small this season.... Many of the fans are staying away because there is no League." Rossiter also found it "practically impossible to bring more than one or two teams in that" would "really give some worthwhile competition."[117]

The consequences were predictable: "Crowds have been so small at Maryland Park this season, that the Black Sox owner, in an effort to cut expenses, was forced to let Mule Suttles, crack first baseman and homerun king, go back to St. Louis." Fats Jenkins, the team's star outfielder, was also released.[118] Satchel Paige and Rap Dixon followed. Paige returned to Birmingham, and Dixon, "a dangerous man on offense and defense," left for the Chicago American Giants.[119] The team's on-field performance also suffered. In the first two weeks of July, they lost as many games as they had in the first two and a half months of the season.[120] "The lack of a league bled Baltimore white."[121] The club remained in the doldrums through August. There were some signs that Rossiter was attempting to field a more competitive team: Satchel Paige, reportedly, was back with the club in late July, but by August, he was once again pitching for the Birmingham Black Barons.[122]

In September, a flurry of moves transformed the Black Sox. To reinvigorate the pitching staff, Rossiter acquired Webster McDonald, the "submarine ball artist, who has been playing with a white club in Minnesota," and Sam Streeter, who had been pitching for Birmingham. To replace Jenkins, Rossiter signed William McNeil, who had been with Louisville.[123] The new stars paid immediate dividends. The Black Sox swept a doubleheader from Hilldale with McDonald pitching a four-hit shutout and striking out nine in the first game and Streeter allowing just three hits in the second.[124] Rossiter was not finished making his team better. He acquired Ted Page from the Brooklyn Royal Giants, and reacquired

Rap Dixon.[125] Bill Gibson declared that the "present team appears equally as strong, as least defensively, as it did at the beginning of the season."[126] There would be no African American professional championship in 1930, but George Rossiter was loading up his Black Sox to play a series of games against a major-league all-star team, packed with players from the Philadelphia Athletics, fresh from their world championship.

The Black Sox dominated the All-Stars in the 10-game series, winning eight and losing one; another game was called for darkness. C. M. Gibbs, of the *Baltimore Sun*, wrote that he "didn't know whether the All-Stars are convinced that they can't beat the Black Sox but everybody else is."[127] Seven thousand fans came to Maryland Park for the opening game of the series. They saw Webster McDonald strike out eight en route to a 5–3 victory. Jud Wilson proved the offensive star, with timely hits and a stolen base.[128] After the Black Sox swept the subsequent doubleheader, Jesse Linthicum, the *Sun's* sports editor wrote, "Fans who have watched the Sox batter down the Stars ... are beginning to take seriously the claims of followers of the Negro athletes that they are the equal of many Major Leaguers."[129] Eddie Rommel, a Baltimore native, was the only major-league pitcher to defeat the Black Sox, winning 1–0.[130] He would go on to lose to Webster McDonald in his next start. The all-star team included Hall of Famers Frankie Frisch, who would earn the MVP in 1931; Mickey Cochrane, who batted .357 in 1930 and would win two league MVP awards; Jesse Haines, who was a crucial member of the Cardinals' National League pennant-winning pitching rotation in 1930; and Hack Wilson, who hit 56 home runs, drove in a major-league record 191 runs, and batted .356 for the Chicago Cubs in 1930. The Black Sox had not simply defeated the white all-stars, they had pummeled some of the best the major leagues could offer. It was nonetheless a bittersweet close of the 1930 season for a team that had the talent to rival any professional club in the country. The Black Sox, even without future Hall of Famers Satchel Paige and Mule Suttles, had proven themselves as masters of the white-professional all stars.

1931: "Which team is in the lead?"

In April, the *Pittsburgh Courier* reported that Frank Warfield had been "building up another strong baseball team for the Oyster City fans's entertainment this season."[131] In truth, Warfield and Rossiter had been busy restructuring the club and in ways that would be of interest to Pittsburgh fans. In March, the *Courier* carried the news that Ted Page would join the

Homestead Grays. Also leaving Baltimore for Pittsburgh was Jud Wilson, a fixture in the Black Sox lineup for a decade. The *Courier* was ecstatic: "Wilson is one of the hardest sluggers in Negro baseball.... In addition to being a four-base clouter, Wilson has established an unusual record for consistent, timely batting."[132] The *Afro-American* regarded Jud Wilson as "the best player in the East."[133] The *Harrisburg Telegraph* called him "the best hitter in baseball."[134] Ben Taylor, Wilson's former manager in Baltimore, observed that his departure "will make a big hole in the Sox machine, one that hardly can be filled."[135] His absence would mean more than just the loss of his bat. He was also the last remaining link with the Black Sox' early history. Wilson had been discovered by Charles Spedden and J. D. Hairstone playing semipro ball in Washington, D.C., and Scrappy Brown recruited him to head Baltimore's push into professional African American baseball. He had been the team's leader through the tumultuous mid–1920s, culminating in the 1929 championship. He could not be replaced.

The Black Sox also lost Rap Dixon and Webster McDonald to Hilldale. Simply put, ownership could not compete financially. The team had spent a fortune in assembling and fielding the 1929 and 1930 clubs. Rossiter and Warfield were trying, nonetheless, bringing back Crush Holloway and John Beckwith. They were veterans and showing their age. Holloway was 33 and had lost a step in the outfield. Beckwith, now 31, had put on some weight. Dick Lundy, their star second basemen, also reported in less than ideal physical condition.[136] The Opening Day lineup would see Holloway as the Black Sox' leadoff hitter, followed by Warfield, Beckwith, and Washington; Bill Thomas, the new first baseman; Mickey Casey, the catcher; and veteran Dick Jackson. The *Afro-American* called Thomas and Casey the "best youngsters who have broken in around here in many months."[137] Thomas would bat just .205 that year, and Casey would relinquish starting duties to veteran Bob Clarke by midseason. The year of 1931 was not off to a good start.

There also would be no league for the eastern clubs. There had been "some talk about the Sox and Hilldale in a four-club, colored-white Pennsylvania League."[138] An integrated league would raise fan interest and plans advanced. The proposed league expanded to include Hilldale and the Black Sox, competing with teams from Trenton, Wilmington, Camden, Chester, Newark, and Philadelphia. The "Mixed League plan fail[ed] at parley." In the end, the white teams' "inability to measure up to the standard of the two colored clubs was partly cause of their failure to agree."[139] Ironically, because of the Depression, major-league attendance was also down. The St. Louis Browns would draw, on average, less than 2,400 fans per game. The Phillies drew about 3,700 per game.[140] If major-league baseball had integrated it would have meant a financial boon. Instead, African American teams in the east were left with no option but to barnstorm.

The Black Sox would take to the road, playing games in Wilmington, Delaware; in Washington, D.C.; in New York; and throughout Pennsylvania and Virginia. The newspapers publicized them as entertainment events; Bojangles Robinson even performed during a game against the Harlem Stars.[141] For a scheduled game between Hilldale and the Black Sox in Washington, D.C., the papers proclaimed that it "is creating more interest than any other event that has appeared here recently. John Beckwith ... hard hitting third baseman, is just one of the stars in the Sox line-up and the fans are anticipating that ... he will show his prowess. Planted on the Sox first base is Bill Thomas who is a trickster with a pellet. Dick Lundy, shortstop, has been playing sensational ball with the Sox in the several encounters they have had with Hilldale at Forbes Field, Pittsburgh, the Polo Grounds, and Yankee Stadium."[142] The ballclubs, in essence, had no home, and, consequently, could not cultivate a local following.

Any enthusiasm the entertainment events generated in the spring died as the season progressed. Bill Gibson asked, "Which team is in the lead? ... I don't answer. Now, if there were a league, with standings, etc., we might get somewhere."[143] Echoing the fans' disappointment and their hopes, Gibson would go on to write as the 1931 season drew to a close that if "Hilldale, [the] Black Sox, Harlem Stars, Bacharachs, and some other teams were in a loop, the parks would not be as deserted as they are."[144] For those who cared or who could find the records, the Black Sox finished the season with 20 wins and 36 losses.[145] For Baltimore fans, the season ended with as much disappointment as it had begun. Jud Wilson was playing ball in Pittsburgh, and he had taken with him, it seemed, the heart of the Black Sox. Wilson batted .442 and led the Grays to a 22–13 record. Webster McDonald and Rap Dixon led the Hilldale Daises to the best record in the east, with 30 wins against 11 losses. Even more changes were on the horizon. Before the Black Sox would take the field in 1932, they would have new ownership, be a part of the new East-West League, and begin playing in a new ballpark.

"The first night game played by a colored club in the east"

George Rossiter's tenure as the principle owner of the Black Sox produced some of the most gifted teams in baseball history, regardless of race.

He developed an eye for talent and ultimately demonstrated the type of "baseball intelligence" that Rube Foster had spoken about in the stands at the old Westport Baseball Grounds. Rossiter engineered trades and signings that created the 1929 and 1930 Black Sox and that recreated the 1930 team in time for the series against the white professional all-stars. He put together the Million Dollar Infield. He signed Satchel Paige, Mule Suttles, and Ted Page. He became a brilliant baseball executive, but his treatment of the African American community and his neglect of Maryland Baseball Park ensured that he would not achieve the stature that Charles Spedden earned as Black Sox owner.

Eventually, the Black Sox did play a night game in Westport. Rossiter played up the drama, announcing that on August 30, 1931, Maryland Baseball Park would host the "first night game played by a colored club in the east."[146] It was to be the second game of a doubleheader against the House of David, a white semi-pro team. The Black Sox won the first game. The night contest started at 8:00. It was a clean game; the Black Sox committed no errors and the House of David just one. The Black Sox scored five runs on five hits, but the Baltimore starter would make history. The metaphor was complete. Under a lighting system that had to be installed because the previous system failed and in a deteriorating ballpark, John Wesley "Neck" Stanley, signed by George Rossiter, pitched a no-hitter. Night baseball would prove to be lucrative for the game, but it was not enough to save the team nor the ballpark. The economic effects of the Great Depression would prove too much for the franchise.

8

◇◇◇◇◇◇◇◇◇◇◇◇◇◇◇◇◇◇◇◇◇

The Now Extinct
Baltimore Black Sox:
1932–36

At the outset of the Great Depression, William Broening, a Republican, was serving his second term as mayor. In 1930, he expressed optimism about an economic recovery, telling a gathering of business leaders, "If there were a depression, ... it would be brief, and Baltimore had little to fear."[1] By 1932, however, the economic downturn was beginning to take effect, and, although the "city's situation was not so dire as that in other parts of the country," jobs in manufacturing and in the unskilled labor force had disappeared at an alarming rate.[2] Because of discriminatory policies in education and in housing, those economic losses hit the African American community particularly hard.

Appreciating the economic realities, the owners of seven eastern clubs met in August 1931, to lay "the foundations for general welfare in baseball."[3] Understanding that the survival of African American professional ball was at stake, they would meet again in October and in January.[4] The East-West League emerged from those sessions. It was broader in geographic scope and more ambitious than the Negro American League or the Eastern Colored League. The East-West League would include the itinerant Cuban Stars, in addition to teams from Detroit, Cleveland, Baltimore, Pittsburgh (Homestead), Hilldale, Newark, and Washington, D.C. The owners decided on a daily schedule of games, allowing time for travel between cities.[5] They formed a ballpark committee, to ensure safe playing conditions for the players and attractive accommodations for the fans. They instituted a temporary moratorium on trades, "to get the game to a point where it will become a stable business project" for each club and drafted "uniform league contracts" to be used by all the teams.[6] The league hired umpires and held a general meeting in Philadelphia for them to develop a rule book.[7] As Bill Gibson noted in the *Afro-American*, the

East-West League was "off to an auspicious start," writing that he can "see nothing but a bright future."[8]

Changes were in store for the Black Sox as well. Retaining a limited financial interest in the team, George Rossiter stepped back from day-to-day operations. Joe Cambria became the principal owner and general manager. Cambria was born in Messina, Italy, and immigrated to America when he was just a few months old. He grew up in Boston and played semipro and minor-league ball in New England. After service in the First World War, he bought the Bugle Apron and Laundry Company in Baltimore, which proved to be a lucrative investment.[9] Profits financed Cambria's purchase of string of minor-league teams, including clubs in Albany, Harrisburg, St. Augustine, Salisbury, and Youngstown.[10] Contemporary reports reflect astonishment at his devotion to baseball. He is, the newspapers told their readers, "unmindful of the financial beating he has taken in minor league ball.... His love for the game more than the hope that he will get his money back is urging him on."[11] In a further example of his generous spirit, he sponsored the Bugle Laundry team in Baltimore's semipro league and purchased the Label Men's Oval to serve as their home, christening it Bugle Field.

The Black Sox would make Bugle Field their home grounds for night games during the 1932 season, playing day games in Maryland Park. In anticipation of larger crowds than would come to watch his Bugle Laundry team, Cambria "greatly improved" the ballpark: He ordered the installation of "seats for four-thousand fans" and instructed that the infield and outfield be leveled and put in an ideal playing shape, even hiring "steam shovels" to help.[12] Cambria also had "the

Crush Holloway takes batting practice before a preseason game at Bugle Field in March 1932 as Mick Casey looks on. The photograph is the earliest known image of Bugle Field (*Afro-American*).

145

finest lighting equipment" installed. The city improved access to the ballpark. They repaved Federal Street and "widened" Looney's Lane; it would be renamed Edison Highway. Cars and public transportation would have easy access to Bugle Field, which offered free and ample parking.[13] Paul Menton, in the *Evening Sun*, proclaimed it "a fine baseball spot."[14] The ballplayers and fans very quickly began to prefer Bugle Field to Maryland Park, where some of "the benches had been painted."[15]

1932: "Mythical champions"

There were changes on the field as well. Before relinquishing control, George Rossiter fired Frank Warfield, replacing him with Dick Lundy. Even though the owners of the Washington Pilots hired Warfield to manage their ballclub in the East-West League, he was understandably upset and determined to go "back to show the fans what a whale of a mistake Rossiter has made."[16] Dick Lundy, for his part, busied himself in remaking the ballclub and establishing good relations with the fans. He signed on to write a regular column in the *Afro-American* called "Dick's Diamond Dope," that promised readers "the real low down on what's what."[17] His first column gave his perspective on the new East-West League. He wrote that "the public can look forward to a banner year," that the players will have a "more serious attitude," and that fans will enjoy the regular publication of "standings and stats."[18] Lundy also met the challenges of forming a ballclub head-on. The team would need "two infielders, a second baseman and a third sacker." Lundy, himself, would continue to play short, and Dave Thomas would return at first. Dick Jackson would return as the team's utility man. The club still needed another outfielder to join Crush Holloway and Pete Washington but did have two veteran catchers on the roster, Bob Clarke and Mickey Casey. The Black Sox would need to rebuild their pitching staff, with Willis Flournoy the only reliable starter returning, although Laymon Yokely, plagued by arm trouble, was ready to make a "desperate comeback."[19] Adding to Lundy's difficulties, the team could not acquire players by trade: The best players in the East were under contract, and the best professional teams not in the East-West League had formed the Southern League. It was next to impossible to pry players away from other East-West or Southern League clubs. Nonetheless, Lundy was determined "to build a 1932 club equal to or surpassing the 1929–30" Black Sox teams.[20]

Joe Cambria and Dick Lundy relied on scouting and on their connections with independent teams. They persuaded former Black Sox second baseman Dick Seay to return; Seay had most recently played for the now independent Brooklyn Royal Giants. Lundy recruited Buddy Burbage as the third outfielder. He was from Salisbury, Maryland, and had previously played for Hilldale and the Pittsburgh Crawfords. Lundy described Burbage as a "fine all around ballplayer," a "good hitter," and a "fast base runner."[21] Tom Finley joined the team as their new third baseman. He had played for the Harlem Stars in 1931 and made an impression on Lundy. For pitchers, the club would rely on "the work of youngsters." Cambria and Lundy discovered Lefty Holmes, pitching for the Cuban House of David, and Dizzy Cooke, starting for the Norfolk Pennsylvania Red Caps. Cooke was described as having a "powerful physique."[22] In contrast, Half Pint Allen, another rookie left-hander, weighed just 123 pounds. Apart from Yokely, Herb Smith, another rookie, was the only right-hander in the rotation.

Despite having a young and relatively inexperienced ballclub and despite Frank Warfield's revenge (his Washington team shut out the Black Sox in their home opener and won the opening series), Baltimore played exceptional baseball during the first half of the season. Leading the way, Allen pitched a one-hitter against Hilldale to rally the team after the "Blankety-Blank" games against the Pilots.[23] The Black Sox would go on to sweep Hilldale and Washington, avenging that opening series in the first night games at Bugle Field.[24] They finished the first month of the season in third place but just a game behind Detroit and a half-game behind Pittsburgh. The *Afro-American* hailed "the sensational hurling of [the] rookie pitchers," who "have been blazing a trail through the ranks of the Eastern clubs."[25] Capping their achievement, Allen pitched a 13-inning complete game against the Washington Pilots at Bugle Field. After a dramatic walk-off win, Joe Cambria "doused Allen with water."[26]

The league published its first-half statistics, which reveal a well-rounded ballclub. The Black Sox were third in the league in hitting, with a .291 team average. They were third in stolen bases, second in home runs, but fifth in runs scored. They were second in fielding percentage but had committed the fewest errors in the league.[27] It was pitching that set them apart. Ironically, Flournoy was the only starter with a losing record. Laymon Yokely had won a game in relief. The rookie pitchers, as the papers had suggested, were sensational. Allen was 3–1. Homes was 4–2. Cook was 2–0, and Smith was 4–0.[28] By mid–June, the Black Sox were in first place, with a 17–8 record, two games ahead of the Homestead Grays.[29] Baltimore continued their phenomenal pace. With three games remaining in the first-half schedule, they were three games in front of Homestead, but, simultaneous with the Black Sox' surge, disaster struck.

News reports indicated that, due to financial issues, the Pittsburgh and Detroit teams had merged.[30] At about the same time, the league's owners met for an all-night emergency session in Philadelphia. They concluded that "only radical changes would permit any of the clubs to continue." The owners instituted three: (1) The clubs would make "drastic cuts in salaries and overhead operating expenses." Players would be paid from shares of the gate receipts, and all players were then free agents. (2) The teams' schedules would be revised, meaning the "discontinuance ... of everyday baseball." (3) The league would no longer employ "monthly salaried umpires."[31] The league was down to six teams by the end of the first half. The Newark Browns folded. The Cubans were also in danger of disbanding. A season that had begun with such promise was now in disarray.

The obituaries listed numerous causes of death. The *New York Amsterdam News* blamed the continuing Depression, citing "unemployment" and the "congested circulation of money."[32] The *Philadelphia Tribune* reported, simply, that "the receipts from operations" were "insufficient to meet carrying charges."[33] The *Washington Tribune* saw lack of "publicity" and marketing as the cause.[34] Bert Gholston, an umpire and Baltimore native, offered a cogent analysis in the *Afro-American*, citing the "inability of the owners to cooperate" and the failure of ownership to "understand the fundamental principles of the game as a business."[35] Syd Pollock, the Cubans' owner, offered his views in the *Kansas City New Journal and Guide*. He pointed out, "Baseball in general has been dealt a severe blow by the existing depression" that can be seen in attendance "in all parks white and colored." He added, perhaps stung by criticism like that in the *Washington Tribune*, that "no one can blame the promoters." He offered no hope for a league until "the baseball fan goes back to work." In the end, he thought the East-West League was a good idea but one that was attempted in "the wrong year."[36] No matter the causes, the East-West League was no more. The papers, throughout the former league's cities, assumed that the Baltimore Black Sox would "naturally be conceded the winner" of the pennant.[37] In mid–July, the vestiges of the league owners declared the Homestead Grays the champions. The *Chicago Defender* used the word "given" rather than earned or won to describe the league's actions.[38] The gift to the Grays points to, perhaps, another cause for the league's demise. Bert Gholston also attributed the East-West's failure to the lack of a president who has "no connection with any team."[39]

With players no longer under contract, many switched teams. Judy

Johnson left Hilldale for Pittsburgh, joining former Black Sox Satchel Paige.[40] In Baltimore, Thomas, Holloway, and Burbage "jumped the club." Lefty Cook departed in such "haste" that he "is said to have taken a team uniform with him."[41] The Black Sox were able to persuade most of their former players to return, but they returned to an environment that resembled barnstorming more than an organized baseball season. For publicity, Pittsburgh and Baltimore staged a "Baseball Players Frolic," that involved fungo hitting contests, accurate throwing competitions, and sprints around the bases.

There was even a "special backward race" scheduled between "Satchel Paige and an opponent yet to be selected."[42] Games more often involved white semipro teams than professional African American clubs. Not as promising as league play, the post–East-West games and events enabled teams to make a small profit, and players were able to earn somewhat of a living. The strain proved too much for former Baltimore manager Frank Warfield. His Washington Pilots were in Pittsburgh, and while traveling from his hotel to a game, he suffered a fatal heart attack.

The Black Sox under Cambria and Lundy were able to survive financially and to mold an accomplished team. By mid–July, they had won eight consecutive games, including two against Hilldale.[43] After losing one game (out of four) to a white semipro team in Philadelphia, the Black Sox went on to win 18 games in a row, including sweeping the Homestead

Frank Warfield played for 10 different clubs over a 19-year career. He spent six years with Hilldale and four with Baltimore, managing the Black Sox to the 1929 Negro American League championship (illustration courtesy Gary Joseph Cieradkowski, StudioGaryC. com).

Grays.[44] In September, Joe Cambria, together with the ownership of the Washington Pilots and the New York Black Yankees, decided to play a series of games to determine the "the strongest colored team in the country."[45] The *Afro-American* considered the Black Yankees "on par" with Pittsburgh, the Chicago Giants, and the Kansas City Monarchs. Those clubs, the *Afro* noted, had bigger stars, but Baltimore had a better team, and the team that won the "inter-city baseball series," the paper declared, would be "the mythical champions of the East."[46] In the first match-up, Baltimore "slaughtered the New Yorkers," winning three of four.[47] Against Washington, the Black Sox won two of three games.[48] Bill Gibson summed up the team's season: "The Black Sox were in the lead when the end [of the East-West League] came." Further, the "three cornered inter-city baseball series" was "a fair means" for determining the championship. As the Black Sox won both series, they were then the champions.[49]

The team would end their season with the annual series against a white all-star team. For the first time, Bugle Field would play host. Joe Cambria added bleacher seating and took out ads in the local papers. He offered the "lowest prices in years" for admission and added attractions: A "rodeo" and a "cow-girl band" performed between innings and before the games.[50] A "capacity crowd" jammed the ballpark. The "All Star" team was dominated by Orioles from the city's International League team, who had finished their season with a 93–74 record and in second place. For the first time in the history of the series, the *Sun* reported, the All Stars swept a doubleheader from the Black Sox.[51] G. M. Gibbs, in his *Sun* daily column, pointed out that "the Negro team usually knocks the wadding out of the so-called All Stars."[52] Adding to the Black Sox' troubles, as the major-league season ended, more talented players bolstered the All Stars lineup. Hack Wilson would join the team. Fred Frankhouse, a pitcher for the Boston Braves, also arrived. Frankhouse had a mediocre season in 1932, but he would pitch in the major-league All-Star Game in 1934. The Dodgers' Van Mungo also agreed to pitch for the local All Stars. He had won 13 games for Brooklyn that season and would pitch for the National League All-Stars from 1934 through 1937. The Black Sox also called in reinforcements. Mule Suttles and Jud Wilson returned to Baltimore. It was also rumored that Satchel Paige would make an appearance.[53] Although he did not come, the return of Suttles and Wilson must have offered the Black Sox and their fans thoughts of what might have been, if the economic realities had not upended the franchise and African American professional ball midway through the 1930 season. The Black Sox dominated the remaining games of the series, although they did drop the final contest, 13–9.[54]

In evaluating the season, Bill Gibson noted, "had it not been for the rescue work of Manager Cambria, Baltimore would have been without a baseball team." Gibson added that Cambria "had spent much time and money in trying to give the fans a run for their money," and that in his "dealings with athletes and the paying public," he has "always been above board."[55] Based on Cambria's influence on the team and city, Gibson noted that "there are indications of a bright future ahead."[56] By the end of the year, Gibson would temper his view, not blaming Cambria, but rather seeing the demise of baseball, "the sick man of sports." It had, in Gibson's view, "suffered a serious relapse after an emergency operation designed to save its fast ebbing life."[57] In retrospect, Gibson proved prescient. Cambria would find success, and Bugle Field would, by 1938, play host to a very successful Baltimore franchise, the Elite Giants. The intervening years would witness the slow death of the Black Sox. Fans could not have known that 1932 would be the last full season for the franchise.

1933: "The city has two clubs"

The year did not start nor did it end well for the Black Sox: "Rumors had been current that for this season at least the Sox would not operate."[58] They had been owner's meetings and the news of a "new baseball association."[59] Baltimore was "not invited" to the discussions.[60] Official word came in early March that "Baltimore [was] out."[61] Dick Lundy, the only remaining member of the Million Dollar Infield and the team's manager, left for Philadelphia; many of the Black Sox starters also left the team. Undaunted, Joe Cambria vowed to "put a hustling Black Sox team on the field."[62] He also poured money into Bugle Field: "The "right field fence [was] set back about 20 feet and a press box and club house with showers" were installed.[63] In addition, "all the usable seating equipment from the old Maryland Park" was moved to Bugle Field.[64] He also expanded the grandstand seating by about 900 and added more bleacher seats. In mid–May, Cambria arranged for a meeting in Baltimore with Gus Greenlee and Cum Posey, the new league's officials. Baltimore was then admitted to the league. The other owners scrambled to revise the schedule. Baltimore's season would open on May 20, which meant that they would have a week to assemble a team.[65]

Cambria got to work immediately, naming Jesse Hubbard as the new manager. Hubbard was a veteran ballplayer who had spent most of his career with the Brooklyn Royal Giants, although he had played for the Black

BALTIMORE SOX NATIONAL NEGRO LEAGUE

The Baltimore Sox pose for a photograph in front of their new team bus. Note that the uniforms and the caption carry the name "Sox" and not the "Black Sox." The name was also confusing to out-of-town papers, who continued to use the appellation, Black Sox, to refer to Joe Cambria's club. The players are unidentified.

Sox briefly in 1928. Cambria further promised to "spend money to get a team." To take care of the players, he purchased a "new $7200 Mack bus."[66]

Cambria and Hubbard did assemble a team, comprised in part of veterans who had played for the Black Sox earlier in their careers. Dick Seay would return as second baseman. Namon Washington, Bert Johnson, Crush Holloway, and Babe Milton would anchor the outfield. Mack Eggleston and Tex Burnett would share catching duties. Half Pint Allen and Lamon Yokely would pitch, joined by Leon Day. Dennis Simpson would play first, with Jake Dunn at short.[67] Joe Lewis, the last active member of the 1913 Black Sox, would also return. The men, for the most part, were past their prime, but, given the circumstances, Cambria and Hubbard had done a remarkable job.

Just as they were taking the field, the Black Sox received word that they no longer had the rights to their own team name. J. B. Hairstone, the former Black Sox catcher and manager, had filed suit against the team, alleging that Rossiter (and therefore Cambria) had forfeited the rights to the name after failing to pay taxes in 1930.[68] Hairstone organized his own Baltimore Black Sox, scheduling games against local and regional semipro clubs at Maryland Park, or what was left of the old ballfield.[69] Cambria, for his part, called his team the "Baltimore Sox." Bill Gibson explained the situation to his readers: "The Baltimore Black Sox (notice the Black) are not affiliated with any baseball organization and operate at Maryland Park.... So you see the city has two clubs—the Sox and the Black Sox.

You're welcome, I'm sure."[70] In December, Cambria would win the legal battle for the use of the Black Sox, but for the remainder of the season, his team was the Sox.[71]

Overall, the Sox season was a disappointment. Just before their first game, Jesse Hubbard was admitted to Maryland General Hospital.[72] The team was "crippled by the lack of a regular first baseman, ... as well as suffering from a none-too-strong pitching staff. The Sox have been but a shadow of what the old Black Sox were." There was "none of the walloping of the ball, none of the daring speed that stretched singles into doubles and kept the opposing pitchers on edge." They "stopped playing league ball" in midsummer, "playing, in fact only three games in the second half."[73] After their last game, the Sox had a losing record and were in fifth place, just behind the Nashville Elite Giants.[74] Even the annual series between the (Black) Sox and white all-stars was discouraging. The Sox team was "the weakest offensively that has ever gone into such a series." Bill Gibson noted, "There is a need of a Rap Dixon, an Oscar Charleston, a Mule Suttles." In the first six games, the Sox batted .244 and committed 10 errors. They were "hopelessly outclassed" and the series was "a farce." The league itself did not fare well in 1933. The games were not profitable: "The Sox have made two trips West and lost money on each one." League membership was constantly in flux: "The Greys are out and the Cubans were out before they were in.... The Indianapolis Club moved to Detroit and Chicago moved to Indianapolis and now we have another club—the Akron (Ohio) Grays."[75] The one bright spot for the league was the inaugural "East West Diamond Classic," held at Chicago's Comiskey Park.[76] The one bright spot for Baltimore in 1933 was Dick Seay, who was voted onto the East team.

1934: No More Games Were Played in Baltimore

When the Negro National League's team owners met in February 1934 to plan the season, Baltimore was "not present."[77] Unlike the previous year, when the owners decided not to invite Baltimore, Joe Cambria did not attend because he was "not ready." In fact, "after being admitted as a regular member," Cambria "sought suspension ... until they [the Black Sox could] gain a definite line on what players they can get."[78] He had given "a number of old timers ... the proverbial air," and hoped to "give some sandlot and schoolboy talent an opportunity." Cambria had found success with such a model with his white professional team in Albany, New York, and applied the same formula to the Black Sox. Sadly, the newly assembled squad fared poorly, losing their first game to the Harrisburg Senators, a "local white team," 20–1. The Black Sox had three hits and committed six errors.[79] Witnessing the continued failure of his experiment, and also failing to enter his franchise into the Negro National League, Cambria sold the Black Sox to Jack Farrell, who became the team's first African American owner since 1917.

Farrell was based in Chester, Pennsylvania, and had made a reputation and a good income as a boxing promoter. He had also acquired the Washington Pilots. With his purchase of the Black Sox, Farrell "gained a franchise ... in the National Baseball Association," the Negro National League. He planned to use the Black Sox name and "a nucleus" of players, from "his Washington" team. He appointed Rap Dixon the team's manager and was able to field a club for the second half of the League's 1934 season.[80] Paul Dixon, dubbed the "most dangerous batsmen in baseball" was the star. Tom Dixon served as catcher, with Casey Jones and Hack Cunningham in the outfield.[81] Despite Farrell's determination, his Black Sox lost their opening doubleheader to the Nashville Elite Giants by scores of 10–9 and 7–3.[82] On-the-field issues were not Farrell's chief concern.

In July, just as he was assembling his club, the Baltimore City police arrested him for larceny. J. B. Hairstone filed the complaint in a dispute over thirteen of the club's uniforms. Hairstone, not conceding his court case of the previous year, also contended that he was the rightful manager and president of the Black Sox. The court dismissed the charges against Farrell, but the incident represented "another chapter in a series of difficulties which have beset the Baltimore Black Sox baseball team for more than a year."[83] Troubles continued to mount. A dispute over a game between the Pittsburgh Crawfords and Philadelphia Stars, scheduled to take place at Bugle Field but cancelled, caused the league to cancel all scheduled games in Baltimore.[84]

Farrell responded by moving the Black Sox to Chester, Pennsylvania. They became, for a short time, the Chester Baltimore Black Sox, playing their home games at the ballpark on Front and Edwards streets, opposite the Chester-Bridgeport Ferry Terminal. The locals embraced the team and they had begun to jell, dominating the local semipro competition.[85] In terms of their league schedule, they played in 11 games, winning just three. They would not play another season in the Negro National League.[86]

There was one final series against the white professional All-Stars in Baltimore. Whereas, just two years previously, the Black Sox had sold out Bugle Field with a team packed with stars from the Negro Leagues, the

1934 version of the Black Sox could draw just 2,000 fans to the opening game.[87] As they had in 1933, the All-Stars won the series from the Black Sox. The games were unremarkable, with the exception that they were the last games the Baltimore Black Sox would play in the city.[88] The next spring, the *Afro-American* declared the team "extinct."[89]

Black Sox Now Extinct

Even though there was "no Black Sox team in Baltimore," Farrell's Chester Baltimore Black Sox continued to play ball against semipro and sandlot teams throughout Pennsylvania, Southern New Jersey, and into Delaware.[90] Box scores from August 1935 show the same players that Farrell had recruited to play for his 1934 team.[91] The Baltimore Black Sox, who had begun life as the Weldons on the Number 1 diamond in Patterson Park, likely played their last game at Pennsy Field in Wilmington, Delaware, on July 18, 1936, against the Royal Dukes, a "local Negro team."[92]

The paper did not record the results of that game. Thunderstorms rolled along the Christina River that Saturday evening. The weather was remarkably like the Weldons' game against Joe Gans' team that 1905 afternoon in Patterson Park thirty-two years earlier. It is possible the game was rained out. It would have been a fitting end.

"5 Major Clubs"

By 1936, African American professional baseball was on the threshold of its Golden Age. The Negro National League, which had included the Baltimore Black Sox as a charter member, would provide stability and leadership for professional clubs in the east. In 1937, the Negro American League would offer the same for clubs in the west. For the first time since the mid–1920s, African American professional baseball had stabilized to the point where it could serve as a showcase for the elite talents of its members, leading to the integration of professional baseball. Baltimore would become a prominent member of that league structure, but it was not the Black Sox that would hold that place. They had been reports of a reorganized Black Sox team, joining the NNL for the 1937 season, with Oriole Park as their home.[93] The plan failed to develop beyond the speculative stage.

The Black Sox demonstrated the viability of African American

The Baltimore Tigers were an African American semipro team that played in the Southern Colored Baseball Association and against semipro teams in the Baltimore area. Top row, from left: Dixie Walker, Herb Young, Slim Slaughter, Luke Hall, Red Wyn, and "Tex"; seated, from left: J. Shallington, Hawkins, Davis, Scott, and Barry Luke. The boys holding the championship trophy are not named. The club's offices were at 307 Cross Street in Federal Hill (South Baltimore).

baseball in the city. That viability led to a myriad of "colored" teams that sprouted up through the city, but particularly in South Baltimore. The South Baltimore Giants and the reorganized Weldons played their home games in Port Covington, but the most intriguing of the African American teams to play there was the Baltimore Tigers.

The team's headquarters was at 307 East Cross Street in South Baltimore.[94] Charter members of the Southern Athletic Association, they were a powerhouse club, earning the 1935 championship. Formed at a time when the Negro Leagues had established themselves, the Southern Association offered men of color the opportunity to develop their skills in what was, essentially, a minor-league system.

8. The Now Extinct Baltimore Black Sox: 1932–36

In 1938, the Elite Giants would move to Baltimore and deliver championships in 1939 and 1949. Men such as Roy Campanella, Leon Day, Thomas Butts, Bill Byrd, Henry Kimbro, Jim Gilliam, and Joe Black would represent Baltimore on Negro League All-Star teams for the next decade. Many would play in the major leagues. Roy Campanella, Biz Mackey, Willie Wells, and Leon Day are members of the Hall of Fame in Cooperstown. Bob Luke tells their story in *The Baltimore Elite Giants*.

If they could have survived a few more seasons, the Black Sox may have played a more prominent role in Negro League history. As it stands, they played a key role the development of African American professional baseball, even if the team is now largely forgotten or misunderstood. Their prominence can be measured in the names adopted by the employees of the Harlem YMCA for their membership drive in 1932. The Black Sox' importance can also be seen on the field in the inaugural Negro League All-Star game, known as the "East-West Classic," and played in Comiskey Park in 1933. It was the Negro Leagues' counterpart to the major-league All-Star game played that year for the first time. Dick Seay represented the Baltimore Black Sox, one of the "5 Major Clubs" in the east, according to the headline in the *Pittsburgh Courier*. Of the seventeen players on the East's team, ten had spent part of their careers in a Baltimore uniform. In addition, Mule Suttles, who had been a Black Sox in 1930, started for the West team. Like Suttles, Satchel Paige, Sam Streeter, and Ted Page had only spent a season or less in Baltimore. The others (Jud Wilson, Dick Lundy, Rap Dixon, George Britt, Dick Seay, Fats Jenkins, and James Mackey) had spent a considerable part of their careers as members of the Black Sox. Baltimore had witnessed the development of these men as ballplayers just as the city had witnessed the birth of major-league African American professional baseball.

9

"Called on account
of darkness"

Before the Great Depression, white unemployment in the city was comparable to black unemployment, "albeit in poorly paid, unskilled jobs." With the onset of the economic downturn, "the lives of Baltimore's African American citizens had become totally circumscribed by racial restraints."[1] Forty percent of the city's African American population was on some form of government relief. The realities of the 1930s created a "nightmare world"[2] for the African American community. They were "trapped in substandard employment resulting in inordinately high mortality, crime, and dependency rates…. Blacks were segregated by law into separate schools, hospitals, jobs, parks, restaurants, and railroad cars," and "Separate toilets and water fountains were provided."[3] Those restraints, and media distortions and racism, encouraged the "segregationists' conflation of African Americans with community degradation and plummeting property values. These 'pernicious associations long outlived the [segregation] ordinances themselves and continued to fuel efforts at restricting African Americans' residential options well into the twentieth century.'"[4]

To combat the effects of segregation, exacerbated by the Depression, new leaders began to emerge, including Carl Murphy, owner of the *Afro-American*, and Carroll Jackson, head of the Baltimore chapter of the NAACP. Together, they "championed a series of successful legal, political, and economic challenges to … segregation."[5] They founded the "Citywide Young People's Forum," which hosted Friday night lectures from W. E. B. DuBois, Walter White, and James Weldon Johnson.[6] The forum led to boycotts of industries that did not employ African Americans and to campaigns to end lynching.

Many of the men associated with the Black Sox also fought for the rights of African Americans. Doc Sykes, for example, was a key witness in the "Scottsboro Case," which involved a trial of nine teenaged African

Institutionalized racism and inequality in vocational education, combined with the restrictive "Segregation Ordinances," ensured that African Americans would live in the poorest sections of the city and in houses that were crumbling, such as these on South Spring Street, ca. 1933 (A. Aubrey Bodine).

American men accused of raping a white woman.[7] "Because he had the courage and honesty to go on the stand," Sykes endured the "burning of crosses before his office and home."[8] Like Sykes, Howard Young, the team's first owner, was active in the civil rights movement. He played an important role in Baltimore's branch of the NAACP. He "brought suit against the city for equalization of colored and white teachers's salaries," and he "agitated for an end to segregation."[9] Other figures from the Black Sox' early days also went on to play an active role in the civil rights movement.

After his work as the team's secretary, John R. Williams studied at Brown University, majoring in journalism; he was the only African American on the college paper's staff.[10] After graduating, he enlisted in the army, trained at Fort Mead, and served on the Western Front.[11]

Williams published a short monograph about his experiences in the army: *A Trench Letter* speaks of his hopes for international cooperation and of the promise of democracy.[12] Following his discharge, he moved

to Washington, where he promoted baseball and set up a game
between the Brooklyn Royal
Giants, the club the Black Sox
had played to open their inaugural season, and Judge's All
Stars, a team of major-league
players.[13] He then moved to Los
Angeles, Detroit, and then back
to California. Among other jobs,
he was the Detroit correspondent for the *Pittsburgh Courier*.
He espoused integration, particularly in baseball, and visited
Baltimore frequently. He passed
away on July 13, 1968.

Other men who played with
those Black Sox teams would
continue their baseball careers.
Walter Williams, the team's
first manager, would become
the first professional African
American "official scorer" work-

Carl Murphy, publisher of the *Baltimore Afro-American*, was a leader in the civil rights movement in Baltimore in the 1930s (*Baltimore Afro-American*).

ing for the Black Sox, the Chicago American Giants, and the Bacharach Giants into the 1920s.[14] Joe Lewis, who was a member of
the 1913 team, would go on to have a long career in the Negro Leagues,
playing for Hilldale and then the Bacharach Giants before retiring in
1934. June Matthews, the team's star shortstop from its days as the Weldons in 1905, would, after returning from the war, become manager for a
new incarnation of the Weldon Giants, recruiting his old teammate O. J.
Barbour to play center field.[15] When his playing days ended, Blainey Hall
went on to manage a local semipro team, the Lincoln Reds, in the late
1920s.[16]

Members of that first Black Sox team, who had played for the Weldons and Baltimore Giants, would settle in the city. Charles Evans went to
work in the Sparrows Point shipyards and managed the steel mill's semipro
team, the Bethlehem Black Sox.[17] After leaving the team, Charles Thomas
took a job as a laborer at the American Sugar refinery on Key Highway,
where he would work for the next thirty-seven years, eventually becoming
a foreman.[18] Joe Lewis supervised the baseball field and related facilities in

Portsmouth, Virginia. He also managed Portsmouth's local team.[19] Lewis and Evans remained lifelong friends. Joe Lewis died in 1975 and Charles Evans passed away in 1977. He was the last living link to the 1913 Black Sox and the original Weldons.

Wallace Smith, the Weldons' founder, and his brother Thomas continued to play a central role in the franchise. As James Bready points out, "Many of black baseball's greatest stars took the field in South Baltimore. They and many of the Black Sox, stayed at Smith's Hotel."[20] It is likely that Wallace Smith regaled them with stories of the franchise's early days, and Thomas had erected a shrine to Joe Gans in the hotel's lobby. When Thomas Smith died of natural causes in 1938, the governor, mayor, both of Maryland's senators, and 1,500 citizens paid their respects.[21] His brother's death would not be as peaceful and his life not as celebrated. Just before Christmas in 1939, two African American men forced their way into the front room of a house on Druid Hill Avenue, a few blocks from Smith's Hotel. They ordered all the men present into an adjoining room, except for the 75-year-old Wallace Smith. Witnesses reported hearing two gunshots. Smith was hit in the arm and chest. Rumors spread of connections with organized crime. The house was "said to be used for horse race betting."[22] Wallace died on the scene. He had risen from slavery to become a successful business owner and founded the team that would become the Black Sox. No politicians came to his funeral, and there was no outpouring of public grief. The hotel he and his brother founded was sold off and razed in 1957. Gone was the intricately carved wooden bar, the memorial to Joe Gans, and the legacy of African American entrepreneurship. The *Afro-American* put it succinctly: "Smith's Hotel to become a Parking Lot."[23]

For the most part, the men who later ran the team that Wallace Smith founded also remained in Baltimore. Charles Spedden, after his forced exile, worked in sales, quietly raising a family. He passed away in March 1960.[24] None of the papers carried an obituary. Like Wallace Smith's, Spedden's legacy was largely forgotten. George Rossiter's lengthy obituary never mentions the Black Sox by name. Instead, it notes that he "owned a Negro baseball team and ballpark in Westport."[25] It is William Brauer's obituary that mentions the Black Sox. Brauer and Spedden had purchased the team in 1917 and Brauer was the epitome of a silent partner. In contrast, the headline for his obituary reads, "Ball team's founder dies." The article goes on to detail how he "started the city's Black Sox."[26] Joe Cambria, who had built his fortune in Baltimore, would not remain rooted to the city. Instead, among his many accomplishments, he "opened Cuba" to major-league baseball and "re-engineered the art of scouting," introducing a battery of tests and scientific evaluations.[27] Jack Farrell, the Black Sox' last owner, opened a hotel. Like Smith's Hotel, the Moonglo, on Market Street in Chester, catered to African American travelers.

Many of the other men who played for the Weldons and Black Sox in the 1910s, 1920s, and 1930s would also settle in Baltimore. Crush Holloway opened a "cleaning and pressing store" on Edmondson Avenue and "umpired Elite Giant games."[28] Scrappy Brown, the slick-fielding shortstop from Sparrows Point, played semipro basketball and managed prizefighters after his baseball career ended. When he died in 1951, young men in the "Northwest Baltimore" community where he lived mourned him as their "idol."[29] Ed Wise, the Weldons' catcher, managed a semipro team, the Silver Moons, in the 1930s.[30] He also owned and operated a "bootblack stand" on East Lombard Street, where members of the African American community would gather to socialize and to hear stories of Wise's playing days. He passed away in 1944.[31] Laymon Yokely ran Yokely's Shine Parlor on the west side of town, decorating his business with mementos from his playing days and other baseball memorabilia.

He spoke of his career in an interview with John Holway, recalling how, when he first joined the team, in 1926, he could not control his pitches. Ben Taylor "put a match box on the ground for me to throw over. After a while I felt I could throw it through a needle's eye."[32]

Crush Holloway and Laymon Yokely would join some of their former teammates for a "reunion game" at Memorial Stadium in 1951. In between games of an Elite Giants' doubleheader they played a two-inning exhibition. Joining Holloway and Yokely were George Ford, Cleo Smith, Script Lee, Buck Ridgely, Goose Curry, Eggie Clark, Nick Logan, Jud Wilson, and Doc Sykes.[33] There would be no other such games, and the Baltimore Black Sox would fade from memory. In 1971, Crush Holloway noted, "It's just lost history.... Nobody is going to dig it up."[34]

Holloway was largely right. For many years, the exact location of Maryland Park and the Westport Baseball Grounds remained lost. Additionally, despite the work of Daniel Nathan, the error that the Black Sox "organized in 1916 ... under the ownership of two white businessmen, George Rossiter and Charles Spedden," and that Jack Farrell was the club's "only Black owner" persists.[35] Nathan points out the difficulties in writing the history of the club: "there are no known business records, and no surviving ballplayers." He notes that few players gave interviews, and, in any case, such oral history is "sometimes factually suspect, especially regarding particulars from long ago."[36] Moreover, even though respect

Laymon Yokely stands outside of his business on North Avenue, ca. 1970. Yokely played for the Baltimore Black Sox from 1926 to 1933. In 1944, he attempted a comeback with the Baltimore Elite Giants (*Baltimore Sun*).

for the Negro Leagues and the accomplishments of the men who played professional African American baseball has increased, much still needs to be done. There are players who wore the Black Sox uniform and deserve recognition in the Hall of Fame, including Fats Jenkins, Dick Lundy, Rap Dixon, Laymon Yokely, and John Beckwith.

There is cause for optimism. Cooperstown includes men who played for the Black Sox such as Satchel Paige, Leon Day, Mule Suttles, Jud Wilson, Ben Taylor, Pete Hill, and Biz Mackey. Advances in technology and digital archives have enabled historians to discover the exact location

of the team's ballparks in Westport.[37] As additional archival
material comes online, the
details of the Baltimore Black
Sox history and the individ-
uals who contributed to the
club will become more widely
available. Still, much of the
team's history, as Daniel Nathan notes, lies in darkness.

An apt metaphor for our
understanding of the Black Sox
occurred in October 1927.

Laymon Yokely, just 21,
was on the mound for the
Black Sox, pitching against
a white professional all-star
team. Hack Wilson, the Cubs'
star outfielder, approached
the batter's box. He "came up,
swinging his bat in big league
style and setting his spikes."
Yokely "wound up leisurely
and Wilson swung. The ball,
however, was someplace else.

Crush Holloway, ca. 1970. Holloway
played for a number of Negro League
teams including the Black Sox (1924–28,
1931, and 1933) and the Baltimore Elite
Giants (1939).

Yokely snapped another hot one over and Wilson timed this one better,
swinging only a fraction of a second too late. The Black Sox pitcher, with
his deceptive slow wind up, whirled his arm and the ball cut the plate."
Wilson "stood with his bat on his shoulders and heard the umpire call him
out." Yokely "indulged in a majestic grin, Wilson grinned back, while the
5,000 fans went wild. A moment later the game was called on account of
darkness."[38] It's a beautiful and memorable moment.

Two men, at the top of their profession, exchanging smiles, with Hack
Wilson enjoying the moment perhaps as much as Yokely and the fans...
Because of the racial barriers in baseball, they would never face one another in a major-league game. No box score survives from this game, and
it was not even an official game. Nonetheless, the image remains because
a sportswriter for the *Baltimore Sun* decided to tell the story. Ironically,
it was the *Sun* that published the caricature of Doc Sykes just four years
previously. Both writers cast some light into the darkness that continues

to obscure the history of the Black Sox. It is stories such as these from the *Sun,* the *Afro-American,* the *New York Age,* the *Pittsburgh Courier,* the *Philadelphia Tribune,* the *Wilmington News Journal,* and other papers that enable us to trace a history of the team and to illuminate the stories of the men who played for the Baltimore Black Sox.

Appendix:
Black Sox Team Records,
1913–36

Team records for 1913–17 and 1935–36 are not available. For 1918–21, the local Baltimore papers offered the team's records. For 1922–34, seamheads.com offers the team's official records in various leagues and in independent ball. Where Seamheads differs from newspaper reports, I place the record from Seamheads first, followed by the reports from the newspapers in parenthesis. I also combine records for a year where Seamheads offers separate records for multiple leagues for a given year. In 1922, 1928, and 1932, the newspapers reported the team's overall record whereas Seamheads records only the league records or games against independent professional teams for those years.

Year	Wins–Losses	Titles	League (Place)
1913	No records available	Colored Champions of the South	
1914	No records available	Colored Champions of the South	
1915	No records available	Colored Champions of the South	
1916	No records available		
1917	No records available		
1918	88–23	Colored Champions of the South	
1919	47–6	Colored Champions of the South	
1920	1–1 (66–29)		

Appendix

Year	Wins-Losses	Titles	League (Place)
1921	4–7 (88–32)	*Colored Champions of the South*	
1922	25–26 (52–19)		
1923	23–35 (19–30)		Eastern Colored League (6)
1924	39–24 (35–19)		Eastern Colored League (2)
1925	36–33 (30–19)		Eastern Colored League (3)
1926	22–38 (18–33)		Eastern Colored League (6)
1927	34–36 (32–29)		Eastern Colored League (4)
1928	29–29 (52–19)		Eastern Colored League (2)
1929	61–28 (46–20)	*American Negro League Champions*	American Negro League (1)
1930	24–20		
1931	22–38 (20–36)		
1932	33–34 (52–14)		East-West League (3)
1933	20–23		Negro National League (4)
1934	4–9		Negro National League (6)
1935	No records available		
1936	No records available		

Chapter Notes

Preface

1. "Y.M.C.A. Picks Membership Drive Heads," *New York Age*, October 8, 1932, 2.
2. Daniel A. Nathan, "The Baltimore Black Sox and the Perils of History," in *Baseball in America and America in Baseball*, edited by Donald G. Kyle and Robert B. Fairbanks (Austin: University of Texas Press, 2008), 52–87.
3. James Bready, *Baseball in Baltimore: The First 100 Years* (Baltimore: Johns Hopkins University Press, 1998), 171.
4. Michel Foucault, *Power/Knowledge: Selected Interviews and Other Writings, 1972–1977* (New York: Pantheon Books, 1980), 82.
5. Richard Kearney, *Poetics of Modernity: Towards a Hermeneutic Imagination* (Amherst, NY: Humanity Books, 1998), xii.

Chapter 1

1. "Fans to Have Plenty of Good Baseball," *Baltimore Afro-American*, May 4, 1913, 8; "Baseball in the Air," *Baltimore Afro-American*, March 15, 1913, 8.
2. "Suffering is Law," *Baltimore Sun*, February 8, 1904, 6.
3. *The Baltimore Conflagration: Report of the Committee on Fire-Resistive Construction* (Chicago: The National Fire Protection Association, 1904), 6–8.
4. Matthew A. Crenson, *Baltimore: A Political History* (Baltimore: Johns Hopkins University Press, 2017), 332–333.
5. *Ibid.*, 335.
6. Carl Schoettler, "Lost in the Great Fire," *Baltimore Sun*, February 5, 2004, E1.
7. Crenson, 335.

8. "The Men Who Sail the Seven Seas," *Baltimore Sun*, October 23, 1932: MA7.
9. *Ibid.*
10. *Ibid.*
11. *Ibid.*
12. "Arrived on Saturday," *Baltimore Sun*, February 15, 1915, Arrived," *Baltimore Sun*, November 7, 1915, 6; "Arrived," *Baltimore Sun*, January 29, 1916, 10; "I Remember … When the Dreamland Came to Baltimore," *Baltimore Sun*, August 9, 1959, M2.
13. "New Elevator Hailed as Good Omen for Post," *Baltimore Sun*, August 8, 1921, 7; "Western Maryland to Build New $1,000,000 Grain Elevator," *Baltimore Sun*, August 7, 1921, ES6; "Rich in Factory Sites," *Baltimore Sun*, December 11, 1909, 9.
14. "Great Power Station," *Baltimore Sun*, April 16, 1906, 9.
15. "Work on the Hanover Street Bridge Being Pushed to Completion," *Baltimore Sun*, June 29, 1915, 8.
16. "Appomattox," *Baltimore Afro-American*, April 17, 1915, 4.
17. "Negro Education: Its Necessities and Limitations," *The Journal of Education* XXXV (1892): 94.
18. "The Growth of Popular Interest in Athletic Contests," *Baltimore Sun*, January 1, 1898, 6.
19. "In the World of Sports," *Automobile Topics*, Vol. 17, No. 7 (January 1909): 1481.
20. *Ibid.*
21. "'Fan,' Appropriately Came from Fanatic," *Baltimore Sun*, June 1, 1913, SSS8.
22. James C. Summers, "The World of Sports," in *Journalism* (New York: New York Press Club, 1905), 148.
23. James Roscoe Day, "The Function

of College Athletics," *American Physical Education Review* Vol. 15 (1910): 95.

24. "Profits in the Field," *Hardware and House Furnishing Goods*, Vol. 8, No. 1 (September 1920): 47.

25. Norris Arthur Brisco, *Retail Salesmanship* (New York: The Ronald Press Company, 1920), 256.

26. Howard Palmer Young, *Character Through Recreation* (Philadelphia: American Sunday School Union, 1915), 171.

27. *Ibid.*, 90.

28. Allan Freeman Davis, *Spearheads for Reform: Social Settlements and the Progressive Movement* (New Brunswick, NJ: Rutgers University Press, 1994), 62.

29. Jacob Riis, *How the Other Half Lives* (New York: Charles Scribner's Sons, 1890), 295.

30. John Thomas Scharf, *History of Baltimore City and County, from the Earliest Period to the Present Day, Including Biographical Sketches of Their Representative Men* (Philadelphia: L. H Leverts, 1881), 273.

31. "Our Suburban Parks," *Baltimore Sun*, July 26, 1881: 1.

32. *Ibid.*

33. Ken Mars, *Baltimore Baseball: First Pitch to First Pennant, 1858–1894* (Baltimore: Private Printing, 2018), 23.

34. "More Athletic Fields," *Baltimore Sun*, July 18, 1900, 6.

35. "Playground Cause," *Baltimore Sun*, March 22, 1900, 6.

36. *Ibid.*

37. "South Baltimore Glad," *Baltimore Sun*, March 26, 1901, 6.

38. "Inspect Sites for Parks," *Baltimore Sun*, March 15, 1901, 12; "Want Park at Locust Point," *Baltimore Sun*, September 24, 1901, 12.

39. "Laying out a Diamond," *Baltimore Sun*, April 29, 1902, 12.

40. *Ibid.*

41. "South Baltimore Anxious," *Baltimore Sun*, May 20, 1902, 6

42. "South Baltimore Field," *Baltimore Sun*, August 28, 1902, 6.

43. *Ibid.*

44. "An Athletic Triumph," *Baltimore Sun*, April 17, 1903, 9.

45. "Want Athletic Field," *Baltimore Sun*, November 14, 1903, 9.

46. "Plans for Other Equipment, Park Names Changed," *Baltimore Sun*, January 30, 1904, 12. Olmstead died in 1903, so it is believed that this solicitation was for work performed by his son.

47. *Ibid.*

48. "Parks Surely Popular," *Baltimore Sun*, July 18, 1915, 13.

49. Burt Solomon, *Where They Ain't: The Fabled Life and Untimely Death of the Original Baltimore Orioles, the Team That Gave Birth to Modern Baseball* (New York: Free Press, 1999), 4.

50. Bill Ferber, *A Game of Brawl: The Orioles, the Beaneaters and the Battle for the 1897 Pennant* (Lincoln: University of Nebraska Press, 2007), xxi.

51. *Ibid.*

52. "Many Clubs Are Hit," *Baltimore American*, February 14, 1919, 14.

53. "Baseball Games Today," *Baltimore Sun*, June 8, 1913, 7.

54. "Baseball Games Today," *Baltimore Sun*, June 21, 1913, 7; "Baseball Games Today," *Baltimore Sun*, July 13, 1913, SS1; "Gossip of Baltimore's Amateur Balltossers," *Baltimore Sun*, April 7, 1915; "Some Baseball Games Today, *Baltimore Sun*, May 9, 1920,15.

55. "The Growth of Popular Interest in Athletic Contests," 6.

56. *Ibid.*

57. "Baseball Team of Calumet," *Baltimore Sun*, October 11, 1908, 10.

58. "Summer Program for Baltimore Folks," *National Electric Light Association Bulletin*, Vol. 8, No. 7 (July 1921): 437.

59. "A Year in the Baltimore Section," *National Electric Light Association Bulletin*, Vol. 7, No. 8 (September 1920): 587.

60. "Amateur Ball Clubs," *Baltimore Sun*, May 10, 1909, 10.

61. "No. 48 Is 'Champ' Again," *Baltimore Sun*, June 24, 1915, 7.

62. "Afro Baseball League," *Baltimore Afro-American*, May 13, 1921, 7.

63. "Baltimore Giants Beaten," *Baltimore Sun*, July 17, 1904, 10.

64. "Sports Miscellany," *Baltimore Sun*, September 8, 1902, 2.

65. "White Players and Black," *Baltimore Sun*, July 5, 1901, 6.

66. "Yannigans and Colored Giants," *Baltimore Sun*, September 3, 1900, 6.

67. Harold McDougall, *Black Baltimore: A New Theory of Community* (Philadelphia: Temple University Press, 1993), 41.

68. Garret Power, "Apartheid Baltimore Style: The Residential Segregation Ordinances of 1910-1913," *Maryland Law Review*, Vol. 42, No. 2 (October 2012): 289–90.

69. *Ibid.*, 295.

70. "Dr. Young Expects All to Help," *Baltimore Afro-American*, Dec. 6, 1913, 1.

71. *Ibid.*

72. "To Make a Protest," *Baltimore Afro-American*, October 25, 1913, 1.

73. Dean William Pickens, "The Evil Influences of Jim Crowism," *Baltimore Afro-American*, March 15, 1918, 1.

74. "Up in Arms against B&O Railroad," *Baltimore Afro-American*, Feb 3, 1912, 1.

75. Power, "Apartheid Baltimore Style," 289–90. http://digitalcommons.law.umaryland.edu/cgi/viewcontent.cgi?article=2498&context=mlr

76. Antero Pietila, "History of Baltimore's Racial Segregation Includes a Hard Look at Newspapers's Role," *Baltimore Sun*, March 15, 2010.

77. "Wants Segregation of Street Cars," *Baltimore Sun*, August 12, 1913, 6.

78. "Wouldn't Play Blacks," *Baltimore Sun*, August 2, 1908, 5.

79. *Ibid.*

80. *Ibid.*

81. "Correspondent Thinks Negro Baseball Players Drink in Druid Hill," *Baltimore Sun*, August 2, 1908, 22.

82. "Weldons 8; Blackstockings, 2," *Baltimore Afro-American*, August 19, 1908, 9.

83. "Capt. Ward Leads Raid," *Baltimore Sun*, July 27, 1902, 14. "Receiver for Billiard Rooms," *Baltimore Sun*, January 28, 1903, 6.

84. "Colored Southern Ball League," *Baltimore American*, March 20, 1903, 10.

85. "Baltimore Giants Beaten," *Baltimore Sun*, July 17, 1904, 10.

86. "Sporting Miscellany," *Baltimore Sun*, July 9, 1901, 6; Mark Kram, "It Seemed Like It Happened in Another Country," *Baltimore News American*, August 9, 1981, 2E.

87. "Gans Arranging Ball Schedule," *Baltimore Sun*, July 5, 1905, 8; "Busy Time for Gans's Nine," *Baltimore Sun*, July 14, 1905, 8.

88. "Games for Gans's Team," *Baltimore Sun*, August 13, 1905, 10; "Gans Nine to Play Georgia Team," *Baltimore Sun*, July 8, 1905, 8.

89. "Gans Team," *Baltimore Sun*, July 16, 1905, 10.

90. "Crack Negro Teams to Play," *Washington Post*, June 25, 1905, SP2; "Gans's Team Defeated," *Washington Post*, July 1, 1901, 8; "Joe Gans a Ball Player," *Washington Post*, July 1, 1901, 8.

91. "Protests Against Fights," *New York Times*, April 11, 1916, 14.

92. "Boxing as Builder of Character," *Washington Post*, April 11, 1915, M2.

93. "Pugs Draw Color Line," *Washington Post*, January 17, 1909, S2.

94. "To Exclude Revolting Show," *Baltimore Sun*, July 6, 1910, 14.

95. Colleen Aycock and Mark Scott, *Joe Gans: A Biography of the First African American World Boxing Champion*, (Jefferson, NC: McFarland & Company, 2008), 13.

96. "Timely Boxing Talk," *Baltimore Sun*, January 29, 1906, 8.

97. Aycock and Scott, 200.

98. Lawrence D. Hogan, *Shades of Glory: The Negro Leagues and the Story of African American Baseball* (Washington: National Geographic Society, 2006), 106.

Chapter 2

1. "Amateur Ballclubs," *Baltimore Sun*, April 28, 1917, 8.

2. There is no additional extant information available on the "white ownership" that assumed controlled of the Baltimore Giants. Available sources do not list names or any other identifying information.

3. "Amateur Ballclubs," 8.

4. "Thomas R. Smith: Biography," Maryland State Archives, http://msa.maryland.gov/msa/stagser/s1259/121/6050/html/12418100.html.

5. *History and Roster of Maryland Volunteers, War of 1861–5.* (Baltimore: Press of Guggenheim, Weil & Co., 1899), 239.

6. "Democratic Negroes," *Baltimore Sun*, May 2, 1903, 1.

7. "Joe Gans Baseball Team," *Baltimore American*, June 25, 1905, 18.

8. "Amateur Ballclubs," 8.

9. "Weldons," *Baltimore American*, August 10, 1905, 11.

10. "Gans Team Is Ready," *Baltimore Sun*, May 30, 1905, 8.

11. "Baltimore Local Report," *Baltimore Sun*, June 6, 1905, 1; "Forecast for Baltimore and Vicinity," *Baltimore Sun*, June 6, 1905, 1.

12. "Amateur Ballclubs," 8.

13. *Ibid.*, 10.

14. *Ibid.*

15. "Victory for Gans's Nine," *Baltimore American*, June 29, 1905, 12.

16. "The Gans and Weldon Nines," *Baltimore American*, July 17, 1905, 21.

17. "The Weldons and Gans's Nine," *Baltimore American*, August 29, 1905, 10.

18. "Two Games for the Weldons," *Baltimore American*, June 6, 1906, 12.

19. Frederick N. Rasmussen, "Steamboats Meant Vacation," *Baltimore Sun*, June 19, 1999, 60.

20. "Weldons after Cuban X Giants," *Baltimore Sun*, September 9, 1909, 10; "Weldons," *Baltimore American*, August 8, 1906, 5.

21. "Weldons Win the Series," *Baltimore Sun*, August 10, 1908, 10; "Weldons Play Fine Ball," *Baltimore Sun*, September 6, 1908, 10.

22. "New Baseball League," *New York Times*, December 17, 1907, 7.

23. Union League Park's grandstands and bleachers were dismantled after the 1920 season. However, the field continued to be a center for Baltimore's semipro and amateur teams well into the 1930s, and there was some discussion about the site hosting another team from an upstart league, the Continental Baseball Association.

24. Helen Granger Boss, "I Remember ... Riverside Scenes in Old South Baltimore," *Baltimore Sun*, May 30, 1965: SM2.

25. "Weldons Play Fine Ball," 10; "Weldons to Play Turners," *Baltimore Sun*, September 1, 1908, 9.

26. "Amateur Ball Clubs," *Baltimore Sun*, August 26, 1907, 10.

27. "Weldons Land Pennant," *Baltimore Sun*, September 8, 1908, 9; "Weldons to the Top," *Baltimore Sun*, September 20, 1908, 10.

28. "Weldons Land Pennant," 9.

29. "Weldons and Cuban Giants," *Baltimore Sun*, September 21, 1908, 10.

30. Hogan, *Shades of Glory*, vii–viii.

31. *Ibid.*, 116.

32. "Weldons Will Have to Work," *Baltimore Sun*, September 23, 1908, 10.

33. "Baltimore Local Report," *Baltimore Sun*, September 23, 1908, 1.

34. "Cuban Giants, 4; Weldons, 2," *Baltimore Sun*, September 24, 1908, 10.

35. "Weldons Snowed Under," *Baltimore Sun*, September 25, 1908, 10.

36. "Weldons to Lose Players," *Baltimore Sun*, October 13, 1908, 10.

37. "Colored Players Ready," *Baltimore Sun*, May 10, 1909, 10.

38. "Forecast for Baltimore and Vicinity," *Baltimore Sun*, May 10, 1909, 1.

39. "Colored Players Ready," 10.

40. Power, "Apartheid Baltimore Style," 289–90.

41. Ordinance 692, Baltimore, MD. (May 15, 1911).

42. "Segregation in Force," *Baltimore Sun*, December 20, 1910, 20.

43. "Two Games at Ball Parks," *Washington Herald*, July 3, 1909, 9.

44. "Weldons Now Baltimore Giants," *Baltimore American*, May 23, 1909, 22.

45. "Weldons Prepare for Season," *Baltimore Sun*, May 3, 1909, 9.

46. "Weldons Release Players," *Baltimore Sun*, May 3, 1909, 12.

47. "Baltimore Giants Win," *Washington Herald*, May 13, 1909, 9.

48. "Weldons Initial Practice," *Baltimore American*, March 21, 1909, 21.

49. "Quarters for Weldons," *Baltimore Afro-American*, March 20, 1909, 8.

50. "Weldons Initial Practice," 21.

51. "Baltimore Weldons," *New York Age*, April 1, 1909, 6.

52. "1812 Society Observes," *Baltimore Sun*, January 9, 1906, 7.

53. "Loyal to Lost Cause," *Baltimore Sun*, January 21, 1906, 16.

54. "Pleads for the Annex," *Baltimore Sun*, August 24, 1906, 7; "Suggests Mr. R. E. Lee Hall as Next Mayor," *Baltimore Sun*, October 30, 1916, 6.

55. Sherry Olson, *Baltimore: The Build-*

ing of an American City (Baltimore: Johns Hopkins University Press, 1997), 375.

56. "Baltimore Giants New Players," *Baltimore American*, July 5, 1909, 6.

57. "The Weldon Giants to Play the LaFayettes of Washington," *Baltimore Afro-American*, July 17, 1909, 5.

58. "Signs with Weldons," *Baltimore American*, July 25, 1909, 7.

59. "Giants to Play at Oriole Park, "*Baltimore Sun*, June 7, 1909, 10.

60. "The Weldon Giants to Play the LaFayettes," 5.

61. "Easy for Philadelphia Giants," *Baltimore American*, May 25, 1909, 6; "The Weldon Giants to Play the LaFayettes," 5.

62. "Joe Gans to Umpire," *Baltimore American*, July 26, 1909, 6.

63. "Gans, After a Merciless Beating," *San Francisco Examiner*, September 10, 1908, 8.

64. "Gans Puzzles Sports," *Baltimore Sun*, March 13, 1909, 10.

65. Aycock and Scott, *Joe Gans*, 221.

66. "Joe Gans Joins Ball Team," *Baltimore Sun*, August 2, 1909, 9.

67. "Colored Team to Play," *Washington Herald*, July 24, 1910, 31.

68. "Fast Game Today," *Washington Herald*, June 11, 1911, 16.

69. "Washington Giants Winning Games," *New York Age*, June 8, 1911, 6; "New Baseball Manager," *Asbury Park Press*, June 16, 1911, 12.

70. "First Game of Series at Union League Park," *Baltimore Sun*, May 20, 1912, 10.

71. "Vickers May Pitch Here," *Baltimore Sun*, May 17, 1912, 12.

72. "Weldons Are in the Field Again," *Baltimore Sun*, June 27, 1912, 16.

73. "Baseball Notes," *Asbury Park Press*, July 27, 1909, 9.

74. "Good Game Sunday," *Washington Herald*, June 13, 1912, 8; "Giants Split Even," *Washington Herald*, July 8, 1912, 9.

Chapter 3

1. William Stater, "Baseball, His First Love," *Baltimore Afro-American*, April 11, 1959, 5.

2. "Play Black Sox Nine," *Washington Herald*, August 13, 1914, 8; "Member of Pioneer Team," *Baltimore Afro-American*, June 13, 1931, 15.

3. "Boxing, Baseball and Running," *Baltimore Afro-American*, April 4, 1914, 4.

4. U.S. Census Bureau, 1910 Census, Elkridge, Maryland, District 1.

5. "Weldon A. C.," *Baltimore Sun*, August 25, 1905, 8.

6. U.S. Selective Service System, Baltimore, Maryland, Roll 1684192, Draft Board 19.

7. "Colored Baseball Team," *Baltimore Sun*, April 1, 1913, 10.

8. "Baseball," *Baltimore Afro-American*, May 4, 1913, 5.

9. U.S. Census Bureau, 1910 Census, Baltimore, Maryland, 14th Ward, District 235.

10. *Ibid.*

11. "Our High School," *Baltimore Afro-American*, September 28, 1901, 4.

12. *Ibid.*

13. "Good Advice," *Baltimore Afro-American*, July 8, 1899, 1.

14. See Chapter 1, note 1.

15. Elizabeth Dowling Taylor, *The Original Black Elite: Daniel Murphy and the Story of a Forgotten Era* (New York: Amistad, 2017). 3.

16. *Ibid.*, 3–4.

17. The *Afro-American* identifies John R. Williams as the team's "promoter." ("Fans have plenty of good baseball," 8.). Therefore, it is reasonable to conclude that he had a hand in writing both the notices that appeared in the *Sun* and the *Baltimore Afro-American*.

18. "Colored Baseball Team," 10.

19. "Baseball in the Air," 8.

20. *Ibid.*

21. See Chapter 1, note 1.

22. See *The First Colored Professional, Clerical, Skilled and Business Directory of Baltimore City*, 4th ed. (R.W. Coleman Pub. Co., 1916–17).

23. "Dr. Young," *Baltimore Afro-American*, October 13, 1945, 18.

24. N. Louise Young Photograph Collection, Maryland Historical Society, http://www.mdhs.org/findingaid/n-louise-young-photograph-collection-pp283.

25. U.S. Census Bureau, 1880 Census. District 1 (Baltimore).

26. "Black Sox Having a Successful Season," *Baltimore Afro-American*, August 9, 1913, 8; "Black Sox Getting Ready," *Baltimore Sun*, March 1, 1914, 34.

27. Power, "Apartheid Baltimore Style," 289–90.

28. Colonel Midnight, "A Real Hotel in Baltimore," *Baltimore Afro-American*, May 4, 1913, 6.

29. "Democratic Negroes," 1.

30. "Big Crowd Sees Doubleheader," *Baltimore Afro-American*, May 10, 1913, 8.

31. "Plucky Girl Makes Mayor Shake Hands," *Baltimore Afro-American*, July 1, 1911, 4.

32. *Ibid.*

33. "Death Comes to Harry S. Cummings," *Baltimore Afro-American*, September 8, 1913, 1.

34. "Big Crowd Sees Doubleheader," 8.

35. "Sports and Athletics," *Baltimore Afro-American*, July 11, 1914, 4.

36. "Sports and Athletics," *Baltimore Afro-American*, October 2, 1915, 4.

37. "Sports and Athletics," *Baltimore Afro-American*, May 9, 1914, 4.

38. "Baseball," *New York Age*, July 13, 1916, 6.

39. "Local Ball Teams Winding Up Season," *Baltimore Sun*, September 21, 1913, 36; "Gossip of Baltimore's Amateur Balltossers," *Baltimore Afro-American*, September 4, 1914, 8; "YMAA Beats Negro Stars," *Baltimore Sun*, October 4, 1915, 5.

40. "Sports and Athletics," *Baltimore Afro-American*, August 7, 1915, 4.

41. "Baseball Briefs," *Baltimore Afro-American* September 25, 1915, 8.

42. "Baltimore Black Sox Defeat the Bobbitz All Stars in a Double-Header," *Indianapolis Freeman*, June 24, 1916, 7.

43. "Sports and Athletics," *Baltimore Afro-American*, October 2, 1915, 4.

44. "Black Sox Win Two Games," *Baltimore Afro-American*, May 27, 1916, 4.

45. "Black Sox Defeated," *Indianapolis Freeman*, July 15, 1916, 7.

46. *Ibid.*

47. "Two Games at Oriole Park," *Baltimore Sun*, August 2, 1913, 5; "We Will Have Good Baseball," *Baltimore Afro-American*, July 5, 1913, 8.

48. "Sports and Athletics," *Baltimore Afro-American*, June 20, 1914, 4.

49. "We Will Have Good Baseball," 8; Alexander Waters, "Baseball," *New York Age*, April 27, 1916, 7.

50. "Fans Were Disappointed When Team Fails to Appear," *Baltimore Sun*, June 20, 1915, 48.

51. "Personals," *Baltimore Afro-American*, April 7, 1917, 4. In 1916, the Black Sox played two series of games against the Simpson and Doeller Company's team at the company's "grounds on East Federal Street ("Just Baseball," *Baltimore Afro-American*, May 20, 1916, 2.). The Simpson and Doeller Oval, as it was called, would eventually be renamed, Bugle Field, the home field of the Black Sox after the 1932 season and the future home of the Baltimore Elite Giants. James A. Riley writes that the "Black Sox played most of their games on Bugle Field" (*Of Monarchs and Black Barons* [Jefferson, NC: McFarland, 2012], 94). The notice from April 1917 regarding games on East and Federal streets, at what was Bugle Field's predecessor, may be the source for Riley's statement.

52. "YMAA Downs Black Sox," *Baltimore Sun*, April 16, 1917, 7.

53. "Black Sox to Play," *Baltimore Afro-American*, April 28, 1917, 4. The papers did run notices for games involving area teams called the Black Sox, but these clubs were not the Baltimore Black Sox. Those teams included the Mount Winans Black Sox ("Some Baseball Games Scheduled for Today," *Baltimore Sun*, September 9, 1917, SN14.) and the Curtis Bay Black Sox ("Colgates Divide Double Bill," *Baltimore Sun*, July 5, 1917, 8.).

54. Walter Williams lived at 451 Orchard, suggesting that the men were neighbors.

55. The 1910 census does list an H. L. Harris (white) who worked as a bricklayer. However, it is doubtful that this H. L. Harris is the same man who took over management of the Black Sox. (U.S. Census Bureau, 1910 Census, Baltimore, Maryland, Ward 4; Family History Library Microfilm Service, Roll T624_553, Page 7A, Enumeration District 0044, FHL microfilm 1374566.).

Chapter 4

1. "Baseball Needs Brains and Money," *Baltimore Afro-American*, October 29, 1920, 7.

2. Larry Lester, *Rube Foster in His Time* (Jefferson, NC: McFarland, 2012), 67; Henry Williams, "Hits and Runs," *Los Angeles Times*, October 18, 1912, 31.

3. "Baseball Needs," 7.

4. "Shibe Park," *Evening Public Ledger* (Philadelphia), October 6, 1920, 20.

5. "On February 20, 1920, Rube [Foster] called together all the owners of Black baseball teams in the Midwest. They agreed to a set of rules that the league would follow.... They named the league the Negro National League. It had eight teams—the Cuban Stars, the Detroit Stars, the Chicago American Giants, the Chicago Giants, the Kansas City Monarchs, the St. Louis Stars, the Indianapolis ABC's and the Dayton Marcos" (Kadir Nelson, *We Are the Ship* [New York: Hyperion, 2008], 9.).

6. "Chicago Shuts Out Bacharachs," *Baltimore Afro-American*, October 16, 1920, 7; "Baseball Needs Brains and Money," 7.

7. *Ibid.*

8. Williams, "Hits and Runs," 31.

9. "Baseball Needs," 7.

10. Wallace Smith perhaps came closest to Foster's ideal owner, but, ultimately, Smith could not make a long-term success, for whatever reasons, of the Weldons or the Black Sox.

11. "The Mt Clare All-Stars Will Play the Black Sox Two Games Today at Westport," *Baltimore Sun*, September 23, 1917, SO13.

12. "Series to Open Today," *Baltimore Sun*, October 14, 1917, 20.

13. His work in 1917 to rebuild the club is likely the genesis of a partially erroneous report in the *Afro-American* from February 12, 1927. The story accurately states that Spedden "picked up local ball players and whipped them into a team" (14), but the story also inaccurately claims that he "was the owner of the original Black Sox" (14).

14. "Enthusiasm Great for Saturday Game," *Baltimore Afro-American*, November 14, 1919, 7.

15. "Black Sox Get New Players," *Baltimore Afro-American*, January 11, 1924, A14.

16. U.S. Selective Service System, Baltimore, Maryland, Roll 1684143, Draft Board 18.

17. U.S. Census Bureau, 1880 Census, Baltimore, Maryland; Family History Library Microfilm Service, Roll 504, , Page 519A, Enumeration District: 174, FHL microfilm 1254504; B&O employment records; George C. Bauer, "Coal Traffic Department," *Baltimore and Ohio Employees Magazine*, Vol. 8, No.5 (September 1920): 43. B&O employment records indicate that Spedden worked for the railroad from December 27, 1909 through April 7, 1923.

18. "Black Sox Get New Players," January 11, 1924, A14; "Base Ball Notes," *Baltimore Sun*, May 28, 1893, 6; "Pitcher Barker," *Baltimore Sun*, May 16, 1901, 6; "Amateur Ball Clubs," *Baltimore Sun*, May 24, 1904, 9; "Amateur Ball Clubs," *Baltimore Sun*, September 12, 1905, 8; "Amateur Ball Clubs," *Baltimore Sun*, August 22, 1907, 10.

19. U.S. Selective Service System, Baltimore, Maryland, Roll 1654042, Draft Board 1; U.S. Census Bureau, 1910 Census, Baltimore, Maryland, Ward 22, District 0373.

20. Limpert, "Baltimore and Ohio Building," (November 1915):76.

21. Baltimore and Ohio team had been organized in 1910: "B. & O.'s Strong Nine: Manager Phil Wallace Has a Fine Trip for His Team," *Baltimore Sun*, Mar 23, 1910, 12; John Limpert, "Baltimore and Ohio Building," *Baltimore and Ohio Employees Magazine*, Vol. 4, No. 2 (June 1916): 73.

22. "Baltimore and Ohio Team Will Compete in Baltimore Semi-Professional League," *Baltimore and Ohio Employees Magazine*, Vol. 4, No. 11 (March 1917): 41.

23. *Ibid.*

24. Historically, Annapolis Road was also known as Maryland Avenue and Waterview Avenue was known as Fish House Road.

25. "Grand Opening," *Baltimore Sun*, December 13, 1905, 1.

26. "Exhibition Polo Game," *Baltimore Sun*, December 15, 1905, 1.

27. "Basketball on Skates," *Baltimore Sun,* January 24, 1906, 8.

28. "Improvements at Westport Rink," *Baltimore Sun,* January 7, 1906,10; "Fun for the Roller Skaters," *Baltimore Sun,* January 1, 1906, 8.

29. The Westport Palace Skating Rink originally served as a center for the white middle class. It opened in December 1905, just in time for the Christmas season, proclaiming itself the "finest roller-skating rink in the South," with all "modern equipment." The rink was convenient to the streetcar line, with an option for cab service stopping in front of the facility. Patrons could explore the surrounding areas before entering the Rink. Facilities included a park with a fountain, open-green spaces, an abundance of trees, and easy walking distance to the Middle Branch. Patrons could see sailboats skim the surface of the water, far enough away so as to offer an escape from the city, but close enough so as not to make travel prohibitive; the Long Bridge and industrial south Baltimore would have framed the horizon.

30. "Base Ball," *Baltimore Afro-American,* August 2, 1918, 2.

31. See Chapter 1.

32. "Black Sox defeat Yannigans," *Baltimore Afro-American,* June 21, 1918, 31.

33. "Colored Troopers at Camp Meade Drilling," *Baltimore Afro-American,* Aril 5, 1918, 1.

34. "Col. Moss Praises Colored Officers," *Baltimore Afro-American,* January 12, 1918, 1.

35. Emmett Scott, *The American Negro and the World War* (Privately printed: Emmet Scott, 1919), 459.

36. "Says War Has Helped Negro," *Baltimore Afro-American,* March 29, 1918, 1.

37. "Baltimore Boys at Camp Meade Who Are in Training to Make the World Safe for Democracy," *Baltimore Afro-American,* April 12, 1918, 1.

38. "Soldiers Must Not Ask for Legal Rights," *Baltimore Afro-American,* April 12, 1918, 1.

39. "Will Play Irvington," *Baltimore American,* September 22, 1918, 20.

40. "Will Play the Strickers," *Baltimore Sun,* September 7, 1918, 8.

41. "Flag Raising and Baseball," *Balti-* more *Afro-American,* September 20, 1918, 2.

42. Evidence suggests that there were at least three games. The first took place in July ("Black Sox to Play Boys from Camp Meade Sunday," *Baltimore Afro-American,* July 12, 1918, 2.). The teams played two additional games in August: see note 47 and "Baseball," August 2, 1918, 2; "Even Break for the Black Sox," *Baltimore American,* August 5, 1918, 5.

43. "Black Sox to Play Series of Games for Championship," *Baltimore Afro-American,* October 4, 1918, 5.

44. "Games at Westport," *Baltimore American,* October 13, 1918, 19.

45. "Doc Sykes Was a Pitcher and a Fighter against Bigotry," *Baltimore Sun,* April 30, 1990, 7C; "Baseball," *New York Age,* July 13, 1916, 6; Dick Clark and Larry Lester, *The Negro Leagues Book* (Cleveland: Society for American Baseball Research, 1994), 65.

46. "Doc Sykes," 7C.

47. "Play Black Sox Today," *Baltimore American,* September 8, 1918, 18.

48. "Pastor Pareda." Baseball Reference, https://www.baseball-reference.com/bullpen/Pastor_Pareda.

49. "Cuban Will Do Hurling," *Altoona Tribune,* May 25, 1915, 6.

50. "Series with the Black Sox," *Baltimore American,* August 31, 1918, 5; "Black Sox to Play Country Lads," *Baltimore Sun,* June 7, 1918, 8; "Will Play Irvington," 20; "Railroads and Sox to Clash," *Baltimore Sun,* June 23, 1918, C7.

51. "Black Sox Defeat Yannigans," *Baltimore Afro-American,* June 21, 1918, 2.

52. "Black Sox to Play a Series of Games," 5.

53. "Black Sox to Play," *Baltimore Afro-American,* October 11, 1918, 2.

54. "Base Ball," August 2, 1918, 2; "Baseball," *Baltimore Afro-American,* July 19, 1918, 3.

55. "Base Ball," *Baltimore Afro-American,* August 9, 1918, 2.

56. "Base Ball," *Baltimore Afro-American,* July 19, 1918, 3.

57. "Black Sox to Play a Series of Games," 5.

58. "Black Sox to Play Boys from Camp Meade," 2.

59. "Base Ball," *Baltimore Afro-American*, September 20, 1918, 2.

60. "Games at Westport," *Baltimore American*, April 13, 1919, 24.

61. "Colored Troopers Have Returned from Overseas," *Baltimore Afro-American*, April 18, 1919, A6.

62. "Black Sox to Test Their Strength," *Baltimore Afro-American*, July 11, 1919, 2.

63. "Parkside Meets Baltimore Team," *Wilmington Morning News*, June 16, 1921, 9.

64. Draft Registration Cards for Maryland, 10/16/1940–03/31/1947, The National Archives, St. Louis, Missouri Records of the Selective Service System, 147, Box 63.

65. U.S. Census Bureau, 1900 Census, Sparrows Point, Baltimore, Maryland; Family History Library Microfilm Service, Roll 607, Page 5B, Enumeration District 0061.FHL microfilm: 1240607.

66. "Games at Westport," *Baltimore American*, May 4, 1919, 24.

67. William Nunn, "Diamond Dope," *Pittsburgh Courier*, 11 July 1925, 10.

68. "Philly Giants to Play Black Sox," *Baltimore American*, September 7, 1919, 7; "Black Sox Win Two More Games," *Baltimore Afro-American*, June 20, 1919, A6.

69. "Both Ends to Black Sox," *Baltimore American*, September 22, 1919, 6.

70. U.S. Census Bureau, 1900 Census, Martinsville, Henry, Virginia; Family History Library Microfilm Service, Roll 1713, Page 3B, Enumeration District 0053, FHL microfilm 1241713.

71. U.S. Selective Service System, Baltimore, Maryland, Roll 1786820, Draft Board 158.

72. G. L. Mackay, "Sports Mirror," *Baltimore Afro-American*, April 4, 1925, 7.

73. "Black Sox Meet Tigers," *Baltimore Afro-American*, August 8. 1919, 2.

74. "Some Baseball Games Booked for Today," *Baltimore Afro-American*, September 7, 1919, 12; "Wilmington Giants to Play Black Sox on Sunday," *Baltimore Afro-American*, August 15, 1919, 6.

75. "Community League Standings," *Wilmington News Journal*, August 16, 1919, 10.

76. "Black Sox Will Play on Sunday," *Baltimore American*, November 1, 1919, 6.

77. "Black Sox vs. Quakers," *Baltimore Sun*, October 5, 1918, 78.

78. "Black Sox Change Schedule," *Baltimore Afro-American*, July 25, 1919, 6.

79. "Two Big Events," *Baltimore Afro-American*, October 31,1919, 2.

80. "Sporting Dope," *Baltimore Afro-American*, September 10, 1920, 7; "Scrappy Brown Back at Short," *Baltimore Afro-American*, November 12, 1920, 7.

81. "Games at Westport," *Baltimore Afro-American*, April 4, 1920, 14.

82. "Thomas Out of the Game," *Baltimore Afro-American*, July 16, 1920, 7.

83. "Rex Nine Will Play Black Sox," *Baltimore American*, June 25, 1920,4.

84. *Ibid.*

85. "Black Sox Defeat Yannigans," *Baltimore Afro-American*, June 21, 1918, 2.

86. "Black Sox Win Double-Header," *Baltimore Afro-American*, June 13, 1919, 2.

87. "Thomas Out of the Game," 7.

88. "Smith Is Let Go," *Pittsburgh Courier*, June 21, 1924, 6.

89. "Parkside Meets Baltimore Team," *Wilmington Morning News*, June 16, 1921, 9.

90. "Sox Going Strong," *Baltimore Afro-American*, July 16, 1920, 7.

91. U.S. Census Bureau, 1900 Census, Baltimore, Maryland, Ward 17; Family History Library Microfilm Service, Roll 615, Page 12A, Enumeration District 0224, FHL microfilm 1240615.

92. U.S. Selective Service System, Baltimore, Maryland, Roll 1684140, Draft Board 15.

93. U.S. Census Bureau, 1900 Census, Baltimore, Maryland, Election District 1; Family History Library Microfilm Service, Roll 606, Page 8B, Enumeration District 0020, FHL microfilm 1240606.

94. U.S. Census Bureau, 1910 Census, Baltimore, Maryland, Election District 1; Family History Library Microfilm Service, Roll T624_550, Page 19A, Enumeration District 0001, FHL microfilm 1374563.

95. U.S. Census Bureau,1920 Census, Baltimore, Maryland, Election District 1; Family History Library Microfilm Service, Roll T625_654, Page 4B, Enumeration District 2.

96. "Sox Going Strong," 7.

97. "Buck Ridgely," Negro Leagues

Database, seamheads.com, http://seam
heads.com/NegroLgs/player.php?player
ID=ridgl0c

98. "Sox Going Strong," 7.

99. "Colored Stars," *Washington Evening Star*, July 11, 1920, 27.

100. "Rex Nine Will Play," 4.

101. "Baltimore Black Sox Here for Game," *Wilmington Morning News*, August 17, 1920, 9; "Black Sox Take Three," *Baltimore Afro-American*, June 25, 1920, 7.

102. "Rommell In Box against Black Sox," *Baltimore American*, November 4, 1920, 5.

103. "Parker Shuts Out Stars," *Baltimore Afro-American*, July 16, 1920, 7; "Baltimore Black Sox Win," *Washington Evening Star*, July 13, 1920, 19.

104. "Fayetteville BB Club Record," *Fayetteville Observer*, August 27, 1920, 5.

105. "Local Colored Team Takes Remarkable Game, "*Fayetteville Observer*, August 27, 1920, 5.

106. "Colored Stars," 27.

107. "Giants Put Up Good Game," *Baltimore Afro-American*, July 2, 1920, 7.

108. "New York Makes Clean Sweep," *Baltimore Afro-American*, August 13, 1920, 7.

109. "Sporting Days," *Baltimore Afro-American*, August 13, 1920, 7.

110. "New York Makes Clean Sweep," 7.

111. "Pierce Hits Three Homers in One Day," *New York Age*, September 25, 1920, 6.

112. "Hilldale Beaten," *Philadelphia Inquirer*, September 21, 1920, 14.

113. "Washington Letter," *New York Age*, July 17, 1920, 5.

114. "25 Years Ago Today," *News Journal*, June 23, 1942, 6.

115. "Darby Colored Team Drops Close Game to Black Sox," *Philadelphia Inquirer*, September 21, 1920, 14.

116. "Hilldale and Black Sox in Last Ballgame," *Wilmington Morning News*, October 22, 1920, 9.

117. "Black Sox Defeat Harlan Giants," *Baltimore Afro-American*, August 20, 1920, 7.

118. "Black Sox Get on Giants's Neck," *Wilmington Evening Journal*, August 19, 1920, 6.

119. "Sammy Hits Back at Black Sox," *Wilmington Evening Journal*, August 20, 1920, 15.

120. The controversial games in Wilmington also have Cooperstown connections. Baseball Hall of Famer Bill McGowan's older brother served as umpire for the series between Harlan and the Black Sox (both the Wilmington and Baltimore versions). It is also tempting to think that the Black Sox infusion into a local rivalry compelled Hall of Famer Judy Johnson to sign with Hilldale rather than with Baltimore; Johnson was one of the players the Harlan Giants had pulled in from Chester.

121. "Blainey Hall Leads Black Sox Batters," *Baltimore Afro-American*, April 29, 1921, 7.

122. *Ibid.*

123. "New Park for Black Sox," *Baltimore Afro-American*, February 6, 1920, 7.

124. Lester, *Rube Foster in His Time*, 115.

125. *Ibid.*, 114.

126. "Johnson with American Giants," *Washington Post*, October 12, 1920, 8.

127. "Colored Championship," *Evening Journal* (Wilmington, DE), October 9, 1920, 5.

128. "Bacharachs Take Foster's aggregation," *Courier News* (Bridgewater, NJ), October 9, 1923, 11.

129. "Semi-Pro Nines to Play in Flatbush To-Day," *New York Tribune*, October 10, 1920, 22.

130. "Crack Colored Team to Play Series Here," *Washington Herald*, October 12, 1920, 8.

131. "Chicago Shuts Out Bacharachs," 7.

Chapter 5

1. "The Sporting Mirror," *Baltimore Afro-American*, June 9, 1922, 9.

2. "Black Sox Win and Lose," *Baltimore Afro-American*, May 20, 1921, 2.

3. "Base Ball," *Baltimore Afro-American*, May 6, 1921, 7.

4. "Black Sox Win and Lose," 2.

5. "Colored Baseball Team," *Fayetteville Observer*, April 13, 1921, 5.

6. "Black Sox Win Three Games," *Baltimore Afro-American*, June 17, 1921, 2.

7. "Black Sox Win Another," *Baltimore American*, July 26, 1921, 7.

8. "Black Sox Win Three Games," 2.

9. "Parkside Set for Black Sox," *Wilmington Morning News*, May 17, 1921, 9.

10. "Black Sox vs. Aberfoyle," *Wilmington News Journal*, August 22, 1921, 7; "O'Mara Fades Out," *Wilmington Evening Journal*," August 24, 1921, 10.

11. "Wheeler Led Sox Pitchers," *Baltimore Afro-American*, April 14, 1922, 9.

12. "Sox Swamp Tigers," *Baltimore Afro-American*, June 3, 1921, 2; "Twin Bill to Black Sox," *Baltimore Afro-American*, October 14, 1921, 9.

13. "Wheeler Led Sox Pitchers," 9.

14. U.S. Census Bureau, 1900 Census, Marshall, Buckingham, Virginia; Family History Library Microfilm Service, Roll 1702, Page 5A, Enumeration District 0059, FHL microfilm; U.S. Census Bureau, 1910 Census, Baltimore, Maryland, Ward 9; Family History Library Microfilm Service, Roll T624_555, Page 11B, Enumeration District 0125, FHL microfilm 1374568.

15. "Black Sox Win in Sunday Games," *Baltimore Afro-American*, July 23, 1920, 7.

16. "Logan Pitched," *Baltimore Afro-American*, May 27, 1921, 2; "Black Sox Showing Class," *Baltimore Afro-American*, August 26, 1921, 2.

17. "Old Times Beaten," *Philadelphia Inquirer*, August 12, 1921, 14.

18. "Wheeler Led Sox Pitchers," 9.

19. "Sox Swamp Brooklyn Sides," *Baltimore Afro-American*, July 8, 1921, 2; "Braves Defeat Slides," *Washington Herald*, April 30, 1921, 9; "LeDroit Tigers," *Washington Evening Star*, March 20, 1921, 31.

20. "The Black Sox Trim Stentons," *Baltimore Afro-American*, August 26, 1921, 2; "Wheeler Led Sox Pitchers," 9.

21. "Twin Bill to Black Sox," 9.

22. U.S. Census Bureau, 1920 Census, Washington, District of Columbia; Family History Library Microfilm Service, Roll T625_211, Page 10A, Enumeration District 198.

23. "Black Sox Win Three Games," *Baltimore Afro-American*, June 17, 1921, 2.

24. "Black Sox Win and Lose," 2.

25. "Black Sox Win Three Games," 2.

26. "Chick Meade, Ex-Ball Player out of Maryland Pen," *Baltimore Afro-American*, September 24, 1932, 23.

27. Larry Lester, *Black Baseball's National Showcase: The East West All Star Game, 1933–1953* (Lincoln: University of Nebraska Press, 2001), 264.

28. See U.S. Census Bureau, 1900 Census, Fairmont Ward 3, Marion, West Virginia; Family History Library Microfilm Service, Roll 1764, Page 16B, Enumeration District 0052, FHL microfilm 1241764.

29. "'Chick' Meade Is a Native of Fairmont, W.VA.," *Baltimore Afro-American*, July 4, 1931, 4.

30. "Chick Meade, Baseball Star, Gets 18 Months," *Baltimore Afro-American*, June 13, 1931, 15.

31. "'Chick' Meade Is a Native," 4.

32. Harry Stegmaier, *Cumberland, Maryland, Through the Eyes of Herman J. Miller* (Cumberland: Mayor and Council, City of Cumberland, 1978), 241.

33. "1915 Cuban Giants Program Featuring First White Player in Negro Leagues," Huggins and Scott Auctions, http://sep12.hugginsandscott.com/cgi-bin/showitem.pl?itemid=49690.

34. U.S. Census Bureau, 1900 Census, Fairmont Ward 3, Marion, West Virginia.

35. See U.S. Census Bureau, 1880 Census, Weston, Lewis, West Virginia; Family History Library Microfilm Service, Roll 1406, FHL microfilm 1255406, Page 88C, Enumeration District 134; See also U.S. Census Bureau, 1880 Census, Fairmont, Marion, West Virginia; Family History Library Microfilm Service, Roll 1407, FHL microfilm 1255407, Page 400C, Enumeration District 086. The 1870 census does list his paternal grandparents as "W," for White, but that is an aberration as Alfre Meade is listed as "M" on older census forms.

36. U.S. Census Bureau, 1930 Census, Charleston, Kanawha, West Virginia; Family History Library Microfilm Service, Roll 2537, Page 6A, Enumeration District 0046, FHL microfilm 2342271.

37. "Colored Baseball Fans," *Baltimore Afro-American*, June 23, 1922, 9; "Baseball Notes," *Baltimore Afro-American*, May 18, 1923, 15.

38. "Baseball Prices Reduced," *Baltimore Afro-American*, June 16, 1922, 5; "Black

Sox Club," *Baltimore Afro-American*, March 10, 1922, 9.

39. "Baltimore Black Sox," *Wilmington Evening Journal*, August 22, 1921, 9.

40. "Black Sox-SPHA Ready for Tilt," *Wilmington Evening Journal*, September 2, 1921, 14.

41. Ralph Matthews, "Thinking out Loud," *Baltimore Afro-American*, September 12, 1970, 5.

42. "Sport Tidbits," *Baltimore Afro-American*, August 5, 1921, 2.

43. "Black Sox Win and Lose," 2.

44. "Black Sox Open Season," *Baltimore Afro-American*, April 5, 1921, 5.

45. "Black Sox, 5; Norfolk 5," *Baltimore Afro-American*, May 6, 1921, 7.

46. "Logan Pitched," 2.

47. "Two Hit by Batted Balls," *Baltimore Afro-American*, July 25, 1921, 14.

48. "Black Sox Win Three Games," 2.

49. "SPHA Will Meet the Fast Baltimore Black Sox," *Wilmington Morning News*, September 2 1921, 8.

50. "Meet Black Sox Today," *Baltimore American*, October 2, 1921, 2; "The Black Sox Trim Stentons," 2.

51. "Harrisburg Giants," *Harrisburg Telegraph*, September 2, 1921, 17.

52. "Black Sox Take Both," *Baltimore Afro-American*, October 7, 1921, 9.

53. "Black Sox Close Season," *Baltimore Afro-American*, November 11, 1921, 9.

54. "Black Sox Incorporate," *Baltimore Afro-American*, July 29, 1921, 2.

55. "Baltimore Black Sox to Be Real Baseball Team," *Baltimore Afro-American*, March 10, 1922, 9.

56. "Sports Tidbits," *Baltimore Afro-American*, November 18, 1921, 9.

57. "Black Sox Elect Officers," *Baltimore Afro-American*, January 27, 1922, 9.

58. U.S. Census Bureau, 1930 Census, Baltimore, Maryland; Family History Library Microfilm Service, Roll 862, Page 6B, Enumeration District 0295, FHL microfilm 2340597.; "Nite Clubbing in Baltimore," *Baltimore Afro-American*, April 27, 1935, 9.

59. "Numbers Bankers Suffer Big Loss from 'Lucky" Tip," *Baltimore Afro-American*, August 30, 1930, A1.

60. "Black Sox Elect Officers," 9.

61. U.S. Census Bureau, 1910 Census, Baltimore, Maryland, Ward 18; Family History Library Microfilm Service, Roll T624_559, Page 7A, Enumeration District 0307, FHL microfilm 1374572.

62. "Black Sox Elect Officers," 9.

63. U.S. Census Bureau, 1900 Census, Baltimore, Maryland, Ward 23l; Family History Library Microfilm Service, Roll 618, Page 11A, Enumeration District 0298, FHL microfilm 1240618.

64. "Baltimore Black Sox to Be Real Baseball Team," 9; "Special Notice," *Baltimore Afro-American*, June 16, 1922, 3.

65. "Colored Baseball Fans," 9.

66. "Baseball Prices," *Baltimore Afro-American*, June 16, 1922, 5.

67. "Philadelphia Association," *Harrisburg Evening News*, April 5, 1922, 15.

68. "Baseball Association," *Harrisburg Evening News*, March 27, 1922, 13.

69. "Baltimore Black Sox to Be Real Baseball Team," 9.

70. "Richmond Giants to Play Black Sox Today," *Baltimore American*, May 21, 1922, 2.

71. "Play Hilldale Two Games," *Baltimore American*, September 24, 1922, 4; "Black Sox Defeat Hilldale," *Baltimore American*, September 25, 1922, 10.

72. "Baltimore Black Sox to Be Real Baseball Team," 9.

73. "Black Sox Started Season Sunday," *Baltimore Afro-American*, May 5, 1922, 9.

74. "Baltimore Black Sox Play Here Thursday and Friday," *Wilmington Morning News*, July 18, 1922.

75. "Hairstone Leading Black Sox Hitter," *Baltimore Afro-American*, April 14, 1922, 9.

76. "Black Sox Take Both," *Baltimore Afro-American*, April 28, 1922, 9.

77. "Philadelphia Giants Win," *Philadelphia Inquirer*, May 27, 1910, 10; "Lincoln Stars Win," *New York Age*, May 7, 1914, 6; "Steel Company Team Easily Defeats Colored Club," *Allentown Democrat*, August 13, 1917, 3; "'Smokey Joe' Williams to Be Here With Lincolns," *Bridgewater Courier*, August 26, 1921, 18.

78. "The Sporting Mirror," 9.

79. "Three Black Sox Players Quit Team," *Baltimore Afro-American*, May 5, 1922, 9.

80. "Ford Jumps Black Sox," *Baltimore Afro-American*, May 19, 1922, 9.

81. "The Sporting Mirror," 9; "Baltimore Black Sox Play Here Thursday and Friday," *Wilmington Morning News*, July 18, 1922, 7.

82. "The Sporting Mirror," 9.

83. "Ford s Jumps Black Sox," 9.

84. "Brown and Smith Dropped by Sox Club," *Baltimore Afro-American*, June 30, 1922, 9.

85. "Pitches No Hit Game," *Baltimore Afro-American*, August 25, 1922, 12.

86. "Sox Drop Ford," *Baltimore Afro-American*, August 18, 1922, 12.

87. "Bill Gibson, "Hear Me Talkin' to Ya," *Baltimore Afro-American*, August 5, 1933, 21.

88. "Black Sox Grab Two, *Baltimore Afro-American*, September 12, 1922, 10.

89. "Black Sox Had Great Season," *Baltimore Afro-American*, December 8, 1922, 7.

90. "Big Leaguers Shut Out by Black Sox," *Baltimore American*, October 16, 1922, 10.

91. "Black Sox Conquer," *Baltimore Sun*, November 1, 1922, 16.

92. "Black Sox Defeat Chester by One Run," *Philadelphia Inquirer*, September 10, 1922, 20.

93. "Sykes Loses Hurling Duel," *Baltimore Afro-American*, August 13, 1922, 11.

94. "Black Sox Had Great Season," 7; "Submarine Lee Trims Bacharach Giants Twice," *Baltimore Afro-American*, October 27, 1922, 11.

95. "Black Sox Win and Lose in Tilts with Richmond Giants," *Baltimore American*, October 9, 1922, 11.

96. "Five Homeruns Feature Sox Games," *Baltimore Afro-American*, June 23, 1922, 9.

97. "The Black Sox Batting Averages," *Baltimore Afro-American*, July 21, 1922, 9.

98. "Five Homeruns Feature Sox Games," 9; "Black Sox to Play for Championship," *Baltimore Afro-American*, October 8, 1922, S18; "Black Sox Win over Hilldale," *Baltimore Afro-American*, July 21, 1922, 6; "Knight Gives One Hit to Stenton Lads," *Philadelphia Inquirer*, August 19, 1922, 9.

99. "Black Sox Pitching," *Baltimore Afro-American*, August 11, 1922, 9.

100. "Looking Back 22 Years," *Negro Baseball*, 1944, 9.

101. Timothy Gay, *Satch, Dizzy and Rapid Robert* (New York: Simon and Schuster, 2010), 90.

102. U.S. Selective Service System, Draft Cards (Fourth Registration) for the District of Columbia, Records of the Selective Service System, 1926–1975, Record Group Number 147, Box 075, National Archives at St. Louis; St. Louis, Missouri; U.S. Selective Service System, World War I Draft Registration Cards, 1917–1918, Ancestry.com.; U.S. Census Bureau, 1910 Census, Lee, Fauquier, Virginia; Family History Microfilm Service, Roll T624_1628, Page 16A, Enumeration District 0045, FHL microfilm 1375641.

103. "Ben Taylor Says Black Sox Broke Two Records," *Baltimore Afro-American*, January 10, 1925, 7; "Out again, In again," *Baltimore Afro-American*, June 6, 1929, 5; "Looking Back 22 Years," 9.

104. U.S. Census Bureau, 1910 Census, Lee, Fauquier, Virginia.

105. Presentation Made by the Railway Employees' Department of the American Federation of Labor Before the United States Railroad Labor Board, Chicago, Illinois, 1921: In Reply to the Objections of the Railroads as Presented by the Conference Committee of Managers of the Association of Railway Executives; National Agreement, Federated Craft Shops, Part 1: 550

106. "Wanted Positions-Male," *Miami News*, December 25, 1927, 18.

107. Joseph Gerard, "Jud Wilson," Society for American Baseball Research, https://sabr.org/bioproj/person/e8da6967; Steven Clay, "U.S. Army Order of Battle 1919–1941, *Volume 4, The Services: Quartermaster, Medical, Military Police, Signal Corps, Chemical Warfare, and Miscellaneous Organizations, 1919–1941* (Fort Leavenworth, KS: Combat Studies Institute Press, 2010), 1919. https://archive.org/stream/USArmyOrderofBattle1919-1941Volume4/USArmyOrderofBattle1919-1941Volume4_djvu.txt.

108. "Black Sox Trim LeDroit Tigers," *Baltimore Afro-American*, September 8, 1922, 8.

109. "Black Sox Had Great Season," 7.

110. "Big Leaguers Play at Westport Today," *Baltimore American*, October 15, 1922, 3.
111. "Sykes Blanks All-Star Nine," *Baltimore Afro-American*, October 20, 1922, 11.
112. Sherry Olson, *Baltimore: The Building of an American City* (Baltimore: Johns Hopkins University Press, 1997), 326.
113. *Ibid.*
114. *Ibid.*
115. Olson, 326–27.
116. Olson, 326.
117. "Swimming Pool for Negroes Opens with Song and Prayer," *Baltimore Sun*, June 12, 1921, 18.
118. "Black Sox Divide with Bacharachs," *Baltimore Afro-American*, May 19, 1922, 9.
119. "Harrisburg Giants Lose Close Tilt to Black Sox," *Harrisburg Telegraph*, July 31, 1922, 15.
120. "Hilldale and Sox Divide," *Baltimore Afro-American*, July 28, 1922, 9; "Sykes and Cockrell in Pitching Duel," *Baltimore Afro-American*, September 29, 1922, 9.
121. "Black Sox Had Great Season," 7.
122. "1922 MLB Attendance & Team Age," Baseball Reference, https://www.baseball-reference.com/leagues/MLB/1922-misc.shtml.
123. "The Sporting Mirror," 9.

Chapter 6

1. "Spedden, C. P.," Baltimore and Ohio Railroad. 381331. 1942/1922.
2. U.S. Census Bureau, 1920 Census, Baltimore, Maryland, Ward 18; Family History Microfilm Service, Roll T625_665, Page 10A, Enumeration District 306.
3. "Eastern Baseball Clubs Organize," *Baltimore Afro-American*, December 22, 1923, 14.
4. "Sox Sign Catcher and New Pitcher," *Baltimore Afro-American*, February 9, 1923, 11.
5. *Ibid.*
6. "Baseball League War Goes On," *Baltimore Afro-American*, February 22, 1924, 14.

7. *Ibid.*
8. "Winters Sets Black Sox Down with Lone Single as Mates Bombard Sykes," *Pittsburgh Courier*, June 2, 1923, 6.
9. "Year's Review of Sports," *Baltimore Afro-American*, January 4, 1924, A14; "5 Homers Feature in Sunday's Twin Bill," *Baltimore Afro-American*, May 18, 1923, 15; F. William Stahl, "Black Sox Split Bill with Giants," *Baltimore Sun*, May 7, 1923, 12.
10. "Rojo's Triple Wins for Sox," *Baltimore Sun*, May 8, 1923, 12.
11. "5 Homers Feature in Sunday's Twin Bill," 15.
12. "Black Sox Beat Brooklyn Giants," *Baltimore Sun*, May 15, 1923, 12.
13. "Black Sox Batting Average," *Baltimore Afro-American* May 25, 1923, 14.
14. "Black Sox, 5, Royal Giants, 2," *Baltimore Afro-American*, May 18, 1923, 15.
15. "Black Sox Bow Low," *Baltimore Sun*, May 14, 1923, 20.
16. Stahl, "Black Sox Split Bill," 12.
17. "5 Homers Feature in Sunday's Twin Bill," 15.
18. "Cockrell and Mahoney Each Have Bad Inning," *Baltimore Afro-American*, June 1, 1923, 14.
19. "Black Sox Beaten by Hilldale Club," *Baltimore Sun*, May 29, 1923, 14.
20. "Sports Mirror," *Baltimore Afro-American*, June 1, 1923, 15.
21. "Black Sox Lose Final to Hilldale," *Baltimore Afro-American*, June 1, 1923, 14.
22. "Sports Mirror," June 1, 1923, 15.
23. "Final Standings," *Baltimore Afro-American*, October 5, 1923, 14.
24. "Cuban Stars Twice Humble Black Sox," *Baltimore Sun*, July 23, 1923, 10.
25. "Bacharach Giants Shove Sox Further Down in Eastern League Pennant Race," *Baltimore Afro-American* July 20, 1923, 14.
26. "Hilldale Again Is Baltimore's Master," *Philadelphia Inquirer*, June 22, 1923, 21.
27. "Black Sox Still Moving Towards Cellar Position," *Baltimore Afro-American*, July 27, 1923, 14.
28. "Black Sox Lose to Cuban Giants," *Baltimore Sun*, June 5, 1923, 12.
29. "Lincoln Giants Beat Black Sox," *Baltimore Sun*, July 3, 1923, 13.

30. "Professor Fudge Says," *Baltimore Afro-American*, July 27, 1923, 9.

31. "Baseball Sidelights," *Baltimore Afro-American*, June 8, 1923, 14.

32. "Sports," *Baltimore Afro-American*, August 17, 1923, 1.

33. "To My Patients and Friends," *Baltimore Afro-American*, September 7, 1923, 2.

34. "Mackey Leads League in Batting," *Baltimore Afro-American*, November 9, 1923, 15.

35. "Spedden Will 'Junk' Present Black Sox Club," *Baltimore Afro-American*, November 2, 1923, 15.

36. "Many Changes among Managers of Teams in Eastern League," *New York Age*, February 23, 1924, 6.

37. "D.C. and Harrisburg in Eastern League," *Baltimore Afro-American*, December 14, 1923, A15.

38. "Black Sox Get New Players," *Baltimore Afro-American*, November 11, 1924, 14.

39. "Sox to Show a New Line Up," *Baltimore Afro-American*, May 2, 1924, 14.

40. "Practice Starts at Black Sox Park," *Baltimore Afro-American*, April 11, 1924, 14.

41. "Lefthander Signed," *Baltimore Afro-American*, March 28, 1924, 14.

42. "Black Sox Players," *Baltimore Afro-American*, March 14, 1924, 14; "Black Sox Players," *Baltimore Afro-American*, February 29, 1924, 14.

43. "Sox Will Start to Work on April 1st," *Baltimore Afro-American*, March 7, 1924, 14.

44. "Black Sox Players," *Baltimore Afro-American*, February 1, 1924, A14.

45. "Black Sox Get New Players," 14.

46. "Black Sox Players," *Baltimore Afro-American*, February 22, 1924, 14.

47. "Sports Mirror," *Baltimore Afro-American*, October 3, 1925, 2.

48. "Sox to Show a New Line Up," *Baltimore Afro-American*, May 2, 1924, 14; "Black Sox get new players," January 11, 1924, 14.

49. "The Weather," *Baltimore Sun*, April 27, 1924, CA1.

50. "Sox Lose Series to Bacharachs," *Baltimore Afro-American*, May 2, 1924, 14.

51. Ibid; "Black Sox Bow in First Tilt," *Baltimore Sun*, April 27, 1924, S3.

52. "Sox Lose Series to Bacharachs," 14; "Black Sox Drop Pair to Bacharach Giants," *Baltimore Sun*, April 28, 1924, 10.

53. "Black Sox Win Opener; Lose Second on Forfeit," *Baltimore Sun*, May 26, 1924, 11.

54. "Cops Save Ump from Fans," *Baltimore Afro-American*, May 30, 194, A15.

55. "Sox Had Chances to Beat Hilldale," *Baltimore Afro-American*, June 27, 1924, 15.

56. "Beckwith Now Sox Captain," *Baltimore Afro-American*, August 8, 1924, 14.

57. "Beckwith Goes to Baltimore," *Pittsburgh Courier*, June 28, 1924, 6.

58. "Beckwith Released," *Pittsburgh Courier*, June 21, 1924, 6.

59. "Beckwith Goes to Baltimore," 6.

60. "Beckwith Fills Up a Bad Hole," *Baltimore Afro-American*, July 4, 1924, 15.

61. "Bobo Leonard Leads Eastern League Sluggers," *Baltimore Afro-American*, August 8, 1924, A18.

62. "Cuban Stars Bow to Black Sox," *Baltimore Sun*, June 30, 1924, 11; "Black Sox Garner Two More Games," *Baltimore Sun*, July 7, 1924, 8.

63. "Black Sox Second," *Baltimore Afro-American*, August 8, 1924, A18.

64. "Bobo Leonard Leads Eastern League Sluggers," A18.

65. "1,000 Fans Follow Bier of Player," *Baltimore Afro-American*, August 15, 1924, A6.

66. "Ben Taylor Says Black Sox Broke Two Records," 7.

67. "Black Sox Have Fighting Chance to Win the 1924 Pennant," *Baltimore Afro-American*, August 29, 1924, 14.

68. "Baseball Ends September 30," *Baltimore Afro-American*, September 19, 1924, A10.

69. "Ben Taylor Says Black Sox Broke Two Records," 7.

70. In the famous panoramic photo of opening game of the 1924 Series, Spedden stands in the center among the leagues's leadership. In 1926, the joint session of the Negro National League and the Eastern Colored League elected Spedden secretary. ("National Negro Baseball League Meets in Philadelphia," *Kansas City Advo-*

cate, January 15, 1926, 5; Lee Sartain, *Borders of Equality: The NAACP and the Baltimore Civil Rights Struggle, 1914–1970* (Jackson: University Press of Mississippi, 2013) 18.

71. "10,000 See World Series," *Baltimore Afro-American* October 10, 1924, 5.

72. *Ibid.*

73. "Eastern League Clubs Preparing for 1925 Pennant," *Baltimore Afro-American*, February 28, 1925, 8.

74. "Sox Defeat Hamden and Giants Sunday," *Baltimore Afro-American*, April 11, 1925, A7.

75. "Pete Hill, Business Manager," *Baltimore Afro-American*, December 20, 1924, 3.

76. "Sox Defeat Hamden," *Baltimore Afro-American*, April 11, 1925, 7.

77. "The Four Horsemen of the Black Sox," *Baltimore Afro-American*, July 25, 1925, 6.

78. "Black Sox Share Double-Header with Cuban Stars," *Afro-American*, May 9, 1925, 26.

79. "300 Hitters," *Baltimore Afro-American*, June 20, 1925, 6.

80. "Ten Leading Base Stealers," *Afro-American* June 20, 1925, 7.

81. G. L. Mackay, "Sports Mirror," *Baltimore Afro-American*, June 20, 1925, 7; "Sox Are Third," *Afro-American*, July 4, 1925, 7.

82. *Ibid.*

83. "Sox Down Hilldale Club Twice on Sunday," *Baltimore Afro-American*, June 27, 1925, 7.

84. "Sox Grab Twin Bill from Royal Giants," *Baltimore Afro-American*, September 5, 1925, A7.

85. "Sox Get Two Sunday from Wilmington," *Baltimore Afro-American*, July 4, 1925, 7.

86. "Two Black Sox Players Battle with Umpire," *Baltimore Sun*, July 30, 1925, 15.

87. "Beckwith Suspended for Beating Umpire Sewell Last Tuesday," *Baltimore Afro-American*, August 1, 1925, A8.

88. G. L. Mackay, "Sports Mirror," *Baltimore Afro-American*, August 8, 1925, 7.

89. "Beckwith Suspended for Beating Umpire Sewell Last Tuesday," A8.

90. "Sox and Giants to Lock Horns Sunday," *Baltimore Afro-American*, August 8, 1925, 7.

91. "Eastern League," *Baltimore Afro-American*, August 29, 1925, A7.

92. "Sox Drop Double-Header to Harrisburg Giants," *Afro-American*, August 15, 1925, 7.

93. "Cubans Put Indian Sign on Hitters," *Baltimore Afro-American*, August 22, 1925, 7.

94. "Lloyd and Company to Battle Black Sox Twice on Sunday," *Baltimore Afro-American* August 22, 1925, 6.

95. "Eastern League Standings," *Pittsburgh Courier*, September 19, 1925, 12.

96. "Charleston and Beckwith Lead in Batting and Homeruns," *Baltimore Afro-American*, October 15, 1925, 7.

97. "Rojo Is Voted Most-Valuable Player on the Black Sox Team," *Baltimore Afro-American*, October 17, 1925, 7.

98. "Ben Taylor Son of a Methodist Minister in Game for 20 Years," *Baltimore Afro-American*, July 23, 1927, A15.

99. "10,000 See Cubans and Sox Divide Two," *Baltimore Afro-American*, May 8, 1926, 9.

100. "Sports Mirror," *Baltimore Afro-American*, May 15, 1926, 8.

101. "Sox Club Average Is Far Below Par," *Baltimore Afro-American*, May 8, 1926, 12.

102. "Eastern League," *Baltimore Afro-American*, May 8, 1926, 9.

103. "Black Sox Realize Pet Ambition Sunday," *Baltimore Afro-American*, May 15, 1926, 8.

104. "Sports Mirror," *Baltimore Afro-American*, May 22, 1926, 7.

105. "Sox Will Encounter a Team of Hard Hitters in Cuban Stars," *Baltimore Afro-American*, June 12, 1926, 7.

106. "Eastern League," *Baltimore Afro-American*, June 12, 1926, 7.

107. "Black Sox Drop Doubleheader to Cuban Stars," *Baltimore Afro-American*, June 12, 1926, 7.

108. "Hilldale Hands Baltimore Black Sox 17 to 5 Lashing," *Pittsburgh Courier*, July 10, 1926, 15.

109. "Wildness of Sox Pitchers Helps Hilldale Win, 17–5," *Baltimore Afro-American*, July 10, 1926, 9.

110. "Sports Mirror," *Baltimore Afro-American*, July 10, 1926, 8.

111. "Sox Scout Country for Pennant Winning Material," *Baltimore Afro-American*, June 26, 1926, 7.

112. "John Beckwith Is Traded to Harrisburg," *Baltimore Afro-American*, July 10, 1926, 8; "Giants trade three for one," *Mt. Carmel Daily News*, July 8, 1926, 6.

113. "John Beckwith Is Traded to Harrisburg," 8.

114. "Cooper Leaves Sox," *Baltimore Afro-American*, July 17, 1926, 10.

115. "Eastern Colored League," *New York Age*, July 10, 1926, 6.

116. "Harrisburg Wins," *New York Age*, September 25, 1926, 6.

117. "Black Sox Lose Three Games to Lincoln Giants," *Baltimore Afro-American*, July 17, 1926, 8.

118. "Black Sox Bow Twice to Hilldale Nine," *Baltimore Sun*, August 2, 1926, 11; "Baseball," *Baltimore Afro-American*, August 7, 1926, 7.

119. "Sox Argue, Ump Forfeits Game," *Baltimore Afro-American*, August 14, 1926, 9.

120. "Dallard and Strong Dropped from Sox," *Baltimore Afro-American*, August 14, 1926, 8.

121. "Cuban Stars to Play Black Sox Today," *Baltimore Sun*, August 22, 1926, 17; "He'll Be Watching," *Baltimore Afro-American*, April 23, 1927, 14.

122. "World Series," *Baltimore Afro-American*, October 9, 1926, 12. William E. Clark of *The New York Age* estimated the crowd at about 11,000. ("Hilldale Has Advantage," 6.)

123. "Rube Foster to Remain," *Baltimore Afro-American*, January 3, 1925, 5.

124. "Cubans, League Leaders, Here for Seven Games," *Baltimore Afro-American*, August 21, 1926, 11.

125. "Colored Baseball Players Receive Handsome Salaries," *Baltimore Sun*, August 30, 1923, 15.

126. "Ponteu K.O.'s Harry Wills," *Baltimore Afro-American*, March 26, 1927, 15; "Spot Lights," *Baltimore Afro-American*, July 18, 1924, A5; "Sox Practice Held Up by Loss of the Pitcher's Box Key," *Baltimore Afro-American*, April 23, 1927, 14.

127. "Sues Owner of Black Sox Team," *Baltimore Afro-American*, January 16, 1926, 9.

128. "Cubans, League Leaders, Here for Seven Games," 11.

129. "Sues Owner of Black Sox Team," 9.

130. Robert Wilson, "Sports Shots," *Pittsburgh Courier*, February 26, 1927, SM5.

131. "Spedden No Longer Black Sox Boss," *Baltimore Afro-American*, February 12, 1927, 14.

132. "Vote," *Baltimore Afro-American* September 2, 1921, 7.

133. "Wonderland Park," *Baltimore Afro-American*, August 31, 1923, 8.

134. "Black Sox Café," *Baltimore Afro-American*, December 7, 1923, 15.

135. "Special Baseball," *Baltimore Sun*, August 21, 1926, 20.

136. "Colored Baseball Players," 15; "Sports Mirror," *Baltimore Afro-American*, October 3, 1925, O2.

137. "Black Sox Are State Champs," *Baltimore Afro-American*, October 26, 1923, 15; "Sports Mirror," *Baltimore Afro-American*, April 18, 1925, A7.

138. "Oriole Park Insults Patrons with Jim Crow," *Baltimore Afro-American*, April 22, 1933, 17.

139. "Sports Mirror," *Baltimore Afro-American*, October 3, 1925, O2.

140. "Baseball Notes," *Baltimore Afro-American*, 15.

141. Jan Voogd, *Race Riots and Resistance: The Red Summer of 1919* (New York: Peter Lang, 2007), 41–43; Pietila, "History of Baltimore's Racial Segregation."

142. Census figures from 1910 indicate that of the 750 or so residents of Ward 21, district 350, the area immediately surrounding Maryland Baseball Park, none were black. Therefore, on days when the park drew more than 2,000 fans, as it did on most days, blacks would far outnumber whites in that neighborhood.

143. Stephen Grant Meyer, *As Long as They Don't Move Next Door* (Lanham, MD: Rowman & Littlefield, 1999), 18.

144. "Black Sox Get New Players," January 11, 1924, A14.

145. Lester, *Rube Foster in His Time*, 142–43.

146. "Best in the League," *Baltimore Afro-American*, September 11, 1926, 9.

147. The earliest extant box score listing his name appears in 1920 ("Sporting News: Black Sox take two from LeDroit Tigers," *Baltimore Afro-American*, August 20, 1920, 7. However, a 1922 report suggests he served as the Black Sox' umpire since Spedden assumed control in 1917 ("Linden Win Five," *Baltimore Afro-American*, September 8, 1922, 8).

148. "Black Sox Want Cromwell here," *Baltimore Afro-American*, March 30, 1923, 14. Charles Cromwell had ties to the community. He was a champion bowler, and the *Afro American* had asked him to write a regular column on the game. Also, Spedden had hired another "race man" to umpire, luring Henry "Spike" Spencer north from Washington, DC. If Cromwell stayed in Baltimore, he too would be part of an elite umpiring crew. Such a pairing would place him and Baltimore at the top of the profession. Further, he wouldn't have to uproot his family, and it could not have escaped his attention that he would then become a role model for and leading member of Baltimore's African American community. He chose to stay with the Black Sox. There must have been times over the next few years that he regretted his decision. In 1925, the ECL took the job of hiring umpires away from the teams, putting Cromwell out of work for that season. A white sportswriter from Philadelphia made the assignments and did not favor "colored" umpires. The league suspended that practice the following year and Spedden brought Cromwell back in 1926. However, after Spedden was forced to resign from the Black Sox in 1927, George Rossiter, who had been Spedden's partner, took control of the team's business operations. Rossiter chose not to employ African Americans as umpires, firing both Spencer and Cromwell shortly after Spedden left the team. Rossiter "insist[ed] on the use of white umpires" until "Negro umpires ... prove competent." He would eventually hire Cromwell back, but conditions had changed. The ballpark, which had been an impressive facility, was allowed to deteriorate, even as the Black Sox became one of the best teams in the nation, winning the 1929 championship. The Depression further exposed the club's weakened financial position, and the Black Sox would cease to exist as a franchise in the early 1930s. By that time, Cromwell had moved on. In 1932, he would be named lead umpire in the Southern Colored Athletic Association. Later that decade, he would return to the majors, umpiring games for the Baltimore Elite Giants. His name appears in box scores and, occasionally, surfaces because of a controversial call. However, those times are rare, which bodes well for an umpire. He did not infuse his personality into the game, preferring instead a quiet yet rigorous professionalism. In 1941, his doctors strongly advised that he take a break from the game, but he returned a year later. His name last appears in a box score in 1947. His career spanned four decades and at least 31 years. He was reported to be "one of the 'finest' umpires in the East." He also gave back to the community, enlisting in the army during the First World War. He also rushed into a burning building to save a woman's life. If he had taken Foster up on his offer, Charles Cromwell would have likely served with distinction, ranking with Billy Donaldson and Bert Gholston as the best umpires in the NNL. Instead, he chose to stay in Baltimore. As a consequence, his career was twice interrupted because of racism. He persisted, carving a place for himself in the community and in local baseball. His years of service, his distinctions, and his work in the community rival those major-league umpires in the Hall of Fame. Moreover, he worked in a time where a "colored umpire" was often the punchline of a joke. In this context, it is remarkable we know as much as we do about Cromwell. For many of the "race men" hired by Rube Foster or who labored in black baseball we will never know their names. For others, there are a few pictures or the name or partial name in a box score or a rare news story. It's worth remembering those we know: Leon Augustine, Lucian Spaer, Caesar Jamison, William Embry, Frank Forbes, Judy Gans, Cooper, Greenwald, Ben Taylor, Peirce, Brown, Craig, and Moe Harris. In 1932, Bert Ghoston wrote a column calling them "The Forgotten Men." Indeed, they were and are. Like the Black Sox, African

American umpires, particularly those in the first decades of the twentieth century, deserve a book devoted to their struggles and triumphs.

149. "Spedden No Longer Black Sox Boss," 14.

150. Robert Wilson, "Sports Shots," *Pittsburgh Courier*, February 26, 1927, SM5.

151. "Both Colored Baseball Leagues May Have Smashup at Detroit Meeting," *New York Age*, December 25, 1926, 6.

Chapter 7

1. Bill Gibson, "Talking It Over," *Baltimore Afro-American*, March 31, 1928, 13.

2. *Ibid.*

3. "Rossiter Won't Sell Black Sox Local Men Say," *Baltimore Afro-American*, March 9, 1929, 11. At some point, Rossiter did sell a minority stake in the team to one of these investors, Dr. Joseph H. Thomas. ("New Baseball Loop Completes Set Up," *Baltimore Afro-American*, May 6, 1939, 23.)

4. "Can't Secure Good Umpires," *Baltimore Afro-American*, Aug 10, 1929, 15.

5. "Ball Park Jim Crow Denied by Rossiter," *Baltimore Afro-American*, May 17, 1930, 14.

6. Gibson, "Talking It Over," 13.

7. Bill Gibson, "The Passing Review," *Baltimore Afro-American*, June 9, 1928, 12.

8. Gibson, "Talking It Over," 13; "Rossiter Won't Sell Black Sox Local Men Say," 11.

9. Bill Gibson, "The Passing Review," *Baltimore Afro-American*, May 4, 1929, 15.

10. Bill Gibson, "Hear Me Talkin' to Ya," *Baltimore Afro-American*, January 18, 1930, 14.

11. "Special Notice," *Baltimore Afro-American*, August 18, 1928, 10.

12. "Night Baseball Contest Booked at Maryland Park," *Baltimore Sun*, June 23, 1930, 11.

13. "To Light Oriole Park," *Baltimore Sun*, August 23, 1930, 10.

14. "Fans at Night Game Get Their Money Back," *Baltimore Sun*, June 24, 1930, 8.

15. "Sports Mirror," *Baltimore Afro-American*, March 12, 1927, 14.

16. "Thomas R. Smith to Throw Out the First Ball," *Afro-American*, April 30, 1927, 14.

17. "Sports Mirror," March 12, 1927, 14.

18. "Homerun Nick Tries Out for Sox," *Baltimore Afro-American*, April 2, 1927. 15.

19. "Fan-Sees," *Baltimore Afro-American*, July 7, 1928, 12.

20. "Yokely and Strong Sox Dependables," *Baltimore Afro-American*, February 12, 1927, 15.

21. "Yokely's Fresh Delivery Made Him 1927 Sensation," *Baltimore Afro-American*, December 17, 1927, 12.

22. "Yokely and Strong Sox Dependables," 15; "Yokely's Fresh Delivery Made Him 1927 Sensation," 12.

23. "Rojo Traded By Sox to the Lincoln Giants," *Baltimore Afro-American*, February 12, 1927, 15.

24. "Tasco and Joe Gans Draw," *Baltimore Afro-American*, April 16, 1927, 15.

25. "In Baseball," *Baltimore Afro-American*, May 7, 1927, 14.

26. "Giants Divide with Black Sox," *Baltimore Sun*, May 2, 1927, 12.

27. "Baltimore Black Sox Smother Cuban Stars in Battle at Norfolk," *Baltimore Sun*, May 13, 1927, 15.

28. "Eastern League Standings," *Baltimore Afro-American*, June 25, 1927, 14.

29. "Leading Pitchers," *Baltimore Afro-American*, June 25, 1927, 14.

30. "Leading Hitters," *Baltimore Afro-American*, June 25, 1927, 14.

31. "Play Ball, Stop Arguing, the Fans Will Come Out," *Baltimore Afro-American*, June 18, 1927, 14.

32. "Ryan Shut Out Sox as They Win and Lose," *Baltimore Afro-American*, July 23, 1927, A15.

33. "Baseball and the Big Time," *Baltimore Afro-American*, July 30, 1927, 14.

34. "Eastern League," *Baltimore Afro-American*, August 13, 1927, 14.

35. "Sox $9,800 Motor Coach Wrecked," *Baltimore Afro-American*, August 13, 1927, 14.

36. "Sox Players Cut by Flying Glass," *Baltimore Afro-American*, August 13, 1927, 14.

37. "Injured Sox Are Slipping Badly," *Baltimore Afro-American*, August 20,

1927, 15; "Black Sox Get New Outfielder," *Baltimore Afro-American*, August 27, 1927, 15.

38. "Injured Sox are Slipping Badly," 15.

39. "Bees and Black Sox Split Sunday bill," *Baltimore Afro-American*, September 10, 1927, 15.

40. "Black Sox Blank Cubans," *Baltimore Sun*, September 12, 1927, 10.

41. "Baltimore Hickest of Hick Towns," *Baltimore Afro-American*, September 17, 1927, 8.

42. "Black Sox Plan Boosters Day August 28," *Baltimore Afro-American*, August 20, 1927, 15.

43. "Black Sox in Double Win," *Pittsburgh Courier*, May 5, 1928, A6.

44. "Cubans Give Rossiter Clan Stiff Opposition before Losing," *Philadelphia Tribune*, May 3, 1928, 11.

45. "Black Sox in Double Win," A6.

46. "Cubans Give Rossiter Clan Stiff Opposition before Losing," 11.

47. W. Rollo Wilson, "Sports Shorts," *Pittsburgh Courier*, June 23, 1928.

48. "Col. Struthers Defunct Harrisburg Giants Was a Top Notch Ball Club," *Philadelphia Tribune*, July 26, 1928, 11.

49. Robert Ball, "Those Black Sox," *Philadelphia Tribune*, July 25, 1928, 10.

50. "Bacharach Giants Added to Black Sox Victims," *Baltimore Sun*, May 7, 1928, 13.

51. "Sox Open Season with Victory," *Baltimore Afro-American*, April 13, 1929, 18. The photo accompanying the article shows the Black Sox in spring training in 1928. The team would have new uniforms for the 1929 season. Those uniforms sport the familiar team colors of black and orange.

52. "Black Sox Sported New Uniforms," *Baltimore Afro-American*, May 26, 1928, 12.

53. "Fan-Sees," *Baltimore Afro-American*, June 9, 1929, 13.

54. "Black Sox Open League with Double Victory," *Baltimore Sun*, April 30, 1928, 12.

55. "Eastern League Goes on Rocks," *Baltimore Afro-American*, April 21, 1928, 1; W. Rollo Wilson, "Eastern League Will Continue," *Chicago Defender*, April 28, 1928, 9.

56. "Pompez-Keenan Latest Moguls to Quit League," *Baltimore Afro-American*, June 6, 1928, 12.

57. *Ibid.*

58. Bill Gibson, "The Passing Review," *Baltimore Afro-American*, July 21, 1928, 12.

59. Bill Gibson, "The Passing Review" *Baltimore Afro-American*, June 23, 1928, 12.

60. "Three Black Sox Players Hitting .400 or Better," *Baltimore Afro-American* August 25, 1928, 13.

61. Bill Gibson, "The Passing Review," *Baltimore Afro-American*, September 15, 1928, 13; "Homestead Grays Here Sunday," *Baltimore Afro-American*, September 15, 1928, 13.

62. "Black Sox and Grays Divide Double Bill," *Baltimore Afro-American*, September 22, 1928, 13; "Black Sox to Flash Young Mound Stars," *Pittsburgh Courier*, September 18, 1928, 17.

63. "Black Sox Share Honors with Homestead Grays," *Baltimore Sun*, September 17, 1928, 12.

64. "Sox Drop Three to Homestead Grays," *Baltimore Afro-American*, September 29, 1928, 13.

65. Bill Gibson, "The Passing Review," *Baltimore Afro-American*, January 12, 1929, 9.

66. "Six Eastern Clubs Form New Baseball League," *Baltimore Afro-American*, January 29, 1929, 1.

67. *Ibid.*

68. "Sox and Hilldale Complete Trade," *Baltimore Afro-American*, February 2, 1929, 10.

69. "Rossiter Won't Sell Black Sox," 11.

70. Bill Gibson, "The Passing Review," *Baltimore Afro-American*, April 13, 1929, 19.

71. "They Stop 'Em, and How," *Baltimore Afro-American*, June 1, 1929, 20.

72. Gibson, "The Passing Review," April 13, 1929, 19.

73. "Meet Sir Richard," *Baltimore Afro-American*, May 18, 1929, 1.

74. John Holway, "Baltimore's Great Black Ball Team," *Baltimore Sun*, August 28, 1977, 117.

75. "Black Sox Boss," *Baltimore Afro-American*, May 11, 1929, 1.

76. "Black Sox Million Dollar Infield," *Afro-American*, April 13, 1929, 18; Holway, "Baltimore's Great Black Ball Team," 117.

77. Bill Gibson, "The Passing Review," *Baltimore Afro-American*, April 20, 1929, 17.

78. "Eastern Ball Clubs Await Opening Day," *Baltimore Afro-American*, April 13, 1929, 22.

79. Bill Gibson, "The Passing Review," *Baltimore Afro-American*, March 23, 1929, 12.

80. "Sox Swamp Cubans in Opener," *Baltimore Afro-American*, May 4, 1929, 14.

81. "Black Sox Take Two from Darby Daisies," *Baltimore Afro-American*, May 11, 1929, 14.

82. "Hubbard Stars Afield as Black Sox Win Pair," *Baltimore Sun*, May 13, 1929, 11.

83. "Black Sox Share Pair with Lincoln Giants," *Baltimore Sun*, May 27, 1929, 15.

84. "Wilson and Dixon," *Baltimore Afro-American*, June 15, 1929, 16.

85. "Wilson's Bat Death to Hilldale," *Baltimore Afro-American*, June 8, 1929, 16.

86. Bill Gibson, "The Passing Review," *Baltimore Afro-American*, June 29, 1929, 15.

87. "Wilson Benched as Sox Twice Stop Bees," *Afro-American*, June 22, 1929, 14.

88. Gibson, "The Passing Review," June 29, 1929, 15.

89. "Homestead Grays Bow Twice to Black Sox," *Baltimore Sun*, July 1, 1929, 10.

90. Bill Gibson, "The Passing Review," *Baltimore Afro-American*, July 6, 1929, 14.

91. "Black Sox Win Shutout Victory over Hilldale," *Baltimore Sun*, July 15, 1929, 11.

92. "Chicks Meet Pittsburgh," *Wilmington Evening Journal*, July 27, 1929, 14.

93. "Sox Take Series from Homestead," *Baltimore Afro-American*, July 27, 1929, 14.

94. *Ibid.*

95. "Dixon Makes Fourteen Straight Hits," *Baltimore Afro-American*, August 10, 1929, 15.

96. "Boy, What an Arm," *Baltimore Afro-American* June 29, 1929, 15.

97. Nathan, "The Baltimore Black Sox and the Perils of History," 52–87.

98. James Bready, *Baseball in Baltimore: The First 100 Years* (Baltimore: Johns Hopkins University Press, 1998): 164.

99. "Black Sox Gain Half of Spoils," *Baltimore Sun*, October 7, 1929, 14.

100. Bready, *Baseball in Baltimore*, 164.

101. W. Rollo Wilson, "New American League Completes Schedule," *Pittsburgh Courier*, September 28, 1929, A4.

102. "Charlie Smith Tops East in Hitting," *Baltimore Afro-American* September 28, 1929, 14.

103. Wilson, "New American League Completes Schedule," A4.

104. Paul Menton, "It's All in the Viewpoint," *Baltimore Evening Sun*, April 3, 1930, 33.

105. "Invader," *Pittsburgh Courier*, September 13, 1930, A5.

106. "Black Sox Player Jailed Following Fight in Cuba," *Baltimore Afro-American*, February 8, 1930, 14.

107. Bill Gibson, "Hear Me Talkin' to Ya," *Baltimore Afro-American*, March 1, 1930, 14.

108. "St Louis Stars Play Two Game Series Here," *St. Louis Post Dispatch*, April 18, 1930, 31.

109. "All Ready," *Baltimore Evening Sun*, April 3, 1930, 33.

110. "New Talent in Sox Line-Up for Opening Games Sunday," *Baltimore Evening, Sun* April 9, 1930, 28.

111. Bill Gibson, "Hear Me Talkin' to Ya," *Baltimore Afro-American*, May 3, 1930, 14.

112. Bill Gibson, "Hear Me Talkin' to Ya," *Baltimore Afro-American*, January 18, 1930, 14.

113. "Eastern Magnates Disband," *Baltimore Afro-American*, March 1, 1930, 14.

114. "Sox Victors over Cubans, to Play Hilldale on Sunday," *Baltimore Afro-American*, May 3, 1930, A14.

115. "Sox Celebrated Easter by Lambasting Bugle Outfit," *Baltimore Afro-American*, April 26, 1930, 15.

116. "Black Sox Share Two with Hilldale Club," *Baltimore Sun*, May 5, 1930, 13.

117. Bill Gibson, "Hear Me Talkin' to Ya," *Baltimore Afro-American*, June 7, 1930, 14.

118. Bill Gibson, "Hear Me Talkin' to Ya," *Baltimore Afro-American*, July 5, 1930, 14.

119. "Heeds Call of West," *Baltimore Afro-American*, July 19, 1930, 14.

120. "Local Nine, Revamped," *Baltimore Afro-American*, July 12, 1930, 14.

121. Bill Gibson, "Hear Me Talkin' to Ya," *Baltimore Afro-American*, July 12, 1930, 14.

122. "New Scoring Mark Set Up by Lincolns," *Philadelphia Tribune*, July 24, 1930, 11; "Birmingham beaten by Detroit Stars," *Baltimore Afro-American*, August 30, 1930, A5.

123. "Get Star Players," *Baltimore Afro-American*, September 6, 1930, A15.

124. "Black Sox Twice Trounce Hilldale in Twin Bill," *Baltimore Sun*, September 8, 1930, 13.

125. Ben Taylor, "Jud Wilson Is Best Player in the East," *Baltimore Afro-American*, February 21, 1931, 14. There is some mystery surrounding Ted Page and his place on the 1930 Black Sox. His name appears in box scores as "Paige," inviting speculation that Satchel Paige had rejoined the team and was playing in the outfield. However, the *Detroit Free Press* ran a story titled, "Satchel Paige will hurl for the Stars" (October 5, 1930, 19) on the same day "Paige" appeared in the Black Sox lineup. Further, Ben Taylor, in the February 1931 story (see above) spells Ted Page's name as "Paige" and places him in the Black Sox outfield; "Black Sox and All Stars Start Annual Series with Twin Bill Today," *Baltimore Sun*, September 28, 1930, S3.

126. Bill Gibson, "Hear Me Talkin' to Ya," *Baltimore Afro-American*, September 13, 1930, 14.

127. C. M. Gibbs, "The SUNdial," *Baltimore Sun*, October 28, 1930, 14.

128. "Sox Win First 5 to 3," *Baltimore Afro-American*, October 4, 1930, 1.

129. Jesse Linthicum, "Black Sox Take Two from All Star Nine," *Baltimore Sun*, October 6, 1930, 10.

130. "All Stars Get Half of Spoils," *Baltimore Sun*, October 20, 1930, 11.

131. "Builder," *Pittsburgh Courier*, April 18, 1931, 14.

132. "Wilson to Play Third for Grays," *Pittsburgh Courier*, March 7, 1931, 14.

133. "Jud Wilson Is the Best Player in the East," *Baltimore Afro-American*, February 21, 1931, 14.

134. "Klein Chocolate Team Has Open Date for Games," *Harrisburg Telegraph*, June 29, 1931, 14.

135. "Ben Taylor Tells How Trades Are Effected," *Baltimore Afro-American*, March 14, 1931, 14.

136. *Ibid.*

137. "Sox, Daisies to Clash Over Weekend," *Baltimore Afro-American*, May 2, 1931, 5.

138. "Batter Hit Homerun but Failed to Score," *Baltimore Afro-American*, March 21, 1931, 14.

139. "Mixed League Plans Fail at Parley," *Baltimore Afro-American*, March 28, 1931, 14.

140. "1931 MLB Standings," Baseball Reference, https://www.baseball-reference.com/leagues/MLB/1931-standings.shtml.

141. "Harlem Stars," *Baltimore Afro-American*, August 1, 1931, 12.

142. "Sox Meet Hilldale in DC Stadium," *Baltimore Afro-American*, May 16, 1931, 15.

143. Bill Gibson, "Hear Me Talkin' to Ya," *Baltimore Afro-American*, July 25, 1931, 12.

144. Bill Gibson, "Hear Me Talkin' to Ya," *Baltimore Afro-American*, August 22, 1931, 12.

145. "1931 Baltimore Black Sox," Negro Leagues Database, seamheads.com, http://www.seamheads.com/NegroLgs/team.php?yearID=1931&teamID=BBS&LGOrd=1.

146. "Coming," *Baltimore Afro-American*, August 29, 1931, 12.

Chapter 8

1. Matthew Crenson, *Baltimore: A Political History*. (Baltimore: Johns Hopkins University Press, 2016), 390.

2. *Ibid.*

3. "Baseball Moguls Meet in Capital," *Baltimore Afro-American*, August 22, 1931, 13; "New League Plans Daily Schedule," *Philadelphia Tribune*, February 4, 1932, 11.

4. "Baseball Heads Decide Upon Eight-Club League," *Baltimore Afro-American*, October 24, 1931, 14; "Negro Owners Convene in Cleveland to Formu-

late East-West Baseball Loop," *Philadelphia Tribune*, January 21, 1932, 10.

5. "New League Plans Daily Schedule," 11.

6. Lloyd Thompson, "No Trades in Sight at the Meeting of East-West League," *New York Amsterdam News*, March 2, 1932, 13.

7. "League Umps in Meeting," *New York Amsterdam News*, May 4, 1932, 13.

8. Bill Gibson, "Hear Me Talkin' to Ya," *Baltimore Afro-American*, May 14, 1932, 14.

9. Tom Deveaux, *The Washington Senators, 1901–1971* (Jefferson, NC: McFarland, 2005), 144.

10. Nick Wilson, *Early Latino Ballplayers in the United States* (Jefferson, NC: McFarland, 2005), 176; Deveaux, 144.

11. "Joe Sephus's Callings," *Cumberland Sunday Times*, March 6, 1932.

12. *Ibid.*

13. Bill Gibson, "Hear Me Talkin' to Ya," *Baltimore Afro-American*, June 4, 1932, 14.

14. Paul Menton, "It's All in the Viewpoint," *Baltimore Evening Sun*, April 1, 1932, 46.

15. "Fan-Sees," *Baltimore Afro-American*, May 14, 1932, 14.

16. "Washington Ball Club Getting Ready," *New York Amsterdam News*, April 6, 1932, 12.

17. "Lundy to Write About Baseball," *Baltimore Afro-American*, March 19, 1932, 15.

18. Richard Lundy, "Dick's Diamond Dope," *Baltimore Afro-American*, April 2, 1932, 14.

19. "Black Sox Face Problems of Bolstering Infield," *Baltimore Afro-American*, March 19, 1932.

20. Richard Lundy, "Dick's Diamond Dope," *Baltimore Afro-American*, March 26, 1932, 14.

21. Richard Lundy, "Dick's Diamond Dope," *Baltimore Afro-American*, April 9, 1932, 14.

22. Bill Gibson, "Hear Me Talkin' to Ya," *Baltimore Afro-American*, April 9, 1932, 14.

23. "Washington Pilots Shut Out Black Sox," *Baltimore Sun*, May 8, 1932, S6; "Black Sox Climb Peg in East-West

League," *Baltimore Sun*, May 16, 1932, 8; "Blankety-Blank," *Baltimore Afro-American*, May 14, 1932, 14.

24. "Black Sox Lead League," *Baltimore Sun*, May 18, 1932, 14.

25. "Rookie Moundsmen Place Sox in Temporary Lead," *Baltimore Afro-American*, May 28, 1932, 16.

26. "Fan-Sees," *Baltimore Afro-American*, May 28, 1932, 15.

27. "E-W League Features," *New York Amsterdam News*, June 8, 1932, 12.

28. "Baltimore Hurlers Top East-West Mound Results," *Atlanta Daily World*, June 5, 1932, 5.

29. "East-West Standings," *Pittsburgh Courier*, June 18, 1932, A4.

30. "Judy Johnson Bolts Hilldale for Crawfords," *Philadelphia Tribune*, June 23, 1932, 11.

31. "East-West League Introduces Drastic Changes," *Baltimore Afro-American*, June 11, 1932, 15.

32. "Second Half in East-West to See Many Drastic Changes," *New York Amsterdam News*, July 6, 1932, 9.

33. "EWEE League 'On Rocks' with Club Teams Deep in Debt," *Philadelphia Tribune*, June 30, 1932, 10.

34. Garland Mackey, "East-West League in Trouble," *Washington Tribune*, July 2, 1932, 13.

35. Bill Gibson, "Hear Me Talkin' to Ya," *Baltimore Afro-American*, June 25, 1932, 14.

36. Syd Pollock, "What's Wrong with Baseball," *Kansas City New Journal and Guide*, July 2, 1932, 13.

37. "EWEE League 'On Rocks' with Club Teams Deep in Debt," 10.

38. "Homestead Grays Given Pennant in East-West League," *Chicago Defender*, July 16, 1932, 9.

39. Gibson, "Hear Me," June 25, 1932, 14.

40. "Judy Johnson Bolts Hilldale for Crawfords," *Philadelphia Tribune*, June 23, 1932, 11.

41. "Fan-Sees," *Baltimore Afro-American*, July 2, 1932, 15.

42. "Baseball Player Frolic," *Philadelphia Tribune*, July 28, 1932, 10.

43. "Frank Warfield, Ball Player, Dies," *Chicago Defender*, July 30, 1932, 8.

44. "Sox Snare Three of Four," *Baltimore Afro-American*, July 30, 1932, 15; "Black Sox Defeat Homestead Grays," *Baltimore Afro-American*, September 3, 1932, 17.

45. "Black Sox Will Battle New York Black Yankees Tonight," *Baltimore Sun*, September 11, 1932, S5.

46. Bill Gibson, "Hear Me Talkin' to Ya," *Baltimore Afro-American*, September 17, 1932, 16.

47. "Black Sox Win Series from Black Yankees," *Baltimore Afro-American*, September 17, 1932, 22.

48. "Black Sox Cop Two of Three from Washington Pilots," *Baltimore Afro-American*, September 24, 1932, 16.

49. Gibson, "Hear Me," September 17, 1932, 16.

50. Bill Gibson, "Hear Me Talkin' to Ya," *Baltimore Afro-American*, October 22, 1932, 16.

51. "All Stars Take Two from Black Sox Nine," *Baltimore Sun*, September 26, 1932, 7.

52. G. M. Gibbs, "The Sundial," *Baltimore Sun*, September 25, 1932, S3.

53. "Black Sox Take Double-Header," *Baltimore Sun*, October 3, 1932, 11.

54. "All Stars Beat Black Sox," *Baltimore Sun*, October 31, 1932.

55. Gibson, "Hear Me," October 22, 1932, 16.

56. Bill Gibson, "Hear Me Talkin' to Ya," *Baltimore Afro-American*, September 3, 1932, 16.

57. Bill Gibson, "Plenty of Drama, Little Money, in 1932 Sports," *Baltimore Afro-American*, December 31, 1932, 16.

58. Bill Gibson, "Hear Me Talkin' to Ya," *Baltimore Afro-American*, May 13, 1933, 16.

59. "New Baseball Association Formed in Mid-West," *Baltimore Afro-American*, January 21, 1933, 16.

60. "Black Sox Not to Disband," *Baltimore Afro-American*, February 18, 1933, 17.

61. W. Rollo Wilson, "Eastern Ball Moguls Gather," *Baltimore Afro-American*, March 11, 1933, 16.

62. "Black Sox Not to Disband," 17.

63. Bill Gibson, "Hear Me Talkin' to Ya," *Baltimore Afro-American*, April 15, 1933, 16.

64. Bill Gibson, "Hear Me Talkin' to Ya," *Baltimore Afro-American*, March 4, 1933, 17.

65. "Black Sox Have Berth in League," *Baltimore Afro-American*, May 13, 1933, 16.

66. "Baltimore Black Sox," *Central New Jersey Home New*, September 14, 1933, 16.

67. W. Rollo Wilson, "Sports Shorts," *Pittsburgh Courier*, June 3, 1933, 13.

68. "Seek to Enjoy Team from Use of Black Sox," *Baltimore Afro-American*, May 27, 1933, 16.

69. Professional soccer made its home in Baltimore at Maryland Park (Black Sox Park) in the 1920s. One of the fledgling semiprofessional/professional leagues, the Southeastern Soccer League, was an inter-city (Baltimore/Philadelphia) league. The teams in the league would play a schedule of non-professional games in addition to a league schedule. The Patapsco Rangers, one of two Baltimore teams in the league, made Maryland Park their home during their first season (1923–24). They lost the championship match in February 1924 to a team from Philadelphia. The Rangers would continue to play select home matches at Maryland Park throughout the 1920s and in the early 1930s, and those matches attracted good crowds. These early attempts at professional soccer failed. Nonetheless, Maryland Park holds a significant place in Baltimore's soccer history.

70. Bill Gibson, "Hear Me Talkin' to Ya," *Baltimore Afro-American*, June 17, 1933, 17.

71. Bill Gibson, "Hear Me Talkin' to Ya," *Baltimore Afro-American*, December 9, 1933, 20.

72. "Advanced Guard of Sox Here," *Baltimore Afro-American*, May 20, 1933, 17.

73. Bill Gibson, "Hear Me Talkin' to Ya," *Baltimore Afro-American*, September 9, 1933, 21.

74. "1933 Season: Negro National League II," Negro Leagues Database, seamheads.com, http://www.seamheads.com/NegroLgs/year.php?yearID=1933&lgID=NN2.

75. Bill Gibson, "Hear Me Talkin' to Ya," *Baltimore Afro-American*, July 29, 1933, 16.

76. "East West Diamond Classic," *Pittsburgh Courier*, September 9, 1933, A5.

77. "Baseball Men Meet in Philly, Favor League," *Baltimore Afro-American*, February 17, 1934, 19.

78. "Baltimore Unready as Club Owners Organize," *Baltimore Afro-American*, March 17, 1934, 18.

79. "Black Sox Bow to Harrisburg," *Baltimore Afro-American*, May 5, 1934, 18.

80. Bill Gibson, "Hear Me Talkin' to Ya," *Baltimore Afro-American*, July 7, 1934, 18.

81. "Black Sox Secure League Franchise," *Baltimore Afro-American*, July 7, 1934, 19.

82. "Sox Make Late Bow by Losing Pair to Nashville Giants," *Baltimore Afro-American*, July 14, 1934, 19.

83. "Jack Farrell Let Go upon Larceny Count," *Baltimore Afro-American*, July 14, 1934, 15.

84. "Sox Boss Tells Why No More Games Were Played in Baltimore," *Baltimore Afro-American*, August 25, 1934, 18.

85. "Black Sox Win Pair on Local Diamond," *Delaware County Daily Times*, August 27, 1934, 11.

86. "1934 Season," Negro Leagues Database, seamheads.com, http://www.seamheads.com/NegroLgs/year.php?yearID=1934.

87. "2,000 See Black Sox Take Two Games from All Stars," *Baltimore Afro-American*, September 29, 1934, 20.

88. "All Stars Bunch Hits to Nip Black Sox, 10–9," *Baltimore Afro-American*, October 15, 1934, 10.

89. "Brooklyn Gets Lundy in Trade," *Baltimore Afro-American*, May 25, 1935, 20.

90. "Editor's Note," *Baltimore Afro-American*, July 27, 1935, 20.

91. "Homestead Grays Register 8–3 Win over Baltimore Black Sox at Pennys Field," *Wilmington News Journal*, August 24, 1935, 11.

92. "Baltimore Black Sox Will Oppose Royal Dukes Today," *Wilmington Morning News*, July 18, 1936, 14.

93. "Dial," *New York Age*, December 5, 1936, 8.

94. "Baltimore Tigers Organize Ball Club," *Baltimore Sun*, February 22, 1931, 23.

Chapter 9

1. Sherry Olson, "Old West Baltimore: Segregation, African American Culture, and the Struggle for Equality," in *The Baltimore Book*, Elizabeth Fee, Linda Shopes, and Linda Zeidman, eds (Philadelphia: Temple University Press, 1991), 57.

2. Hayward Farrar, *The Baltimore Afro-American, 1892–1950* (Westport, CT: The Greenwood Press, 1998), 89–90.

3. Ibid.

4. Dennis Halpin, *A Brotherhood of Liberty: Black Reconstruction and its Legacies in Baltimore, 1865–1920* (Philadelphia: University of Pennsylvania Press, 2019), 146.

5. Ibid., 67.

6. Ibid., 69.

7. "Ex Baltimorean Testifies in Scottsboro, Alabama Case," *Baltimore Afro-American*, April 8, 1933, 11.

8. "Decatur Dentist Says, 'Air Still Hot in Alabama Town,'" *Norfolk Journal and Guide*, May 6, 1933, 8.

9. "Dr. Young, Veteran Pharmacist, Dies at 70," *Baltimore Afro-American*, October 13, 1945, 18.

10. "Colored Cops, Firemen Common on the West Coast," *Baltimore Afro-American*, April 2, 1938, p. 24.

11. *Brown Alumni Monthly* Vol. XX, No. 1, June 1919, http://www.archive.org/stream/brownalumnimonth201brow/brownalumnimonth201brow_djvu.t xt.

12. John R. Williams, *A Trench Letter* (Baltimore: William B. Hamer, 1918), 4.

13. *Washington Bee*, October 2, 1920, 5; *Washington Times*, October 6, 1920, 15.

14. "Black Sox Win Double-Header," *Baltimore Afro-American*, June 13, 1919, 2.

15. "Victory for Weldon Giants," *Baltimore Sun*, September 11, 1919, 13.

16. "Lincoln Reds Open at Ellicott City," *Baltimore Afro-American*, July 14, 1928, 13.

17. "Charles Evans Rites Tomorrow: Ballplayer and Steelworker," *Baltimore Sun*, November 9. 1977, A17.

18. Stater, "Baseball, His First Love," 5.

19. "Homestead Grays Select Camp Site," *Pittsburgh Courier*, March 14, 1942, 17.

20. Bready, *Baseball in Baltimore*, 166.

21. "Hundreds View Smith's Remains," *Afro-American,* August 20, 1938, 8.

22. "Negroes Murder Brother of Smith," *Baltimore Sun,* December 17, 1939, 26.

23. "Smith's Hotel to Become a Parking Lot." *Baltimore Afro-American,* July 20, 1957, A3.

24. "Spedden," *Baltimore Sun,* April 2, 1960, 20.

25. "Obituary-Rossiter," *Baltimore Sun,* July 2, 1950, 16.

26. "Ball Team's Founder Dies," *Baltimore Sun,* May 29, 1969, A11.

27. Nick Wilson, *Early Latino Ballplayers in the United States* (Jefferson, NC: McFarland, 2005), 176.

28. John Holway, "I Remember Baseball with Baltimore's Black Sox," *Baltimore Sun,* July 11, 1971, SM2.

29. "Scrappy Brown Captains Jersey Basketball Pros," *Baltimore Afro-American,* November 22, 1930, 15; "Ex-Amateur Champ Seeks Pro Fights," *Baltimore Afro-American,* March 2, 1940, 21; "Watching the Big Parade," *Baltimore Afro-American,* May 27, 1944, 4; "Scrappy Brown Dies," *Baltimore Afro-American,* September 15, 1951, 16.

30. "Moons Answer Piedmont Tigers," *Baltimore Afro-American,* November 22, 1930, 15.

31. "Oldest Bootblack Stand Is Still Going Strong," *Baltimore Afro-American,* September 5, 1953, 5.

32. John Holway, "I Remember Pitching Six No-Hitters for the Black Sox," *Baltimore Sun,* July 19, 1970, SM2.

33. Sam Lacy, "From A to Z," *Baltimore Afro-American,* July 7, 1951, 16.

34. Carleton Jones, "Back Tracks: Lost Leagues and Unsung Heroes," *Baltimore Sun,* May 6, 1990, SM27.

35. Nathan, "The Baltimore Black Sox and the Perils of History," 52–87; Riley, *Of Monarchs and Black Barons,* 94.

36. Nathan, "The Baltimore Black Sox and the Perils of History," 73.

37. Bernard McKenna, "A Field of Their Own: The Baltimore Black Sox and Maryland Park." *Black Ball: A Negro Leagues Journal* 7 (2014), 99–113.

38. "Negro Pitcher Uses 3 Strikes to Reprove Big League Star," *Baltimore Sun,* October 24, 1927, 20.

Bibliography

Baltimore (General)

Crenson, Matthew. *Baltimore: A Political History.* Baltimore: Johns Hopkins University Press, 2016.

Halpin, Dennis. *A Brotherhood of Liberty: Black Reconstruction and Its Legacies in Baltimore, 1865–1920.* Philadelphia: University of Pennsylvania Press, 2019.

McDougall, Harold. *Black Baltimore: A New Theory of Community.* Philadelphia: Temple University Press, 1993.

Meyer, Stephen Grant. *As Long as They Don't Move Next Door: Segregation and Racial Conflict in American Neighborhoods.* Lanham, MD: Rowman & Littlefield, 1999.

Olson, Sherry. *Baltimore: The Building of an American City.* Baltimore: Johns Hopkins University Press, 1997.

_____. "Old West Baltimore: Segregation, African American Culture, and the Struggle for Equality" in *The Baltimore Book,* edited by Elizabeth Fee, Linda Shopes, and Linda Zeidman. Philadelphia: Temple University Press, 1991.

Pietila, Antero. "History of Baltimore's Racial Segregation Includes a Hard Look at Newspapers' Role." *Baltimore Sun,* March 15, 2010.

Power, Garret. "Apartheid Baltimore Style: The Residential Segregation Ordinances of 1910–1913," *Maryland Law Review* Vol. 42, No. 2 (October 2012): 289–328.

Baseball in Baltimore

Bready, James. *Baseball in Baltimore: The First 100 Years.* Baltimore: Johns Hopkins University Press, 1998.

Felber, Bill. *A Game of Brawl: The Orioles, the Beaneaters and the Battle for the 1897 Pennant.* Lincoln: University of Nebraska Press, 2007.

Henneman, Jim. *Baltimore Orioles: Years of Orioles Magic.* San Rafael, CA: Insight, 2015.

Mars, Ken. *Baltimore Baseball: First Pitch to First Pennant, 1858–1894.* Baltimore: privately printed, 2018.

Nathan, Daniel A. "The Baltimore Black Sox and the Perils of History" in *Baseball in America and America in Baseball,* edited by Donald G. Kyle and Robert B. Fairbanks. College Station: Texas A&M University Press, 2008.

_____. "Satchel Paige, the Black Sox, and Politics" in *Satchel Paige and Company: Essays on the Kansas City Monarchs, Their Greatest Star, and the Negro Leagues,* Edited by Leslie A. Heaphy. Jefferson, NC: McFarland, 2007.

Patterson, Ted. *The Baltimore Orioles: Four Decades of Magic from 33rd Street to Camden Yards.* Lanham, MD: Taylor Trade, 1994.

Bibliography

Solomon, Burt. *Where They Ain't: The Fabled Life and Untimely Death of the Original Baltimore Orioles, the Team That Gave Birth to Modern Baseball.* New York: Free Press, 1999.

Stinson, David. *Deadball: A Metaphysical Novel.* Baltimore: Huntington Park Publications, 2011.

Negro Leagues

Burgos, Adrian. *Cuban Star.* New York: Hill and Wang, 2012.

Clark, Dick, and Larry Lester, eds. *The Negro Leagues Book.* Cleveland: Society for American Baseball Research, 2012.

Gay, Timothy. *Satch, Dizzy and Rapid Robert: The Wild Saga of International Baseball Before Jackie Robinson.* New York: Simon & Schuster, 2010.

Hauser, Christopher. *The Negro League Chronology: Events in Organized Black Baseball, 1920–1948.* Jefferson, NC: McFarland, 2008.

Heaphy, Leslie A. *The Negro Leagues, 1869–1960.* Jefferson, NC: McFarland, 2013.

Hogan, Lawrence D. *Shades of Glory: The Negro Leagues and the Story of African American Baseball.* Washington, DC: National Geographic Society, 2006.

Holway, John, et al. *The Complete Book of Baseball's Negro Leagues.* Fern Park, FL: Hastings House, 2001.

Lanctot, Neil. *Fair Dealing and Clean Playing: The Hilldale Club and the Development of Black Professional Baseball, 1910–1932.* Syracuse: Syracuse University Press, 2007.

_____. *Negro League Baseball: The Rise and Ruin of a Black Institution.* Philadelphia: University of Pennsylvania Press, 2008.

Lester, Larry. *Baseball's First Colored World Series: The 1924 Meeting of the Hilldale Giants and Kansas City Monarchs.* Jefferson, NC: McFarland, 2014.

_____. *Black Baseball's National Showcase: The East-West All-Star Game, 1933–1953.* Lincoln: University of Nebraska Press, 2001.

_____. *Rube Foster in His Time.* Jefferson, NC: McFarland, 2012.

Loverro, Thom. *The Encyclopedia of Negro League Baseball.* New York: Facts on File, 2003.

Luke, Bob. *The Baltimore Elite Giants: Sport and Society in the Age of Negro League Baseball.* Baltimore: Johns Hopkins University Press, 2017.

McNeil, William. *Black Baseball Out of Season: Pay for Play Outside of the Negro Leagues.* Jefferson, NC: McFarland, 2012.

Nelson, Kadir. *We Are the Ship: The Story of Negro League Baseball.* New York: Hyperion, 2008.

Overmyer, James E. *Black Ball and the Boardwalk: The Bacharach Giants of Atlantic City, 1916–1929.* Jefferson, NC: McFarland, 2014.

Peterson, Robert. *Only the Ball Was White: A History of Legendary Black Players and All-Black Professional Teams.* New York: Oxford University Press, 1992.

Powell, Larry. *Black Barons of Birmingham: The South's Greatest Negro League Team and Its Players.* Jefferson, NC: McFarland, 2012.

Reisler, Jim. *Black Writers/Black Baseball: An Anthology of Articles from Black Sportswriters Who Covered the Negro Leagues.* Jefferson, NC: McFarland, 2007.

Ribowsky, Mark. *A Complete History of the Negro Leagues, 1884–1955.* New York: Birch Lane, 1995.

Riley, James A. *The Biographical Encyclopedia of the Negro Baseball Leagues.* New York: Carroll and Graf, 1994.

Bibliography

_____. *Of Monarchs and Black Barons: Essays on Baseball's Negro Leagues.* Jefferson, NC: McFarland, 2012.

Rogosin, Donn. *The Complete Book of Baseball's Negro Leagues.* Lincoln, NE: Bison Books, 2007.

Snyder, Brad. *Beyond the Shadow of the Senators: The Untold Story of the Homestead Grays and the Integration of Baseball.* New York: McGraw-Hill, 2003.

Wilson, Nick. *Early Latino Ballplayers in the United States.* Jefferson, NC: McFarland, 2005.

Journals

Black Ball: A Negro Leagues Journal

Newspapers

Allentown Democrat
Altoona Tribune
Atlanta Daily World
Baltimore Afro-American
Baltimore American
Baltimore Evening Sun
Baltimore News
Baltimore Sun
Central New Jersey Home News
Chicago Bee
Chicago Defender
Cleveland Gazette
Courier News (Bridgewater, NJ)
Cumberland Sunday Times
Delaware County Daily Times
Detroit Free Press
Fayetteville Observer
Harrisburg Evening News
Harrisburg Telegraph

Indianapolis Freeman
Kansas City Advocate
Kansas City New Journal and Guide
New York Age
New York Amsterdam News
New York Tribune
Norfolk Journal and Guide
Philadelphia Inquirer
Philadelphia Tribune
Pittsburgh Courier
Richmond Planet
St. Louis Post Dispatch
Washington Evening Star å
Washington Herald
Washington Post
Washington Times
Washington Tribune
Wilmington Morning News
Wilmington News Journal

Index

Numbers in *bold italics* indicate pages with illustrations

Index

Index

Index

Index

203

Index